GUIDE TO PRODUCING A
FASHION SHOW
THIRD EDITION

GUIDE TO PRODUCING A
FASHION SHOW
THIRD EDITION

JUDITH C. EVERETT
Northern Arizona University

KRISTEN K. SWANSON
Northern Arizona University

Fairchild Books | New York

This book is dedicated to all our students who have
made our fashion shows better with their
commitment and endless enthusiasm.

Fairchild Books
An imprint of Bloomsbury Publishing Inc

175 Fifth Avenue
New York
NY 10010
USA

50 Bedford Square
London
WC1B 3DP
UK

www.fairchildbooks.com

First edition published 1993
Second edition published 2003
This edition published 2013

Library of Congress Cataloging-in-Publication Data
A catalog record for this book is available from the Library of Congress.
Library of Congress Catalog Number: 2012945035

ISBN: 978-1-60901-506-0

Typeset by Progressive Publishing Alternatives
Cover Design by Sarah Silberg
Cover Art: Getty Images; Courtesy of Fairchild Archive
Printed and bound in the United States of America

CONTENTS

Preface   xi

Acknowledgments   xiii

How to Use the CD-ROM   xv

List of Forms on the CD-ROM   xv

Chapter 1   The Fashion Dolls, Supermodels, and Celebrities   2

Chapter 2   The Background   34

Chapter 3   The Plan   60

Chapter 4   The Message   102

Chapter 5   The Workroom and Runway   148

Chapter 6   The Catwalk   168

Chapter 7   The Framework and Sound Check   212

Chapter 8   The Show   246

Glossary   282

Index   291

EXTENDED CONTENTS

Preface xi
Acknowledgments xiii
How to Use the CD-ROM xv
List of Forms on the CD-ROM xv

CHAPTER 1   The Fashion Dolls, Supermodels, and Celebrities 2
Fashion Show Defined 5
Fashion Show History 5
Notes from the Runway: My First Fashion Show 28
Fashion Dolls, Supermodels, and Celebrities—A Recap 30
Key Fashion Show Terms 30
Questions for Discussion 31
Fashion Show Activity 31
The Capstone Project 31
References 32

CHAPTER 2   The Background 34
Why Produce Fashion Shows? 36
Fashion Show Categories 39
Specialized Fashion Presentations 44
Notes from the Runway: Model Diversity in Fashion Shows 55
The Background—A Recap 57
Key Fashion Show Terms 57
Questions for Discussion 58
Fashion Show Activities 58
The Capstone Project 58
References 59

CHAPTER 3   The Plan 60
Developing Leadership 63
Targeting the Audience 69
Timing the Show 72
Finding a Venue 74
Creating Fashion Show Themes 78
Estimating the Budget 79
Protecting People and Things 87
Finalizing the Fashion Show Plan 89
Notes from the Runway: So, You Want to Be a Fashion Stylist? . . . 93

Notes from the Runway: Budgeting Is Vital for a Successful
    Fashion Show 96
The Plan—A Recap 99
Key Fashion Show Terms 99
Questions for Discussion 100
Fashion Show Activities 100
The Capstone Project 100
References 101

CHAPTER 4   The Message 102
Promotion 105
Advertising 106
Public Relations 114
Direct Marketing 126
Other Forms of Promotion 131
Sponsorship 132
Creative Development of Promotional Materials 135
Promotional Strategies That Will Work for Your Show 139
Notes from the Runway: Branding a Fashion Show 140
Notes from the Runway: Public Relations for a
    Luxury Fashion Retailer 142
The Message—A Recap 144
Key Fashion Show Terms 145
Questions for Discussion 146
Fashion Show Activity 146
The Capstone Project 146
References 147

CHAPTER 5   The Workroom and Runway 148
Merchandise Selection Process 150
Relationships with Merchants 158
Merchandise Pull 158
Merchandise Lineup 158
Merchandise Fittings 159
Notes from the Runway: The Clothing! 164
The Workroom and Runway—A Recap 166
Key Fashion Show Terms 166
Questions for Discussion 166
Fashion Show Activity 166
The Capstone Project 167
References 167

CHAPTER 6   The Catwalk 168
Fashion Models 170
Model Classifications 172
Career Opportunities for Models 177

Modeling Agencies 179
The Downside of Modeling 182
Professional Versus Amateur Models 187
Number and Rotation of Models 191
Model Responsibilities 194
Beauty on the Runway 197
Choreography 200
Notes from the Runway: Inside a Modeling Agency 204
Notes from the Runway: You Find Amateur Models Anywhere,
   Everywhere . . . 207
The Catwalk—A Recap 209
Key Fashion Show Terms 209
Questions for Discussion 210
Fashion Show Activity 210
The Capstone Project 210
References 211

CHAPTER 7   The Framework and Sound Check 212
Staging 215
The Dressing Area 220
Backgrounds 221
Props 222
Seating Patterns 224
Lighting 225
Music 228
Sound System 234
Verbiage 235
Notes from the Runway: Copyrights and Permissions 241
The Framework and Sound Check—A Recap 243
Key Fashion Show Terms 243
Questions for Discussion 244
Fashion Show Activities 244
The Capstone Project 244
References 245

CHAPTER 8   The Show 246
Rehearsing 248
Preparing Backstage 256
Presenting the Fashion Show 259
Closing the Show 261
Striking the Show 262
Being Professional 264
Canceling a Show 265
Wrapping Up 266
Evaluating 266
Specific Elements to Evaluate 270

Measuring Success 277
Notes from the Runway: Nothing Can Beat the Feeling
   of Watching Fashion Unfold! 278
The Show—A Recap 280
Key Fashion Show Terms 280
Questions for Discussion 280
Fashion Show Activity 281
The Capstone Project 281
References 281

Glossary 282
Index 291

PREFACE

The fashion show should be an entertaining and rewarding experience for show producers, participants, and the audience. It is an exciting and theatrical presentation of apparel and accessories on live models conducted by many different market levels—from haute couture designers presenting their latest innovations, to the ultimate consumer extravaganza held by community groups and retail stores. The purposes of the third edition of *Guide to Producing a Fashion Show* are to lead individuals through the process of planning and presenting a fashion show, and to outline the steps necessary for organizing a successful event.

Public interest in supermodels and celebrities, as well as media coverage, contributes to the popularity of the fashion show in the 21st century. This third edition has changes that reflect the changing nature of fashion shows as a business practice and as an entertainment vehicle. We have incorporated many real-world examples into every chapter, and included a new feature, Notes from the Runway—writings from students and professionals who have experienced the joys and pitfalls of producing fashion shows. Additional changes include a more comprehensive discussion of online and social media. We have also incorporated Fashion Show Activities and the Capstone Project at the end of each chapter. Accompanying the Capstone Project is a CD-ROM that has several forms that you might find helpful as you produce your own show. We hope that by following the Capstone Project you can guide your students in producing their own successful fashion show! In addition, we have made other changes to this edition. We have combined staging and music into one chapter because they are integrally linked in fashion show production. Since we wrote the first edition over 20 years ago, commentary has fallen out of favor, to be replaced by music as the key element that sustains the flow and energy of the show. We have also combined the show and the wrap-up. Through our many years of directing student-produced shows, we have realized that if we do not talk about the wrap-up and evaluation BEFORE the show is presented, it gets lost in the afterglow of the performance.

We begin this edition with a discussion of the history of fashion shows. Fashion shows began over two centuries ago as displays of fashion on dolls. In the 21st century, fashion shows have become a multimillion dollar business for fashion designers, supermodels, and celebrities alike. The first chapter of the book also traces the history of the fashion show through a review of designers, special events, and associations that influenced its advancement. The chapter concludes with a discussion of the business of fashion shows and their relevance today.

In the second chapter, we continue the discussion on background and development of the various types of fashion shows. This framework includes the primary purpose of producing a show—to sell merchandise, detailing the various types of shows. European fashion shows have set the pace for innovation and theatrical presentations. The unique styles of the French, Italian, British, and American retailers and designers—couture and ready-to-wear—are thoroughly reported in this chapter along with emerging fashion-conscious countries, such as Canada, Brazil, Denmark, Spain, and others.

The next section of the book outlines the steps in planning the fashion show, beginning with the first stages of planning—establishing the audience, type of show, site, theme, and budget. The message—presented through promotional activities—is fully discussed. Preparation of media materials and advertising for newspapers, magazines, television, and radio, as well as for online and social media venues, is investigated. We have provided examples of news releases and photographs, as well as step-by-step instructions on how to write a news release, which we know will assist fashion show planners with this activity. Social media has become an important communication tool since the writing of the first edition and a discussion of its use is also part of this chapter.

The merchandise selection process involves pulling, fitting, and preparing merchandise. The workroom and runway chapter highlights these important tasks. Grouping merchandise in a creative and interesting lineup that fits the theme is also part of this activity and is fully examined. The role of the models, who display the merchandise on the catwalk, is an important feature of how the show looks. Therefore, both selecting and training models are critical to the overall success of any show. We have considered advantages of and the differences between using professional or amateur models in a fashion show and the responsibilities of all the models during the fittings, rehearsal, and show. Choreography sets the dramatic opening, pace, and finale for the models and concludes this chapter.

In the next chapter, "The Framework and Sound Check," we discuss staging, which consists of the theatrical stage and runway design that can enhance the image or theme established in the early stages of planning. Distinct patterns for runways, seating arrangements, and the appropriate use of lighting and props are featured. Music has taken center stage in fashion show production. Show planners and the audience know that music can enhance or detract from the ambiance of a show more than almost any other theatrical element. Using music is one of the major focuses of this chapter.

The last chapter in the third edition of *Guide to Producing a Fashion Show* outlines the rehearsal, show, and wrap-up. All of the advance preparation pays off on the day of the show. Rehearsal is complete and participants are excited to see everything pulled together, finally having the opportunity to introduce the show to the target audience. The thrill of all activities coming together results in a truly rewarding experience for the fashion show organizers, models, designers, technical staff, and audience. We also discuss the often-neglected portion of producing a fashion show—striking the stage and returning merchandise to the designers, manufacturers, or retailers. Another responsibility at this point is addressed—sending thank you notes and paying promptly for services.

The final step in fashion show production is the evaluation process. This much-overlooked step in fashion show production is really the first step in the production of the next show. Each time a fashion show is presented, the participants learn how to make the next show even better.

Producing a fashion show is a hands-on learning experience. One last feature of this third edition is the use, by example, of student-produced fashion shows, including ours and others that fashion faculty around the United States have willingly shared with us. Producing fashion shows is truly a hands-on learning experience for students who are enthusiastic and proud of their achievements in fashion show production.

It is our hope that the techniques discussed throughout this book will provide a foundation for fashion show planners to organize this enormous project and that the behind-the-scenes photographs support and enhance this information. This in-depth study of fashion show production will serve as a valuable tool for fashion professionals; instructors; students of design, merchandising, and modeling; and charity or community leaders, giving them a view of all the aspects of this dramatic and exciting event. We enjoyed updating this edition and hope that you will find the new information entertaining and helpful as you produce a fashion show.

2012
Judy Everett
Kris Swanson

ACKNOWLEDGMENTS

The authors wish to thank the many business associates and friends who helped to make working on this project a pleasurable and rewarding experience. We appreciate all of the support from those individuals who were eager to answer questions, give counsel, review chapters, and provide entrance backstage to many of their fashion shows.

The authors wish to express deep appreciation to our students whose enthusiasm for fashion show production has always pushed us to do our best in creating a text that would guide them through this exciting and fun process. We would also like to express our deep appreciation for Fairchild's executive editor, Olga Kontzias, who has been our publisher and friend for over 20 years.

We would like to thank Progressive Publishing Alternatives for editing this text and preparing it for publication. We would also like to thank Amanda Breccia, assistant acquisitions editor; Linda Feldman, associate production editor; Sarah Silberg, art director, for her assistance in designing artwork and seeking copyright permissions; Amy Butler, ancillaries editor, who coordinated the instructor's guide; and other members of the Fairchild team.

Our special appreciation goes to Mademoiselle A., Dr. Ben Barry, Reah Norman, Cynthia Tripathi, Patricia Murphey, Miss PR Diva, Cynde Koritzinsky, Sheree Hartwell, Karissa Keiter, Kaci Shields, and Emilee Dunn for contributing "Notes from the Runway" pieces for our text. We would also like to thank Sara Ziff from the Model Alliance for her contributions.

Special appreciation also goes to Christopher Everett who has provided photography for all three editions of this text, and Kristen Sherwin who provided photography for the current edition.

We would also like to thank questionnaire respondents: Tanya Barnes-Matt, instructor, Mesa Community College; Evonne Bowling, fashion program director, Mesa Community College; Natalie Sanger Gendle, lecturer in textiles and clothing; faculty advisor for The Fashion Show, Iowa State University; Debbie Goldberg, director of media relations, Philadelphia University; Clara Henry, fashion design program director and associate professor, Philadelphia University; Cynde Koritzinsky, adjunct professor, University of Bridgeport; and Janice Lewis, professor, chairperson, Moore College of Art and Design.

Additional thanks need to go to the acquisitions reviewers selected by the publisher—Jaylie I. L. Beckenhauer, Baylor University; Sheri Dragoo, Texas Woman's University; Diane Ellis, Meredith College; Nena Ivon, Columbia College; Kristen McKitish, Centenary College; Esther Pariser, Fashion Institute of Technology (FIT); and Pamela Stoessell, Marymount University.

HOW TO USE THE CD-ROM

Guide to Producing a Fashion Show, Third Edition, includes a CD-ROM found on the inside front cover of the book which provides easy access to examples of documents, forms, and templates needed to plan and execute a fashion show.

Forms to coincide with all stages of planning are represented on the CD-ROM, including a budget form, supply checklist, and a post-fashion show evaluation sheet, among others. Helpful templates for keeping track of merchandise and models can be found, as well as forms for promoting the fashion show, such as the news release format and an activity planning calendar.

Look for the CD-ROM icon and note "Please refer to the CD-ROM for tools that may assist you with this section of the fashion show planning process" placed at the end of each chapter.

LIST OF FORMS ON THE CD-ROM

Chapter 3 The Plan
01. Organization Chart Sample
02. Responsibility Sheet
03. Possible Expenses
04. Fashion Show Planning and Final Budget
05. Personal Responsibility Contract
06. Fashion Show Plan
07. Planning Calendar Sample

Chapter 4 The Message

08. Radio Script Sample

09. Media List

10. News Release Sample

11. Cover Letter Sample

12. Basic Fact Sheet Sample

13. Sponsorship Package Sample—Letter

14. Sponsorship Package Sample—Sponsorship Levels

15. Sponsorship Package Sample—Contribution Form

Chapter 5 The Workroom and Runway

16. Ideal Chart Sample

17. Merchandise Loan Record Sample

18. Tentative Lineup Sample

19. Final Lineup Sample

20. Fitting Sheet

Chapter 6 The Catwalk

21. Model Application Form

22. Model Release Form

23. Individual Model Lineup Sample

24. Model List Sample

25. Model Responsibilities Sheet

Chapter 7 The Framework and Sound Check

26. Dressing Room Supply List

27. Music Play List

28. Script Sample

Chapter 8 The Show

29. Show Day Schedule

30. Thank You Letter Sample

31. General Evaluation Form

32. Audience Reaction Form

33. Model Evaluation Form

GUIDE TO PRODUCING A
FASHION SHOW
THIRD EDITION

CHAPTER ONE
The Fashion Dolls, Supermodels, and Celebrities

AFTER READING THIS CHAPTER, YOU SHOULD BE ABLE TO DISCUSS:

- The definition of *fashion show*

- Innovations from influential fashion designers in fashion show history

- Involvement of various associations in fashion show history

- Contributions by retail stores to fashion show development

- The role of fashion models in fashion shows

- The meaning of celebrity participation at fashion shows

- The modernization of fashion shows into alternative presentation methods

Yves Saint Laurent, Spring 1972. *Courtesy of Fairchild Archive*

What do Mary-Kate and Ashley Olsen (Fig. 1.1), Paul McCartney, Blake Lively, Rihanna, and Sarah Jessica Parker have in common? Each of them has attended a runway fashion show as part of the nonstop action that takes place at the semiannual fashion week presentations held in New York, London, Paris, and Milan. Star treatment for sitting in the front row at these events generally includes a gift bag with items from the designer's current line and an invitation to a private party where celebrities have their pictures taken, which will be shown on Style.com or in the pages of *Women's Wear Daily* within hours of the event.

The whirlwind of activities surrounding fashion week brings fashion to the consumer via theatrical presentations staged by designers, performed by supermodels, and attended by celebrities from movies, stage, television, and politics. Fashion shows began as a simple method of presenting new clothes to clients. Today, fashion shows are elaborate productions, regularly featured on broadcasts from television programs such as *Inside Edition*, *Fashion TV*, or *Entertainment Tonight*; via social media, including Facebook and Twitter; or on websites, such as Style.com, mbfashionweek.com, or youtube.com. Fashion consumers have instant gratification by watching runway shows as they take place during fashion week. Consumers in the Middle East or South America do not have to wait months until they see fashion magazine and newspaper articles written by the fashion press about the latest trends in Europe. Fashion-savvy consumers from all over the world can watch the international fashion presentations live via the Internet.

This chapter introduces you to the historical development of the fashion show and will acquaint you with some of the significant people who were involved in its evolution, from simple presentation on fashion dolls to electronic multimedia productions. Public interest in supermodels and celebrities, as

Figure 1.1
As celebrities and designers, the Olsen twins attract attention from photographers as they sit in the front row of a fashion show.

Courtesy of WWD/Steve Eichner

well as other media coverage, contributes to the popularity of the fashion show in the 21st century. Thus, we profile some of the designers, media stars, and models who influence fashion. Finally, we end this chapter with a look at digital fashion show production.

FASHION SHOW DEFINED

Every creative element of theatrical and modern entertainment media is used in a **fashion show**, which is an event where the latest fashion, fabric, and color trends in apparel and accessories are presented, using live models, to an audience. Certainly an advantage of seeing merchandise in an exciting live presentation is that the audience can become involved. They are not seeing a "representation" of a garment in a photograph or in an advertising illustration, nor are they viewing a garment on a hanger. A model on the runway is wearing all the elements of apparel and accessories. The audience members can react to the total look of an outfit and visualize how they might look wearing the newest and latest developments from the fashion world. The models in Color Plate 1 are exhibiting a feeling of whimsy in Paris.

FASHION SHOW HISTORY

The fashion show has been used by dressmakers and clothing designers since the 18th century and by ready-to-wear manufacturers since the start of the mass-production industry in the 19th century as a way to distribute fashion trend information and increase sales of their garments. However, the true inventor of the modern runway fashion show—using live models—is unknown. One of the first methods used by dressmakers to transmit fashion information to reach potential consumers, which at that time (the late 1300s) were the women of the royal courts, was to send fashion dolls (Corinth, 1970).

Fashion Dolls

Fashion dolls are miniature, to scale figures wearing replicas of the latest clothing. The dolls were also known as *puppets, dummies, little ladies, fashion babies, Pandoras, poupées de la mode, poupées de la Rue de Saint-Honoré,* or *les grands courriers de la mode.* Shipping dolls wearing the latest fashion trends from one royal court to another was a common practice in the European monarchy, reaching its peak during the period from the 1640s to the 1790s (Corinth, 1970). Even as early as the 14th century it was recognized that fashion was best shown on a body, even if it was on a lifeless mannequin. One of these fashion dolls is illustrated in Figure 1.2.

Courtesy, Warwick Doll Museum. Copyright © Walter Scott, Bradford, England

Figure 1.2
This fashion doll is shown in Russian court dress of the early 19th century.

According to Kay Corinth (1970), the earliest record of the fashion doll was in 1391 when the wife of Charles VI of France sent a full-size figure wearing the innovative French court fashions of the time to Queen Anne, wife of Richard II, King of England. Although this was more like the modern-day, full-size mannequin, it was called a fashion doll. Queen Anne was able to wear the garment immediately instead of having it reproduced from a miniature scale. Sending small dolls as fashion messengers became common practice in the 17th and 18th centuries.

Olivier Bernier (1981) states that Marie Antoinette, who became Queen of France in 1774, remembered the advice of her mother, Empress Maria Theresa of Austria, which was to pay more attention to her clothes. As a 13-year-old archduchess in Vienna, Marie Antoinette spent countless hours with dressmakers and milliners summoned from Paris to provide her with appropriately luxurious clothing. These female fashion merchants, *marchandes de modes*, showcased their designs on jointed wooden or plaster *poupées de mode*, outfitted in doll-sized versions of the latest Paris fashions (Weber, 2006). The dolls were perhaps the forerunners of contemporary retail store mannequins and runway models. The Queen made it known that her ambition was to be the most fashionable woman in the kingdom.

Marie Antoinette chose Rose Bertin as her personal marchande de mode (Weber, 2006). Although other successful milliners and dress merchants worked in Paris during this era, none of them achieved as much fame as the Queen's dressmaker. With Mademoiselle Bertin's help, the Queen refined her image of power. As the primary fashion adviser to the Queen, Rose Bertin was the first marchande de mode to be recognized by name.

The first "Fashion Parades" attended by the ladies of Louis XVI's court took place at the Galerie des Glaces (Hall of Mirrors) at the Palace of Versailles, according to Michaela Bellisario (2008). These events gave Marie Antoinette and the other ladies of the court the opportunity to display their finest dresses and were perhaps a forerunner to modern fashion shows and red carpet events.

With Marie Antoinette's growing enthusiasm for fashion, the Queen asked Bertin to also dress dolls in the latest French fashions. The Queen had the dolls sent to her sisters and her mother so they could see and copy the latest fashions worn in France. To attract additional customers to her Rue Saint Honoré shop in Paris, Bertin sent dolls to the major European capitals. Despite her creative work for the Queen, Rose Bertin achieved international fame with fashion dolls that she sent to all the capitals of Europe to solicit orders. As a result of her international fame, Bertin was given the nickname "Minister of Fashion" (Corinth, 1970).

The French Revolution did not put an end to the fortunes of Rose Bertin. She opened her business in London for a time to serve her old clients who had emigrated from France. Her fashion dolls continued to circulate to the other European capitals, as far away as St. Petersburg, Russia, and to North America (Bernier, 1981).

Other 18th-century dressmakers also used fashion dolls to communicate fashion trends to distant customers. According to Roselyn Gadia-Smitley (1987), an advertisement in the *New England Weekly Journal* of July 2, 1733, invited customers to view a mannequin brought from London at Mrs. Hannah Teatt's Boston dressmaker's shop. This indicates that fashion dolls were also sent to North America, serving as fashion ambassadors and as the dressmaker's model for dress patterns.

The first doll fashion show in America was sponsored by *Vogue* magazine in 1896, according to Kay Corinth (1970). The event featured approximately 150 dolls that wore dresses reflecting the work of American dressmakers. Society leaders helped support the charity event, which opened with a private preview attended by more than 1,000 people. At the opening, tickets sold for 50 cents and the sponsors raised $500, which is a modest sum compared to the amounts of money raised at modern charity fashion shows and events.

During the 19th century, the doll of choice was the Bébé Jumeau, according to Juliette Peers (2004). These dolls were made by the French firm Jumeau. With a literal translation of *bébé* to "baby," the dolls did not serve the same purpose as 20th-century baby dolls. The French term *bébé* indicated the doll had a younger persona than the fashionable Parisienne of the era. While some of the bébés were dressed in infants' clothes, the majority of them represented girls between the ages of 2 and 12 years. Some bébés were dressed in adult styles. The bébé tells the story of the French haute couture doll from its heyday in the 1870s until its disappearance at the beginning of the 20th century. The dolls provided new channels of information about style in late 19th-century France. Alongside other media, the dolls facilitated modernization of communication about fashion.

Although the practice of sending and displaying fashion dolls gave way to other methods of fashion communication by the 20th century, the *Théâtre de la Mode* was a fashion doll presentation unique to the 20th century, according to Susan Train and Eugène Clarence Braun-Munk (2002). This fashion doll event took place after the end of World War II. Paris designers in a liberated France wanted to let the world know that they were ready to resume

fashion leadership, despite limited resources. Unable to launch a full-scale fashion exhibition, designers, artists, and musicians collaborated to present *Théâtre de la Mode*, allowing the world to see the French spring-summer collection of 1946, the first to be designed for export since the war. *Petits mannequins*, or fashion dolls, were revived for this exhibition. Although the presentation did not use live models, it did present fashion on the human form in the style of a spectacular fashion show.

This project was coordinated through the Chambre Syndicale de la Haute Couture Parisienne (Train & Braun-Munk, 2002). It brought together designers, who otherwise would have concealed their work from competitors, into an unprecedented collaboration never seen before or since. An exhibit of 228 petits mannequins featured the latest work of the French designers. The mannequins were presented in 12 theatrical sets to provide the proper environment for morning, afternoon, and evening attire (Fig. 1.3). Participating couture houses agreed to create from one to five outfits for display. The 27.5-inch wire figurines were built from sketches developed by Eliane Bonabel. Plaster heads constructed by sculptor Joan Rebull were added to the figures so they could have real coiffures and hats. The art director for the project was Christian (Bebé) Bérard, a Parisian artist. He called upon his friends in the arts, theater, and literary world to participate. Balenciaga, Hermés, Balmain, Lanvin, Molyneux, Schiaparelli, Worth, and Ricci were among the fashion designers who were involved.

The show was originally produced to raise money to help war victims. The exhibition traveled to England, Spain, Denmark, Sweden, and Austria. The following year, the show was sent to New York and San Francisco with updated fashions. With

Figure 1.3
Fashion dolls presented at the Thêàtre de la Mode wore fashions created by Paris couturiers, which were placed in sets designed by well-known French artists after the end of World War II.

limited resources, the show's sponsors could not afford to return the mannequins and clothing to Paris. The display was forgotten and it was assumed that the doll collection was lost until it was discovered at the Maryhill Museum of Art in Goldendale, Washington, in 1983 (Train & Braun-Munk, 2002). The garments and accessories were returned to Paris for restoration in 1987. An exhibit featuring 171 dolls opened at the Musée des Arts de la Mode in Paris in 1990. The exhibit moved to the Costume Institute of the Metropolitan Museum of Art in New York City, later that year. The exhibit was later permanently relocated to the Maryhill Museum of Art in the state of Washington.

Perhaps the most well-known fashion doll of the 20th century is Barbie. Mattel Toy Company introduced her in 1959 ("What a Doll," 1998). Barbie was more than a simple toy for girls and boys in the last half of the 20th century: she was a fashion icon. The doll was and continues to be sold with interchangeable fashions of the time, in addition to fantasy, pop culture, historical, and designer dresses. Barbie became a fashion model, wearing Bob Mackie, Ralph Lauren, Donna Karan, Diane von Furstenberg, and other designer-inspired clothing, designed especially for her (Fig. 1.4a). Many youngsters dreamed of becoming fashion designers as they created their original Barbie clothing.

When Barbie turned 50, the Council of Fashion Designers of America celebrated the popular fashion doll by giving Barbie her own runway show during Fall Fashion Week in New York City ("Half-Century Barbie," 2009). Barbie's wardrobe, shown on live models (Fig. 1.4b), was created by 50 top fashion designers, including Tory Burch, Michael Kors, Bryan Bradley, Alexander Wang, Naeem Khan, and Kimora Lee Simmons. The show opened with a model wearing Rachel Roy's retro swimsuit, adorned with sequins, as well as a bedazzled trench coat. Each model wore Pantone Color System's

(a) *Courtesy of WWD*

(b) *Courtesy of WWD/Thomas Iannaccone*

Figure 1.4
(a) Barbie has been dressed by such top designers as Tory Burch. **(b)** Barbie turns 50 in style at her own fashion show at New York Fashion Week

Barbie Pink peep toe pumps, designed by Christian Louboutin.

Fashion dolls inspired Dutch designers Viktor Horsting and Rolf Snoeren (Diderich, 2010). In their 1999 fashion show called *Babushka*, model Maggie Rizer was dressed as a Russian doll (Fig. 1.5). She walked onto the stage wearing a simple tunic and stepped up onto a revolving platform at the center of the stage. Horsting and Snoeren added nine layers of jewel-encrusted, Russian-inspired clothing one piece at a time. The garments engulfed Rizer and the show was a highlight of the fashion season.

While fashion dolls provided a great deal of fashion information and imagery, many fashion designers influenced fashion show development. Next, we look at influential designers and their contributions to fashion show history.

Courtesy of WWD/Stephane Feugere

Figure 1.5
Maggie Rizer as a living Russian doll at the Viktor & Rolf show in 1999.

Influential Designers

The modern runway fashion show has its roots in the French couture that began in the 19th century. Costume historians agree that Charles Frederick Worth, the English-born fashion innovator, was the first couturier in France, opening his Paris fashion house in 1858 (Corinth, 1970). Among Worth's revolutionary ideas was designing clothing for an individual woman, customizing the style, fabric, and trimmings to the wearer. Made-to-order garments were created for his clients from samples in the salon. For his contributions in making the couture world what it is today, Worth was given the nickname "Father of Haute Couture."

Worth worked with fabrics and clothes in London before leaving for Paris in 1845 (Corinth, 1970). One of his first jobs in France was with Gagelin and Opigez, a retailer that sold fabrics, trimmings, coats, and shawls. According to Mary Ellen Diehl (1976), it was the responsibility of the *demoiselle de magasin* (shopgirl) to show customers how the shawls looked on a living form. Marie Vernet, an original demoiselle de magasin who later became Madame Worth, was perhaps the first live fashion mannequin when she showed shawls and the latest Worth creations to clients.

The House of Worth called the women, who wore garments for his clients, **mannequins** (Corinth, 1970). Showing clothing on mannequins allowed clients to see how garments would look on a living and moving person. Up to this point, the term *mannequin* had referred to a stationary doll or dummy used as a display fixture, discussed earlier in this chapter. As Worth became more successful, he hired more young women to model at his *maison*, or fashion house. These mannequins continued to show his collections to his customers.

Before the end of the 19th century, several other designers opened maisons de haute couture in the manner of Charles Frederick Worth. These designers copied the promotion innovations of Worth and featured their designs on live models. During the first two decades of the 20th century, French designers Paul Poiret, Madame Jeanne Paquin, and Jean Patou also made significant contributions to the development of the fashion show.

Paul Poiret, known for liberating women from the corset, opened his couture house in 1903 (Tortora & Eubank, 2010). This designer had a knack for promotion, and among his contributions were his innovative and controversial window displays. Poiret also toured, making personal appearances to show his fashions at chic resorts. Poiret even traveled to Russia with nine mannequins. He was one of the first couturiers to parade his mannequins at the races (Diehl, 1976). Such appearances had a positive impact on his sales and image.

The House of Paquin was known for parading models at the racetrack, but Jeanne Paquin also staged events at the opera. Madame Paquin was the first designer to close her fashion shows with the *finale*. It is said that in one show 20 mannequins were dressed in white evening gowns as a tableau (Diehl, 1976). This created a positive and lasting impression at the end of the show. The **finale**—an exciting conclusion—has become universal and important to contemporary fashion shows.

It was common practice for couture houses to show their latest collections on a predetermined opening day. These dates were established by the Chambre Syndicale de la Haute Couture (discussed in Chapter 2), so that opening times for the important designers would not conflict. After the premiere, the fashion show would be repeated twice each day for a month, with additional smaller shows mounted for private clients. The dress rehearsal, which took place the evening before the premiere, was held with the sales personnel and workers as the audience, giving the employees of the house their only chance to see the presentation of their labors.

Jean Patou (Fig. 1.6), known primarily for his contributions to sportswear and as a rival of Chanel, was associated with two important contributions to the fashion show—the press show and the use of American models in Paris, as discussed by Patou's biographer, Meredith Etherington-Smith (1983). Since 1910, journalists have been invited to fashion shows so that they can report on the latest fashion collections. In 1921, Patou scheduled a special preview showing, the *répétition générale*, a full dress rehearsal for the influential representatives of the press, notable buyers, and exceptional clients on the evening before his regular opening. With the assistance of Elsa Maxwell, a popular party planner of the era and perhaps the world's first press agent, Patou converted the ordinary dress rehearsal into an extraordinary way to introduce the fashion season. The salon was festively decorated with flowers and spotlights. Guests were seated at tables with name cards and were treated to champagne, deluxe cigarettes and cigars, and sample bottles of Patou perfumes. The couturier Patou, his **premier/premiere** (head of the workroom), and his **directrice/directeur** (head of the salon), approved each model before she was allowed to show the garment to the audience. Because some fashion styles were rejected at this program, the audience observed the designer as he made his final eliminations from his collection. Patou's events led the way for the biannual press

shows held by the Paris couture throughout the 20th century and into the 21st century.

An American client complained that she had a hard time visualizing herself in the Patou clothing as it was shown on the French mannequins, whose figures were more mature and round compared to Americans with modern flapper-style figures. According to Caroline Evans (2008), Patou traveled to America in 1924 with the intension of hiring three American models. He was overwhelmed by the response to his advertisement in the *New York Times*, which attracted 500 young, hopeful models to the *Vogue* offices in New York City. With the assistance of a jury consisting of Edna Woolman Chase, then editor of *Vogue* magazine; Elsie de Wolfe, decorator and international socialite; Edward Steichen, photographer; and Condé Nast, publisher of *Vogue*, Patou selected six American models—Josephine Armstrong, Dorothy Raynor, Caroline Putnam, Edwina Pru, Rosalind Stair, and Lillian Farley—to return with him to Paris. The young women

Figure 1.6
The French dress designer Jean Patou, with two women, ca. 1935.

"smart, slender, with well-shaped feet and ankles and refined of manner" (Etherington-Smith, p. 81) gave some prestige to the profession of modeling. They were paid $40 per week and given the opportunity to purchase ensembles from Patou for as little as $25. The use of American models changed the ideal of international physical beauty to the thinner, more athletic shapes that these American women possessed.

If Paquin's contribution to fashion show history was the finale, it was Patou who influenced the dramatic opening. Typically, Patou's first show of the season was presented once in the evening in a party atmosphere for his private clients. For his Spring 1925 opening, Patou had his

French and American models make their first entrance in a single file parade wearing identical check wrappers (Evans, 2008). He demonstrated that the physical form was the same regardless of nationality and it served as the inspiration for his designs. Patou's indistinguishably dressed models must have created the look of a theatrical chorus line on stage. The show featured approximately 350 garments, so each mannequin modeled approximately 18 dresses in a show that lasted over 2 hours. The dramatic fashion show opening was created.

Fashion shows remained as fashion parades through the 1930s and 1940s (Fig. 1.7). Gabrielle Chanel, Alix Grès, Nina Ricci, Elsa Schiaparelli, and Madeleine Vionnet

Figure 1.7
Private clients and influential members of the press were always eager to view the latest French collections. The audience views Jacques Fath's fashion show in the 1940s.

Bettmann/Corbis

were among the popular French couture designers during this era (Tortora & Eubank, 2010). The quality, as well as the technology, of the fashion show productions improved during this time. Many of these shows rivaled Broadway musicals with stage sets, lighting, music, and fabulous mannequins.

Christian Dior was acknowledged by Harriet Quick (1997) for changing the format of the fashion parade with his legendary collection in 1947. Dior asked his models to project the image and lifestyle of the women who wore his clothes, not simply show the cut and cloth. According to then *Vogue* fashion editor Bettina Ballard in her memoirs, "We were given a polished theatrical performance such as we had never seen in a couture house before. We were witness to a revolution in fashion and to a revolution in showing fashion as well" (Ballard, 1960, p. 237). Dior's models entered the salon with an electrical tension, stepping fast, walking provocatively with exaggerated movements, whirling their garments and knocking over ashtrays in a room packed with clients and fashion press (Fig. 1.8). While it might seem tame compared to the energetic fashion shows of the 1960s and into the 21st century, it was a landmark change in fashion show presentation. Dior ruled French fashion between 1947 and 1958, selling more than one and a half times the clothes of all of the other Paris couturiers of the time combined (Quick, 1997, p. 70).

The creativity and energy of the swinging 1960s led to major changes in fashion and the way it was presented. British designer Mary Quant was at the forefront of these changes (Quick, 1997). Certain models were known for their work in the photographic media while other models worked the runway shows. However,

Figure 1.8
Dior encouraged his models to capture an energetic and youthful appearance at his fashion shows after World War II ended.

Bettmann/Corbis

Quant felt that photographic models rather than runway models knew how to move around in clothes, so she selected nine of them to dance down the stairs and runway at her shop, Knightsbridge Bazaar. Since this era, models have worked in each field interchangeably.

Mary Quant discussed her staging, use of innovative props, and dancing, which led to more active fashion shows, in her biography, *Quant by Quant* (1966). Contemporary jazz music was taped for an uninterrupted pace. The show consisted of 40 garments and was shown in 14 minutes. One outfit featured a model wearing a Norfolk jacket and knickers, carrying a shotgun and a dead pheasant for a hunting scene. Models wearing party dresses carried oversized champagne glasses. Absolutely no commentary was spoken. This period marked the elimination of commentary from press and trade shows. Music, dance, and choreography set the mood for these fashion shows.

Figure 1.9
A dress from
Kenzo's 1976
collection.

Courtesy of WWD/Gray Reginald

By the 1970s, French haute couture started to look sadly outdated. Ready-to-wear clothing was quickly becoming popular, overshadowing the expensive made-to-measure couture. Japanese designer Kenzo introduced his extremely successful Jungle Jap label with a fashion show spectacle (Quick, 1997). Kenzo extended the traditional catwalk into a stage performance, attracting an audience almost four times the size of a traditional salon show. Instead of presenting a neat parade, he asked his models to improvise. The girls went wild—clowning, dancing the cancan, doing the rumba, somersaulting, waving sparklers, showering each other with confetti, and baring their breasts. The conservative Parisian and worldwide fashion audience had never seen anything like it before. A dress from Kenzo's 1976 collection is shown in Figure 1.9. After Kenzo, the rules changed. There were no runway rules.

In 1973, Versailles once again became the center of the fashion world's attention at the *Grand Divertissement à Versailles*, which set five young "Studio 54" American ready-to-wear designers against five "French Lions of the French Haute Couture" (Tiffany, 2011). The American designers included Halston, Oscar de la Renta, Bill Blass, Anne Klein, and Stephen Burrows, while the French team included Yves Saint Laurent, Marc Bohan, designer for the House of Christian Dior, Hubert de Givenchy, Emanuel Ungaro, and Pierre Cardin. Many journalists and audience members thought the Americans represented the future wave of fashion, knocking out the declining world of haute couture. Many attendees and journalists suggested that American fashion came of age at that moment, with their bare, modern stage, and their secret weapon, a vibrant group of 36 models, half of them African American and Asian (Fig. 1.10).

The fashion show as a carnival, with punk fashion influenced by street wear, was the atmosphere created by British designer Vivienne Westwood in the 1980s (Quick, 1997). Westwood fused the rebellious styles of the street with tribal and historical costume, attracting a fanatical cult following. Each year the models adopted a different guise, and with that guise the models adopted a different set of poses and gestures.

It was during the 1980s that John Galliano presented his first show. In 1984, Galliano's graduation collection from Central Saint Martins, entitled "Les Incroyables," foretold of how different his approach would be (Quick, 1997).

Helmut Newton/ Vogue © Condé Nast 1973

Figure 1.10
American models helped put American fashion designers on the international fashion map during the Grand Divertissement à Versailles.

His models looked like women resurrected from the French Revolution, as they drifted down the runway barefoot, eyes whitened with pale mascara, in tattered clothes sprinkled with dust and cobwebs. Each season a different set of characters emerged from Galliano. The 1980s were a decade of excess, and everything, including fashion shows, got bigger. Fashion became a global force, with designers licensing their names to perfume, accessories, cosmetics, and even chocolate and wine. The consumer became aware of the biannual fashion events through television coverage, turning the collection presentations into major media events. Satellite and television stations broadcast the collections worldwide, showing celebrities and fashion editors in front-row seats. There were 1,875 journalists and 150 photographers in attendance at the Paris shows in 1986, nearly four times greater than those who attended in 1976 (Quick, 1997). The European fashion shows were no longer the private reserve of the high fashion clients and fashion journalists. Now everyone knew about these exciting presentations.

French designers Thierry Mugler and Claude Montana produced fashion shows of monumental proportions. Dazzling light shows and epic soundtracks sparked their shows. Mugler's shows became so popular that he attracted 4,000 paying guests to a grand spectacular in 1984 (Quick, 1997). Montana sent his battalions of models onto a runway in clouds created by dry ice. Montana's strong silhouette, with "football" shoulders, from his 1984 collection

Figure 1.11
Claude Montana's 1984 fashion show featured models that walked the runway wearing bright colors and strong shapes.

No modeling!
Thank you—you are all beautiful and we love you. (Quick, 1997, p. 174)

Minimalist designers such as Zoran were able to buck the traditional fashion system, gaining success during the end of the 20th century without advertising, courting celebrities, or putting on fashion shows. His styles changed very little in his more than 20 years in business; his line consisted of a collection of minimally cut garments without zippers or buttons in four or five solid colors. Zoran used expensive fabrics, for example, cashmere and Tasmanian wool, to construct separates that cost $3,000 for a two- or three-piece ensemble (Horyn, 1999). Even with those high prices and styles that compared to an upscale Gap, Zoran attracted a loyal following of customers.

In contrast to the minimalist trends of the 1990s, John Galliano led the trend to "over the top" French shows, when he was appointed as the head designer of Dior (Design Museum, n.d.). Galliano's first haute couture collection for Dior was held at the Grand Hotel in Paris in 1997. The ground floor replicated Christian Dior's late 1940s showroom on Avenue Montaigne with 791 gold chairs and 4,000 roses. During his tenure as the couturier for Dior, Galliano created some of the most innovative fashion designs and fashion shows.

is illustrated in Figure 1.11. Fashion shows became increasingly fantastic and ostentatious, as designers were attempting to woo the cameras for publicity. International models on the runway seemed to guarantee camera appeal and media coverage.

Reality hit the fashion scene in the 1990s. Real fashion, consisting of minimal and urban clothes similar to those found at the Gap, was shown on the runway. There was a trend toward using typical-looking girls as models. At his 1996 runway show, American designer Marc Jacobs pinned up the following sign in the dressing room:

> *Boys and Girls*
> *Please walk at a natural pace—not slow, not fast*
> *Please no hands on hips*
> *No "turns"*

Fashion shows at the start of the 21st century became media spectacles again, departing from the minimalist approach taken by many designers in the 1990s. Dutch design team Viktor & Rolf (Viktor Horsting and Rolf Snoeren) shocked their Paris audience with an all-black collection worn by white models painted black (Fig. 1.12). Attempting to delve into the nature of shadow and light, the team did not anticipate the mixed reaction to their show. The girls were said to look beautiful and intriguing, but however unintentional, the connection to blackface and racially insensitive minstrel shows could not be missed (Foley, 2001).

Fashion Associations

As the American ready-to-wear industry was taking shape in the early years of the 20th century, American manufacturers used live models to present the latest collections at the major regional trade marts. The most important trade shows were held in Chicago and New York.

The Merchandise Buyers Exposition and Fashion Show at the New Grand Central Palace, held in 1912 in New York, staged two live fashion parades daily (Diehl, 1976). While a local orchestra played the popular songs of the day, live models walked across a stage carrying cards with simply the manufacturer's name indicated. No evidence of commentary was reported at this time.

In 1914, the Chicago Garment Manufacturers Association presented an elaborate fashion show to the 5,000 people attending this market. One hundred mannequins showed 250 garments in nine scenes. The rehearsal was filmed and distributed to local theaters across the United States. This show used a stage and a large platform or runway to bring the clothing closer to the audience. This was perhaps the first use of a fashion show "runway" (Corinth, 1970).

Edna Woolman Chase, then editor of *Vogue* magazine (Fig. 1.13), combined several elements, including trade shows, society leaders, and a charitable benefit for a wartime cause, into the first major fashion show for the public. On November 4, 1914, the Fashion Fête was produced, featuring

Courtesy of WWD/Giovanni Giannoni

Figure 1.12
Viktor & Rolf created quite a controversy when they painted their models' faces black for their Fall 2001 fashion show.

Conde Nast Archive

Figure 1.13
Vogue editor-in-chief Edna Woolman Chase with Mela Underwood broadcasting on the radio.

American designs at a time when Paris was threatened by World War I. The show was held as a benefit for widows and orphans of the allied countries. With the assistance and patronage of the society women of the day, *Vogue* presented fashions at a gala event held at the Ritz-Carlton hotel. Clothing from Henri Bendel, a leading fashion retailer of the time, was selected by a committee of seven society women as well as Mrs. Chase and Helen Koues, also from *Vogue*. The evening started with dinner, followed by a fashion show and, later, dancing. The show was repeated for two days in the afternoons and evenings.

Vogue advertised for models for the *Fashion Fête*. At this time no formal schools existed for models and dressmaker models. Further, although they were an integral part of French couture, models were employed by only a few New York dressmakers. The applicants were rehearsed by *Vogue* and instructed how to walk, pivot, and show the garments. The following year, partly because of the influence of the first *Fête*, mannequins as models started to become an important factor in the American fashion scene (Chase & Chase, 1954). The use of the fashion show to raise money for philanthropic organizations was common throughout the 20th century and continues in the 21st century.

One group that helped to set high standards for professionalism in the production of fashion shows was the Fashion Group International, which was founded in 1928 by 17 women fashion executives (Corinth, 1970). One of the purposes of the group then, as it is now, was to provide a central source of information on fashion trends. Fashion shows for members and guests were presented almost from the beginning of the organization. The first *Fashion Futures* event was held on September 11, 1935. It was described as the first un-propagandized, un-commercialized, and un-subsidized fashion show ever presented.

The Fashion Group International, Inc., had more than 5,000 members in 33 regional groups by 2011 (Fashion Group International, 2012). Members can be found in various regional groups in the United States, as well

international chapters in Australia, Canada, Columbia, Dominican Republic, Mexico, Korea, Japan, South America, and the United Kingdom. Membership is made up of women and men with executive status, representing the fields of fashion, cosmetics, and the home.

Various volunteer committees provide unique programs. The most important international programs are the multimedia presentations of seasonal fashion trends from New York, Paris, London, and Milan. The visual programs and print *Trend Reports* are available to all members in regional groups who take on fashion leadership roles in the various markets. For example, the Fashion Group International of Dallas has sponsored an annual *Career Day Dallas* for over 40 years. It is the longest-running fashion career event of its kind in the country, attracting more than 1,100 students and faculty. The full day of seminars, exhibits, and keynote speakers culminates with a spectacular runway fashion show featuring professional models wearing the designs of the winners of the fashion design scholarship competition, which comprises several categories. Winners of the various design competitions earn scholarships as well as trips to Paris.

In the late 1930s and early 1940s, the world was facing the start of World War II. The American garment industry and its designers were virtually unknown on the international stage. Eleanor Lambert was the woman who created the job of fashion publicist in the United States. Miss Lambert, who lived to be 100 years old, helped make the American fashion industry and its designers competitive in the international market.

According to John Tiffany (2011), Eleanor Lambert's biographer, she took on her first fashion clients in the 1930s.

Miss Lambert devoted the rest of her life to promoting the American fashion industry and promoting fashion designers as artists. Until then, the industry was disorganized and disjointed. American fashion designers were basically unknown employees in the manufacturing process. Miss Lambert worked with the New York Dress Institute, an unlikely partnership between the International Ladies Garment Workers Union (ILGWU) and Seventh Avenue clothing manufacturers. One of her innovative ideas was to promote the fashion designers at the first American Fashion Press Week, which took place in January 1943. For the first time in history, lifestyle and fashion newspaper editors from around the United States were invited to an organized schedule of fashion shows, introducing the latest fashion designs. The 53 editors, whose expenses were paid by the New York Dress Institute, previewed the collections a full 6 months in advance of the season in which the garments would be worn. The editors were provided press releases and photographs to be included in the stories they wrote for their local papers. Miss Lambert's organization was careful to send different photographs to the various newspapers, ensuring exclusivity and an air of sophistication for the American designers.

The New York Fashion Press Week event initiated the biannual shows, known as New York Fashion Week. By the end of the 20th century, Fern Mallis, who was the executive director of the Council of Fashion Designers of America (CFDA) in the 1990s (discussed in Chapter 2), was playing a role in centralizing the New York fashion shows in the tents at Bryant Park. She has been widely credited for making this week the huge news media spectacle it is today (Morris, 2012). She offered this advice to people entering the fashion business.

Mademoiselle A was a public relations intern for MAO PR during Fall Fashion Week in 2004. She tells us about her responsibilities in Notes from the Runway: My First Fashion Show on page 28.

Another famous organization supporting fashion as art and fashion designers as artists is the Costume Institute of the Metropolitan Museum of Art, founded in 1946 when the Museum of Costume Art merged with the Met (Metropolitan Museum of Art, 2011a). The Costume Institute gained international recognition for its memorable costume exhibitions, which set standards for costume exhibits around the world.

The Costume Institute benefits from strong support from the fashion industry. The annual fund-raising event for the Costume Institute began as a midnight supper in 1948, a publicity idea from Eleanor Lambert. The event, which Miss Lambert called the *Party of the Year*, has grown into one of the most visible and successful charity events in the world, attracting an unsurpassed group of participants from fashion, film, society, business, and the music industry. Now the *Gala Benefit* is held each May and celebrates the opening of the Costume Institute's spring exhibition.

As we discussed earlier, the *Grand Divertissement à Versailles* was a fashion show that

> ATTENTION young fashion designers, editors, bloggers, stylists and others gearing up for New York Fashion Week: "Be Nice. You never know where anyone will end up in this business."
>
> —Fern Mallis, executive director of the CFDA

helped put American fashion designers in competition with the French couture designers. This was another fashion event initiated by Eleanor Lambert, along with Gerald Van der Kemp, the French curator of Versailles, to help raise money for the restoration of Versailles (Tiffany, 2011). *Women's Wear Daily* declared the event was "The Battle of Versailles" on the cover of the November 36, 1973, edition of the paper.

The Costume Institute of the Metropolitan Museum of Art honored the original event on two different occasions. First, in 1993, American fashion designers were featured in the exhibition *Versailles 1973, Top American Fashion on the World Stage* (Morris, 1993). This exhibition was held on the 20th anniversary of the original event and featured 110 styles from the "Versailles Five," as well as other mid-20th-century American designers, including Claire McCardell, James Galanos, Pauline Trigère, and Norman Norell. The second event, *The Models of Versailles 1973 Tribute Luncheon*, was held in 2011 (Metropolitan Museum of Art, 2011b). The contributions of eight of the original multicultural models, including Billie Blair, Jennifer Bryce, Alva Chin, Pat Cleveland, Norma Jean Darden, Charlene Dash, Bethann Hardison, China Machado, and Amina Warsuma, along with designers Oscar de la Renta, Steven Burrows, and Donna Karan, who was Anne Klein's assistant in 1973, were recognized at a luncheon held at the museum.

Fashion Shows at Retail Stores

Retail stores also used the fashion show as a method of promoting the latest fashions to their customers. English dressmaker Lucile, also known as Lady Duff Gordon, used mannequin parades for her clients at her shop in London starting in approximately 1897, according to Christopher Breward and Caroline Evans (2005). Lucile had previously created theater costumes. She used her knowledge of theatrical elements, such as building a stage in her shop and training her mannequins in posture and style, to make her mannequin parades memorable.

In his study on the rise of capitalism in the United States, William Leach (1993) reported that the first fashion shows produced in America were put on at Ehrich Brothers, a retail store in New York City, in 1903. Ehrich Brothers, influenced by the intimate Paris fashion parades, presented live models to upper-middle-class women in the store.

Wanamaker's stores in Philadelphia and New York held many innovative shows. In 1908, the *Fashion Fête de Paris* was held in the Philadelphia store's theater, decorated in gold and red, suggesting the court of Napoleon and Josephine (Leach, 1993). The fashion show's director, Mary Wall, placed giant picture frames trimmed in black velvet on each side of the theater. Inside the frames, live mannequins, wearing the latest Paris gowns, posed. As the script was read to the audience, the models stepped out from the frames, escorted by a child dressed as one of Napoleon's pages. After a walk down the runway to organ music, the models posed. The show's finale was a full-scale re-creation of the coronation of Napoleon and Josephine.

By 1910, many big department stores were holding shows of their own to attract middle-class female customers. Gimbels presented its first *Promenade des Toilettes* in 1910. Thousands of women came into the Manhattan store to watch models parade up and down ramps, wearing the newest Paris fashions. Most department stores highlighted the mannequin parades with music, lighting effects, and sometimes used a specially constructed ramp or stage.

Many retail stores opened in-store tea rooms or restaurants as a service to customers in the 20th century. With ladies stopping for tea or lunch, retailers started offering informal fashion shows for entertainment and to generate interest in the latest fashions. This type of informal fashion show is referred to as **tea-room modeling**. The store selected three to five models, perhaps store employees, who were fitted into outfits prior to the show. During the show, the models walked from table to table showing what they were wearing, careful to interact only with interested patrons. Tea-room modeling remained popular at both in-store eating establishments and independent restaurants during the 20th century.

During most of the 20th century, fashion shows were regularly held at retail stores in the United States, Paris, and London. Fashionable customers enjoyed the entertainment and education provided by these events. Figure 1.14 shows models from a Washington, D.C., clothing shop after they had presented merchandise to the store's customers.

Models and Supermodels

As we previously indicated, Marie Vernet was probably the first fashion model, as the muse of her husband, Charles Fredrick Worth. However, she was accepted into society as Worth's wife, not as a model. Fashion models during the first part of the 20th century were viewed as figures of scorn and scandal (Quick, 1997). It was not until after World War I that the status of fashion modeling improved and was considered an appropriate career for young women.

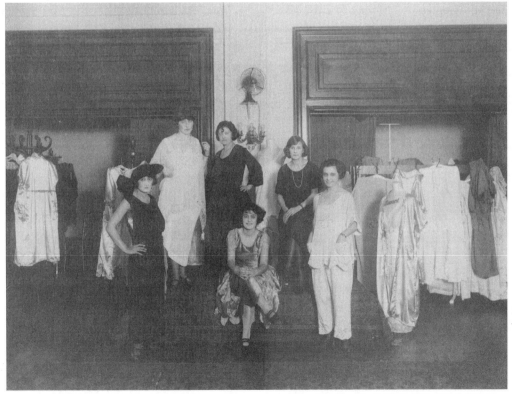

Figure 1.14
Models pose during a 1921 fashion show for the Wells Shop of Washington, D.C. This early specialty store featured corsets, brassieres, hats, and bonnets.

Reproduced from the Collections of the Library of Congress.

High society women, wives of millionaires, and the popular actresses from stage and screen became the fashion models, or **mannequins du monde**, as they were known, in the 1930s. Dressed by couturiers, pressured to appear in the pages of *Vogue* and *Harper's Bazaar*, and complimented in society columns, these women were offered free clothing in exchange for their loyalty and promotion of the designer's clothes (Quick, 1997). Society women were year-round walking advertisements for fashion, resulting in an improved image for fashion models. The professional model was quickly in demand.

The fashion model in the 1950s became the public image of fashion, and girls flocked to New York, London, and Paris to enter the glamorous world of fashion. Names of the popular models of the era, including Suzy Parker and Dovima, were known due to various magazine articles, how-to books, and autobiographies. Models found work as

house or fit models for specific designers, runway models for retail stores such as Harvey Nichols in London and Neiman Marcus in Dallas, or as photographic models.

London was the place to be in the 1960s. Jean Shrimpton and Twiggy became international fashion icons. Models were the center of media attention and the symbol of the pop generation. Rock stars dated and sometimes married the popular models of the era. George Harrison of the Beatles married top model Patti Boyd, which contributed to the growing interdependence of music and fashion.

Starting with Lauren Hutton (Fig. 1.15), who became the face of Revlon cosmetics for a record $400,000 in 1973, American models dominated the fashion scene in the 1970s (Quick, 1997). Cover Girl signed Cheryl Tiegs for a staggering $1.5 million, while Fabergé paid Margaux Hemingway $3 million for an exclusive contract. This media

Figure 1.15
Lauren Hutton (pictured here with Calvin Klein) became the face of the 1970s when her modeling salary skyrocketed after she was offered an exclusive deal from Revlon.

Courtesy of WWD/Pierre Scherman

exposure led these models to acting roles in addition to their lucrative modeling careers.

Fashion in the 1970s also had an appetite for the exotic, as we learned from the fashion show event *Battle of Versailles*, which took place in 1973. Ethnic beauties broke into the business. This led the way for such multicultural icons as Somali-born Iman, the beautiful daughter of a diplomat, who went on to become one of the highest paid models ever. It was reported that she earned $100,000 for doing a Munich runway show, compared to the $1,500 paid to other models at the time (Quick, 1997). Pat Cleveland, one of the models at the Versailles show, was among the first black runway models, and Beverly Johnson became the first black model to appear on the cover of American *Vogue*.

Nearly 100 years after the first models were picked from among the shopgirls and seamstresses working for Charles Frederick Worth and paid wages on a par with a floor sweeper, the celebrity supermodels emerged.

The top fashion models of the 1980s included Kim Alexis, Carol Alt, Christie Brinkley, Gia Carangi, Kathy Ireland, Elle Macpherson, Paulina Porizkova, Brooke Shields, and Cheryl Tiegs. Many of these models became household names after appearing in or on the cover of the *Sports Illustrated, Swimsuit Edition*, which is published annually.

The 1990s supermodels—Naomi Campbell, Cindy Crawford, Linda Evangelista, Christy Turlington (Fig. 1.16), Elle Macpherson, and Claudia Schiffer—became the fashion idols of their time. Their popularity and salaries exceeded those of rock stars and Hollywood celebrities. Linda Evangelista gained a reputation for being arrogant when she remarked, "We have this expression, Christy and I: We don't wake up for less than $10,000 a day" (Quick, 1997, p. 149).

The top five models from the Forbes List of Highest Paid Models include Gisele Bündchen, Heidi Klum, Kate Moss, Adriana Lima, and Alessandra Ambrosio (Blankfeld &

MARKA/Alamy

Figure 1.16
Supermodels from the 1990s pose with Italian designer Gianni Versace.

Bertoni, 2011). Brazilian-born Bündchen was the face of numerous campaigns and endorsements with such firms as H&M, Dior, Procter & Gamble, and Versace, throughout the United States, Europe, Asia, and Latin America, earning her $45 million a year. Heidi Klum, the next-highest-paid model, earned $20 million during the same time period. German-born Klum transformed her traditional modeling days into hosting television shows such as *Project Runway* and *Germany's Next Top Model*, designing activewear, and endorsing brands. British model Kate Moss is a fashion world double threat, landing richly paid modeling jobs as well as designing for TopShop, the UK retailer. Adriana Lima and Alessandra Ambrosio, also born in Brazil, were the fourth- and fifth-highest paid models, known as Victoria Secret's catwalk and catalogue modeling superstars.

Modeling Agencies

John Robert Powers is credited as having started the first modeling agency in 1923. According to Michael Gross (1995), Powers and his wife, Alice Hathaway Burton, were out-of-work actors who were asked to find models to pose for commercial photographers. Realizing that photographers needed models for a rapidly growing advertising industry and knowing many unemployed actors and actresses, they created a business to bring the two together. Powers had pictures taken of his models, put together a catalogue containing their descriptions and measurements, and sent the catalogues to anyone in New York—photographers, department stores, advertisers, and artists—who might be prospective clients. While the first model book contained only 40 models, this project spurred an entire industry of modeling schools and agencies.

In Europe, modeling agencies evolved from charm schools. In 1928, Sylvia Gollidge, a former department store model from Blackpool, England, opened Lucie Clayton, a charm school in London (Quick, 1997). Gollidge charged the girls, or their parents, fees to become more socially proficient. The charm school owner and teacher promised to turn any young girl into a lady through her classes in deportment, basic elocution, and social manners. Such charm schools opened throughout Europe and America, expanding the girls' education into modeling techniques such as posing, applying makeup, and dressing quickly.

American Eileen Ford set up a model-booking agency in 1946 (Gross, 1995). As a former model, Ford and her partner, husband Jerry, recognized the special needs of models and their career development. She provided training and professional advice to her models. With her hands-on management style, Ford turned modeling into a more respectable career, and she turned her modeling agency into a powerful player in the fashion industry. The Ford Agency grew to become one of the largest international agencies, with several offices in the United States, Europe, Canada, and South America. The Ford Agency set the standards in an industry that has become highly lucrative.

The Ford Modeling Agency, founded in New York, and the Marilyn Agency, founded in Paris, were determined to be the most influential modeling agencies in the world (Elliot, 2011). Data were compiled by Klout, a San Francisco company that studies social media. Klout's analysts combed through records from Facebook, Twitter, and Tumblr to determine which modeling agencies had the most influence in the world of modeling that year. Researchers analyzed which agencies provided live tweets from fashion week and were socializing with powerful industry insiders and celebrities. They also looked at which models from each agency were highlighted in social media.

Celebrities and Fashion Shows

Hollywood and the entertainment industry have maintained a symbiotic relationship with fashion since movies became mass distributed. Hair and makeup trends were the primary fashion influence emanating from Hollywood in the 1920s and 1930s. Americans who watched Hollywood movies learned styles from the popular actresses, starting with Clara Bow, and later were influenced by such beautiful women as Joan Crawford, Jean Harlow, Marilyn Monroe, Lauren Bacall, Audrey Hepburn, and Mia Farrow.

Actresses and entertainers learned about the power of clothing from the preeminent Hollywood costume designers, including Edith Head, Adrian, Helen Rose, and Bob Mackie. During the era when powerful movie studios dominated the movie industry, actresses would be dressed for various events by the studios' costume and makeup departments. For Academy Award–winning actress Grace Kelly's 1956 marriage to Prince Rainier of Monaco, Metro-Golden-Mayer left nothing to chance. The studio asked its costume designer, Helen Rose, to create two dresses. She designed a rose-pink taffeta dress covered in Alençon lace for Grace Kelly to wear to the civil ceremony (Diehl & Diehl, 2007). For the Catholic High Mass held on the day after the civil ceremony, Mrs. Rose created Grace Kelly's formal wedding gown. The high-necked, long-sleeved feminine and elegant dress, valued at $7,200, was the most expensive dress Mrs. Rose ever designed.

Another example of the connection between film and fashion is portrayed in the 1957 movie *Funny Face*. Audrey Hepburn portrays a bookstore beauty who becomes a reluctant fashion model. Miss Hepburn's character was inspired by Doe Avedon, a fashion model, actress, and former wife of fashion photographer Richard Avedon (Fox, 2011). This real-life to reel-life depiction of a fashion model also featured Dovima as a ditsy fashion model. The French fashions modeled by Audrey Hepburn in the Paris scenes, as shown in Figure 1.17, were created by Hubert de Givenchy and a friendship developed between the movie star and the fashion designer that lasted until the end of the star's life.

The biggest Hollywood and fashion event held each year is the Academy Awards ceremony, which, in addition to recognizing the outstanding costume design for a movie, prominently portrays the glamorous stars as fashion leaders when they present and receive awards. Leaving nothing to chance,

AF archive/Alamy

Figure 1.17
Audrey Hepburn played a reluctant fashion model in the film *Funny Face*.

the Hollywood studios dressed the actors and actresses for the Oscar ceremony throughout its early years.

Later in the 20th century, international fashion designers started interacting with Hollywood stars more frequently. According to Patty Fox (2000), Italian fashion designer Giorgio Armani had always been a fan of Hollywood and the movies, creating Oscar-night clothing for Diane Keaton in 1978 and designing film images for Richard Gere in *American Gigolo* in 1980. With sales of $90 million the year after that movie was released, Armani and his competitors saw the significance of courting Hollywood stars. Armani went on to dress such stars as Jodie Foster, Mira Sorvino, and Michelle Pfeiffer for their Oscar appearances.

Today, Oscar-nominated actresses and presenters have unlimited choices of dresses and jewelry to wear on such occasions.

Courtesy of WWD/Donato Sardella

Figure 1.18
The Academy Awards' Red Carpet is a fashion runway for celebrities and the designers who create the garments. Actress Milla Jovovich, shown here, is wearing a white gown by Elie Saab Couture.

Academy Awards shows feature celebrities being interviewed on the Red Carpet. This has become a fashion show accessible to anyone with a television or Internet connection. Celebrities are viewed wearing some of the latest designs, many of them transported from the haute couture shows held a month earlier than the television broadcast. When interviewer Joan Rivers began asking celebrities, "Who are you wearing?" the concept of celebrity and fashion designer became forever linked. Figure 1.18 shows Milla Jovovich posing for photographs at the Academy Awards show.

Fashionable actresses realized that by attending the designers' fashion shows, they might end up on the cover of *Women's Wear Daily*, *W*, or *InStyle*, a publicity win for both the actress and designer. Front-row seats at fashion shows, once reserved for significant fashion editors and private clients, are now shared with celebrities such as Penelope Cruz, Uma Thurman, Natalie Portman, Michelle Williams, and Nicole Kidman.

In an ultimate collaboration between celebrity, fashion, and film, Tom Ford decided he wanted to fulfill his lifelong ambition to be a film director (Church Gibson, 2012). Ford had earlier gained celebrity status as the fashion designer for Gucci, created outrageous advertising campaigns, guest-edited *Vanity Fair* magazine, and designed clothing for his extraordinarily expensive menswear shops. He bought the rights to Christopher Isherwood's 1960s novel, *A Single Man*. Ford adapted the book into a film starring Colin Firth. The film was nominated for several awards, including a Best Actor nomination for Colin Firth at the Academy Awards.

With Paul McCartney's daughter Stella gaining an international reputation as a fashion designer, with such models as Heidi

Klum becoming clothing designers, and with fashion designers presenting dramatic and theatrical fashion shows, the interrelationship of the fields of entertainment and fashion are forever dependent upon each other. Exciting fashion design, electrifying music, and fantastic staging are all components of the fashion show in the 21st century.

Digital Fashion Shows

Fashion show audience participation was expanded to anyone with a television or Internet access by the end of the 20th century. Victoria's Secret invited the 1999 Superbowl audience to watch its live fashion show, broadcast on the Internet during the week following the sporting event (Farrell, 1999). More than two million people turned on their computers to watch, causing the system to overload.

Since then, innovators such as Saks Fifth Avenue and Ralph Lauren have expanded the use of virtual fashion shows. Saks Fifth Avenue projected the Spring 2001 New York fashion shows onto the façade of its flagship store on Fifth Avenue. An advertisement in the *New York Times* invited consumers to get a ringside seat to see the shows. Ralph Lauren launched a website to allow customers to look at his fashion shows, hair and makeup trends, and behind-the-scenes activities, and to buy merchandise. Fashion retailer Forever 21 hosted a series of digital fashion shows that used holographic images instead of live models (Irwin, 2011). The first show was scheduled when the retailer opened its flagship store in Vienna. Holographic images walked the runway, wearing the firm's new line. The images disappeared into starbursts and climbed imaginary steps. This holographic show was attended by members of the media as well as consumers, who were invited after becoming "friends" of the retailer on its Facebook page.

Any search for fashion shows on YouTube, Facebook, or Twitter will provide you with access to the latest fashion shows. Some of them are presented as a webcast at the same time they are shown live. The 21st century continues to offer many new ways to become involved in fashion shows and events.

Despite the expense, stress, and overall craziness associated with fashion show production, these events continue to attract media attention and large audiences. Media coverage and consumer accessibility to international fashion productions through the Internet continue to make these events popular.

My First Fashion Show
Mademoiselle A: PR Intern

Courtesy of WWD/John Aquino

For my fifth birthday, my parents had a pool party to celebrate with our family and friends. One would assume that all those attending would be ready to go in a swimsuit, but I (the fashion diva of my family) insisted on wearing a bright red party dress while everyone else swam in the pool. I was incredibly happy watching all my guests swim while I kept my distance to protect my gorgeous party dress. I think most fashionistas are born with a love of fashion in their blood—wanting to explore it and flourish in it!

So let's fast-forward a few years to my college life—I attended the Laboratory Institute of Merchandising (LIM) in New York City. LIM is devoted to the business of fashion and offers majors in fashion merchandising, management, marketing, and visual merchandising. I was a fashion marketing major and was incredibly lucky to experience the most amazing internships. My first one was with a small, up-and-coming public relations firm called MAO PR. At the time, their client list included Heatherette, Gary Graham, DIMMER DVRS, and Duckie Brown. My daily tasks started out quite small—getting coffee, doing mailings, and keeping the showroom clean. As my first fashion week approached, the daily office tasks increased in both scale and importance; as interns we had to ensure that all invitations were sealed and delivered to each guest. Once all invitations were in the mail, we patiently waited for RSVPs to come in. This was an exciting time! The anticipation of who would be attending was quite intense . . . would Anna Wintour come? Would the Olsen twins make an appearance?

One of the first and most important steps in preparing for a fashion show is to confirm a location. This is crucial because of the large amount of factors that tie in with production of the show—seating space, photographer space, lighting, acoustics, backstage, and more. Will the space be able to accommodate every need? Once the location is finalized, it is time for the seating assignments to be completed. This task can be quite difficult because A-list guests must always be given a front row seat! You must be very careful to not upset or offend a stylist, editor, or celebrity. Having the right people, in the right place, at the right time makes all the difference. So, my final task in helping with the seating assignments was calling each guest to let them know where they would be seated. The funniest thing about this is that it was okay to call people at 2 a.m. the same morning as the show to let them know where they would be sitting. Shocking but true!

At the same time the seating charts have been created, model castings and hair/makeup trials have been happening. Weeks before the show, models are in and out of the PR show-room exhibiting their best walk and displaying their best smile for the camera. Models are chosen to show off the best side of a designer's garment. And during my first fashion week, our most important show was for Heatherette, a fashion company and design house located in New York City that was run by Traver Rains and former Club Kid Richie Rich. Heatherette started with a bang in 1999 when they began collaborating on T-shirts and leather goods as a hobby on their living room floor. They were discovered when Richie Rich wore one of their leather tops to a party and a buyer at the downtown Manhattan Patricia Field store noticed and ordered 20 on the spot. For Heatherette, the main model was Anna Nicole Smith. This amazingly voluptuous and stunning woman was able to walk the runway incredibly well. Her passion for fashion and life exuded with every step she took.

Leading up to this main show, the suspense was incredible. Outside the venue, a line formed quickly and the door was carefully guarded so that no guests were let in too early. The finalized guest list was in the hands of the most experienced intern who would make sure that only those on the list were let into the show. (I remember that this intern had her own "assistant intern" who watched her every move, in hopes she would one day be holding a guest list of her own. She eventually did . . . but that is another story.)

While the line was forming, the drama behind the scenes grew! Models were being primped, prepped, and organized. Each garment of clothing was being steamed and meticulously checked for snags, rips, and other imperfections. Photographers were anxiously waiting in their designated spots at the end of the runway. All the interns were checking the seats, gift bags, and anything else they could think of—everything needed to be perfect!

All that show preparation and organization—and then it was over in about 20 minutes! This timing does vary, depending on how many looks a designer will decide to show. Of course, the last look is usually the best! For Heatherettte, Anna Nicole Smith was the final model. She wore a sleek Marilyn Monroe–inspired fuchsia dress and rocked the runway!

After the show, the interns were in charge of getting the venue back into place for the next show to be held. As I walked around and took in the experience of my first fashion show, I knew that I was in the right place and one day my name would be on the guest list . . . receiving that 2 a.m. call with my seating assignment.

After completing several industry internships, Mademoiselle A graduated from Laboratory Institute of Merchandising. She remained in New York and works in fashion marketing as an account manager.

Fashion Dolls, Supermodels, and Celebrities—A Recap

- Fashion shows are events where the latest fashion, fabric, and color trends in apparel and accessories are presented to an audience using live models.
- Fashion dolls are miniature, to scale figures wearing replicas of the latest clothing, even though some of the early dolls were actually full size.
- "Fashion Parades" first took place at the Galerie des Glaces (Hall of Mirrors) at Versailles, during the reign of King Louis XVI and his wife, Marie Antoinette.
- Petits mannequins, or fashion dolls, were revived for the exhibition called *Théâtre de la Mode* after the end of World War II.
- Fashion designers who influenced the history of fashion shows include Charles Frederick Worth, Paul Poiret, Madame Jeanne Paquin, Jean Patou, Christian Dior, Mary Quant, Kenzo, Halston, Oscar de la Renta, Bill Blass, Anne Klein, Stephen Burrows, Vivienne Westwood, Thierry Mugler, Claude Montana, John Galliano, Marc Jacobs, and Viktor Horsting and Rolf Snoeren.
- Fashion associations and events, which influenced the history of fashion show include the Merchandise Buyers Exposition and Fashion Show, Chicago Garment Manufacturers Association, *Vogue* magazine's Fashion Fête, Fashion Group International, the New York Dress Institute, and the Costume Institute of the Metropolitan Museum of Art.
- Retail stores that held innovative fashion shows in the 20th century include English dressmaker Lucile's, Ehrich Brothers in New York, and Wanamaker's in Philadelphia and New York.
- Models and supermodels who have contributed to fashion show excitement include Marie Vernet, Suzy Parker, Dovima, Jean Shrimpton, Twiggy, Patti Boyd, Lauren Hutton, Cheryl Tiegs, Margaux Hemingway, Iman, Pat Cleveland, Beverley Johnson, Naomi Campbell, Cindy Crawford, Linda Evangelista, Elle Macpherson, Claudia Schiffer, Christy Turlington, Gisele Bündchen, Heidi Klum, Kate Moss, Adriana Lima, and Alessandra Ambrosio.
- Modeling agencies that have increased the visibility of models and fashion shows include John Robert Powers, Lucie Clayton Charm School, and the Ford Modeling Agency.
- Celebrities who have contributed to the interaction between fashion, film, and public relations include Clara Bow, Joan Crawford, Jean Harlow, Marilyn Monroe, Lauren Bacall, Grace Kelly, Audrey Hepburn, Mia Farrow, Diane Keaton, Richard Gere, Jodie Foster, Mira Sorvino, Michelle Pfeiffer, Penelope Cruz, Uma Thurman, Natalie Portman, Michelle Williams, Nicole Kidman, Paul McCartney, Blake Lively, Rihanna, Sarah Jessica Parker, as well as Mary-Kate and Ashley Olsen.
- Digital fashion shows have been presented by Victoria's Secret, Saks Fifth Avenue, Ralph Lauren, and many other manufacturers, retail stores, and fashion designers.

Key Fashion Show Terms

directrice/directeur	mannequins
fashion dolls	mannequins du monde
fashion show	premier/premiere
finale	tea-room modeling

QUESTIONS FOR DISCUSSION

1. Did you have a fashion doll that you played with as a child? How do you think that influenced your interest in fashion?
2. Which French designer do you think had the most influence on the historical development of the fashion show?
3. Which American designer do you think had the most influence on the historical development of the fashion show?
4. Other than designers, what kinds of people or groups have contributed to the success of fashion shows?
5. What is the role of a modeling agency in fashion show development?
6. Have you ever watched a fashion show on the Internet? How did you feel about watching the event?

FASHION SHOW ACTIVITY

1. Select two or more fashion show videos from different decades of the 20th century on YouTube or any other websites or resources that are available to you. Write a report that compares and contrasts:
   - The types of clothing worn
   - The stage or lack of stage
   - How the models walk
   - The participation of the designer
   - The finale
2. *About Face: Supermodels Then and Now*, the documentary by Timothy Greenfield-Sanders, profiles some of the most well known fashion models of the 20th century. *Versailles '73: American Runway Revolution*, the documentary by Deborah Riley Draper, profiles *Le Grand Divertissement à Versailles* and features interviews with some of the models. After watching either film, write a one-page summary discussing your favorite model from the documentary and list her contributions to the fashion industry.

THE CAPSTONE PROJECT

It is time to start planning your fashion show. It will be helpful to decide what you want to accomplish with your show. Historical information is a good place to start.

If you are a student enrolled in a fashion show production class, investigate the history of fashion shows that have been held at your school. If you are a member of a charitable organization, investigate the history of your group's prior events. Here are some types of questions that you should be able to answer:

- When was the first show produced?
- What were the reasons for producing the fashion shows?
- What type of merchandise was presented?

- How many people participated in the production and what types of activities did they contribute?
- Where and when was the show (or shows) held?
- How many people attended?

After you have completed your preliminary research, write a report about the background of your school's or organization's fashion show history. Discuss the successes and challenges of doing a live performance to serve as inspiration for your upcoming show.

REFERENCES

Ballard, B. (1960). *In my fashion.* Philadelphia, PA: David McKay.

Bellisario, M. K. (2008). *Guida turistica per fashion victim. La moda a Milano, Firenze e Roma.* [Travel guide for fashion victim. The fashion in Milan, Florence and Rome]. Milan, Italy: Morellini Editore.

Bernier, O. (1981). *The eighteenth century woman.* New York, NY: Metropolitan Museum of Art.

Blankfeld, K., & Bertoni, S. (2011, May 5). The world's top earning models. *Forbes.* Retrieved from http://www.forbes.com

Breward, C., & Evans, C. (Eds.). (2005). *Fashion and modernity.* Oxford, England: Berg.

Chase, E. W., & Chase, I. (1954). *Always in Vogue.* New York, NY: Doubleday.

Church Gibson, P. (2012). *Fashion and celebrity culture.* London, UK: Berg.

Corinth, K. (1970). *Fashion showmanship.* New York, NY: Wiley.

Diderich, J. (2010, April 12). The onion. *WWD Collections,* p. 70.

Diehl, K., & Diehl, D. (2007). *Remembering Grace: 25 years later.* New York, NY: Time.

Diehl, M. E. (1976). *How to produce a fashion show.* New York, NY: Fairchild Books.

Design Museum. (n.d.). *John Galliano.* Retrieved from http://designmuseum.org/design/john-galliano

Elliot, H. (2011, September 13). The most influential modeling agencies. *Forbes.* Retrieved from http://www.forbes.com

Etherington-Smith, M. (1983). *Patou.* New York, NY: St. Martin's.

Evans, C. (2008). Jean Patou's American mannequins: Early fashion shows and modernism. *MODERNISM/ modernity, 15*(2), 243–263.

Fashion Group International. (2012). *Membership directory.* New York, NY: Author.

Farrell, G. (1999, February 8). Victoria's Secret weapon: Ad exec woman behind spots has been to bowl before. *USA Today,* p. B7.

Foley, B. (2001, April). Great expectations with their endless possibilities for intrigue, the collections are a thrill seeker's paradise. *Women's Wear Daily: The magazine,* pp. 45–48.

Fox, M. (2011, December 23). Doe Avedon, fashion model and actress, dies at 86. *The New York Times.* Retrieved from http://www.nytimes.com

Fox, P. L. (2000). *Star style at the Academy Awards.* Santa Monica, CA: Angel City.

Gadia-Smitley, R. (1987). History of the doll. *Dolls' clothes pattern book.* New York, NY: Sterling.

Gross, M. (1995). *Model: The ugly business of beautiful women.* New York, NY: Morrow.

Half-century Barbie. (2009, April 13). *WWD Collections,* p. 19.

Horyn, C. (1999, April 20). Zoran, the master of deluxe minimalism, still provokes. *The New York Times.* Retrieved from http://www.nytimes.com

Irwin, T. (2011, May 2). Forever 21 hosts holographic fashion shows. *MediaPost News.* Retrieved from http://www.mediapost.com

Leach, W. R., (1993). *Land of desire: Merchants, power, and the rise of a new American culture.* New York, NY: Pantheon Books.

Metropolitan Museum of Art. (2011a). *The Costume Institute.* Retrieved from http://www.metmuseum.org/about-the-museum/museum-departments/curatorial-departments/the-costume-institute

Metropolitan Museum of Art. (Producer). (2011b, January 24). *The models of Versailles 1973 tribute luncheon* [Video]. Retrieved from http://www.metmuseum.org/metmedia/video

Morris, B. (1993, September 10). Review/design: When America stole the runway from Paris couture. *The New York Times.* Retrieved from http://nytimes.com

Morris, B. (2012, February 7). Pitching a few new tents of her own. *The New York Times.* Retrieved from http://nytimes.com

Peers, J. (2004). *Fashion doll: From Bébé Jumeau to Barbie.* Oxford, England: Berg.

Quant, M. (1966). *Quant by Quant.* New York, NY: Putnam.

Quick, H. (1997). *Catwalking: A history of the fashion model.* Edison, NJ: Wellfleet Press.

Tiffany, J. A. (2011). *Eleanor Lambert: Still here.* New York, NY: Pointed Leaf Press.

Tortora, P. G., & Eubank, K. (2010). *Survey of historic costume: A history of Western dress* (5th ed.). New York, NY: Fairchild Books.

Train, S., & Braun-Munk, E. C. (Eds.). (2002). *Théâtre de la mode: Fashion dolls; the survival of haute couture.* Portland, OR: Palmer/Pletsch.

Weber, C. (2006). *Queen of fashion: What Marie Antoinette wore to the Revolution.* New York, NY: Holt.

What a doll. (1998, September). *Women's Wear Daily Century,* p. 98.

CHAPTER TWO
The Background

AFTER READING THIS CHAPTER, YOU SHOULD BE ABLE TO DISCUSS:

- Fashion shows as a promotion tool

- Reasons for producing fashion shows

- The differences between production, formal runway, and informal fashion shows

- Various types of specialized fashion presentations within the fashion industry

Alexander McQueen, Spring 2013. *Courtesy of WWD/Giovanni Giannoni*

As a fashion influencer, Miuccia Prada knows how to get attention for her menswear line: invite well-known Hollywood actors including Gary Oldman, Adrien Brody, and Tim Roth, among others, to walk the runway (Fig. 2.1). The show was the talk of Milan during fashion week. The fashion spectacular, dedicated to *power*, had the actors dressed in severe coats evoking Eastern Bloc military dress. The designer described the collection as a riff on powerful men, and on how fashion can telegraph authority, might, or supremacy. In Ms. Prada's words, "Clothing is also a tool of power and a way to express male vanity" ("Alpha Male," 2012, p. 7).

As illustrated in Chapter 1, fashion shows are full of entertainment and excitement. But before readers plunge into the details of producing a fashion show, some background information is necessary to understand the different types of fashion shows and how they are used as promotion tools. This chapter provides needed background information.

WHY PRODUCE FASHION SHOWS?

One of the most important reasons for producing a fashion show is to sell merchandise, as many of the examples in this chapter highlight. The fashion show helps to make an authoritative visual statement about fashion, making it one of the most exciting and dramatic forms of promotion. Each season designers and manufacturers create new lines to present to the buying public. An important step in the production process includes developing promotional materials to get the media's and the public's attention to view and buy the new collections. **Promotion** is a comprehensive term used to describe all communication activities initiated by the seller to inform, persuade, and remind the consumer about products, services, and/or ideas offered for sale (Swanson & Everett, 2007). It is a necessary function for the creators and distributors of fashion items. Fashion shows are important promotion tools used together with advertising, direct marketing and interactive media, sales promotion, public relations, personal selling, special events, and visual merchandising.

Figure 2.1
Actors Tim Roth, Adrien Brody, and Gary Oldman (left to right) wearing Prada on the runway.

Courtesy of WWD/Giovanni Giannoni

Promotion activities function at three market levels—national, trade, and retail, as illustrated in Figure 2.2. **National promotion** involves primary and secondary resources directing promotion activities to the consumer. **Primary resources** are raw materials producers such as textile firms and color agencies. **Secondary resources** are apparel and accessory designers and manufacturers. As part of a national promotion campaign, multiple channel representatives may partner both in financial support and production of a fashion show presentation, termed **cooperative promotion**, or **co-op**.

Manufacturers and retailers will sometimes join together to present a **cooperative fashion show** in which both parties share in the production costs of the show. Major fashion publications such as *W*, *Glamour*, and *Vogue* present fashion shows to consumers as **magazine tie-in** events. This is a cooperative fashion show because the retailer and magazine publisher share the cost of producing the show. These events are generally designed to improve fashion awareness, build loyalty for the brand, or increase the consumer's knowledge of the publication. Many publications have monthly columns dedicated to telling consumers which cities and retailers they will be visiting. *Vogue*'s Haute Stuff is an example of such a magazine feature.

In a unique cooperative venture, The Moms, a multi-platform lifestyle brand; maternity wear designer Shoshanna; national retailer Pea in the Pod; and Mom-entum, a woman-focused marketing channel within the social media agency Big Fuel joined forces to present *Strut: The Fashionable Mom Show* at Lin-

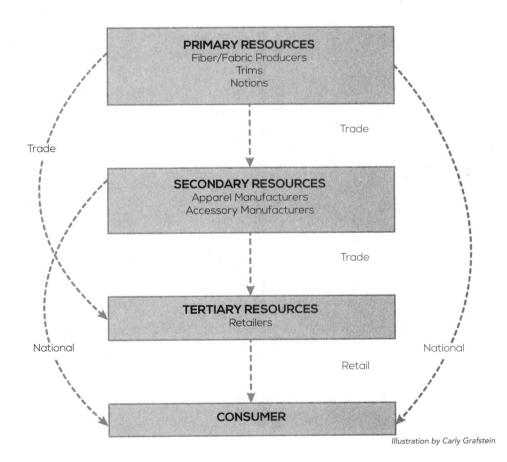

Illustration by Carly Grafstein

Figure 2.2
Market levels of national, trade, and retail promotion activities.

coln Center during Mercedes-Benz Fashion Week (Lockwood, 2012) (Fig. 2.3). The show creators including Denise Albert and Melissa Gerstein of The Moms, and Stephanie Winston Wolkoff, of Lincoln Center, wanted to provide moms with fashion ideas that demonstrated how to transform an outfit worn while hanging out with the kids, into something they could wear to a meeting or out for a night on the town. Real moms served as models.

Trade promotion, also known as *business-to-business (B2B)* promotion, includes activities that promote products from one business to another. Advertisements in *Women's Wear Daily* function as trade promotions, targeting other fashion businesses rather than the consumer market. Trade shows and trade associations, discussed later in this chapter, serve as examples of trade promotion. **Retail promotion** typically involves a retailer (**tertiary resource**) promoting its products directly to consumers, as discussed at the conclusion of this chapter.

Another reason for producing fashion shows is to share information. The latest trends in apparel, silhouettes, fabrics, or color can be communicated to employees or customers through this entertaining format. **In-store training fashion shows** are used to educate sales associates about trends and related promotions intended to highlight new merchandise. These shows may be live, videotaped, or digitally streamed to enable employees to see the trends and adapt the looks to their departments. In-store training shows help improve employee morale in addition to increasing their knowledge about products and upcoming events. Similarly, **instructional videos** are created for in-store training of sales personnel, and may also be given to customers. Customers can replay the video at home and practice the techniques highlighted in the video.

Still other reasons for producing fashion shows include attracting new customers, building traffic, or engaging returning customers. Retailers use fashion shows to solidify their position as a fashion authority and promote goodwill to their patrons. A retailer may invite a designer for a personal appearance in order to promote fashion leadership and increase sales for designer merchandise. Organizations use fashion shows as fundraising activities. Charitable groups use fashion shows for entertainment programming. To promote goodwill within a community, one or more retail stores may support charitable groups by lending clothing and accessories. In addition, a portion of the revenues may be contributed to the charitable group.

Fashion shows are also produced to provide training to fashion students. Nearly every fashion school or department produces a fashion show. This is the opportunity for fashion design students to show their creations. Modeling students have an oppor-

Figure 2.3
Melissa Gerstein and Denise Albert, founders of The Moms and creators of *Strut: The Fashionable Mom Show*, appear with Iman, the show's host, and Stephanie Winston Wolkoff, founding Fashion Director of Lincoln Center, at Mercedes-Benz Fashion Week.

© Everett Collection Inc/Alamy

tunity for practical application of their presentation skills. Merchandising students learn the behind-the-scenes responsibilities for organization, selection of merchandise and models, promotion, presentation, and evaluation of the show.

Students and faculty at the Shannon Rogers and Jerry Silverman School of Fashion Design and Merchandising at Kent State University produce an annual fashion show called *Portfolio*. The show, which features creations made by the fashion design majors, provides an opportunity to learn fashion show production in addition to recognizing outstanding students and alumni. *Portfolio* also raises money for scholarships. According to Lecturer Natalie Sanger Gendle, Iowa State University branded its annual show as *The Fashion Show*. Each spring *The Fashion Show* displays the work and talents of all the students involved, including the student producers, directors, and committee members who plan the event, the student designers who create the runway looks, and the student models who walk the runway.

At schools such as Northern Arizona University and the University of Bridgeport in Connecticut, which have merchandising programs without a fashion design program, students learn the techniques of fashion show production by staging a themed show fusing current fashion trends with merchandise borrowed from local retailers. Northern Arizona University has produced such shows as *Rock the Runway*, *Runway to Wonderland*, and *Get Your Fashion Fix on Route 66*. Adjunct Professor Cynde Koritzinsky reports that recent themes from fashion shows produced at the University of Bridgeport include *NY—A Fashion State of Mind*, *What Happens in Vegas . . .*, and *Seven Deadly Sins of Fashion*. All aspects of fashion show production, from planning to evaluation, are learned by hands-on application.

FASHION SHOW CATEGORIES

As the opening example illustrates, fashion shows are staged to sell a variety of products, including menswear, at various market levels, including international fashion weeks. Shows vary in style based on the desired outcome of the group sponsoring the event. Some shows can be very small, informal activities with limited preparation and casual execution, while other spectacular events take months to prepare and involve a large staff to execute a flawless performance. Fashion shows are defined by production styles. These include production shows, formal runway shows, and informal shows.

Production Shows

The most elaborate fashion show is the **production show**, also called a *dramatized* or *spectacular show* because of the dramatic or theatrical elements used in the performance. The purpose of a production show is to create impact, and to that end fashion trends are emphasized using special entertainment, backdrops or scenery, lighting effects, live or exclusively produced music, and dancing or unique choreography.

Production shows require a great deal of organization and planning. Production shows may be the focus of an evening gala event, complete with cocktails and dinner, with mood-setting preshow entertainment and postevent music, dancing, and frivolity. Models, including guest celebrity models, may walk the runway to emphasize current trends or highlight a designer's contributions to fashion. Often the event is keyed to a special event such as a charity fundraiser.

The fashion industry has always had a fascination with new technology and has aggressively adopted video and interactive technology to create **multimedia production shows**. Whether the show is a spectacular production show, as discussed here, or a formal runway

Macy's Passport

show discussed next, nearly all designers and manufacturers create video productions of their shows for broadcast on media websites such as *Women's Wear Daily* (Fig. 2.4), Style.com, and the *New York Times*; social media sites such as Facebook; and the designers'/manufacturers' home website. In addition, designer showrooms and retailers may project the shows on video walls or interactive kiosks. These digital productions may also be used as **point-of-purchase videos**, presentations acting as a silent salesperson. The consumer is able to take home a copy of the latest show by that designer or manufacturer.

Contemporary fashion show multimedia productions take their cue from music and media. Presented as DVDs or streamed over the Internet, these combine all of the theatrical elements from the entertainment industry.

The modern consumer has grown up with television and digital platforms and expects a sophisticated video broadcast. In a 1970s textbook on fashion show production, the author stated that fashion shows had not yet become major television entertainment (Corinth, 1970). Wow, have things changed! In the 21st century, fashion shows are regularly viewed on television and streamed on the Internet as a contemporary pop culture phenomenon.

An interesting outgrowth of multimedia fashion productions is the fashion documentary, which has become very popular at the beginning of the 21st century. The **documentary video** focuses on the behind-the-scenes activities of designers or manufacturers, runway shows, magazine production, and other aspects of the fashion industry. For example, *The September Issue* took us behind the scenes

Figure 2.4
The Internet is a good source for viewing fashion shows.

Courtesy of WWD.com

of *Vogue* magazine as the biggest issue of the year was put together, while *Valentino: The Last Emperor* illustrated the designer putting together a collection and a museum exhibition. These may be used for training or distributed as point-of-purchase entertainment, or produced for television or movie theaters. *America's Next Top Model* and *Project Runway* are two popular documentary-type television shows featuring behind-the-scenes drama of potential models and fashion designers. Fashion movies abound but a few contemporary ones that belong in any fashionista's library include *The September Issue, Lagerfeld Confidential, Valentino: The Last Emperor*, and *Bill Cunningham New York*, among many other fashion-focused documentaries, and of course the timeless classics *Funny Face* and *Breakfast at Tiffany's*.

Formal Runway Shows

The **formal runway show** is a conventional presentation of fashion similar to a parade in which merchandise is presented in consecutive order (Fig. 2.5). The length of the show is generally 30 minutes to 1 hour and features a series of models walking or dancing down a runway in a sequential manner. Models walk the runway alone, in pairs, or in groups. The main characteristic of this show type is the use of a runway and models coming out one after another. This type of show requires advance planning and organization for a professional appearance and involves the following fashion show elements: theme, location, staging and lighting, models, and music.

A formal runway show may be directed to retailers or consumers. Manufacturers and designers use the runway show as a primary promotional tool during fashion week to show retail buyers and the fashion media the most recently produced lines. In turn, retailers use the formal runway show to entice consumers to buy the latest trends by displaying new colors, fabrics, and silhouettes on the runway. Fashion weeks will be discussed later in this chapter. Formal runway shows may also be reproduced as multimedia production shows. Victoria's Secret produces a live show that is televised a short time

Courtesy of WWD/Jackson Lowen

Figure 2.5
Models parade by fashion media, retail buyers, and celebrities in a formal runway show.

Runway to Wonderland

Figure 2.6
Production and formal
runway shows may be
reproduced in a multi-
media format. Here is a
DVD of a student-
produced show titled *Get
Your Fix on Route 66.*

after the actual fashion show is presented to an
audience each December. Figure 2.6 is a DVD
of a student-produced show titled *Runway to
Wonderland* from Northern Arizona University.

Informal Fashion Shows

A more casual presentation of garments and
accessories on models is an **informal fashion
show**. In this type
of fashion show no
theatrical elements
(music, lighting, or
runway) are used.
Selling is achieved by
the model who walks
through the store
sales floor, manufac-
turer's showroom, or
restaurant display-
ing the merchandise.
Compared to pro-
duction and runway
shows, this type of fashion show requires less
preparation. Informal modeling in a store may
take place in a specific department or throughout the entire store. Store staff will handle
scheduling models and selecting garments and
accessories to achieve a total look and project
the desired fashion statement.

Informal modeling is not restricted to
apparel. Using the movie *Breakfast at Tiffany's* as a theme, the luxury retailer Tiffany's

"Fashion show trends are that
retailers are producing more
shows in their stores and creating
a lot more smaller or informal
events to see a greater return
rather than in the past where
shows were larger with more
special effects and fashion show
budgets were more lucrative."
—Tanya Barnes-Matt,
Mesa Community College

hired models dressed in vintage clothing to
walk around the retail show room displaying
necklaces, bracelets, and earrings that might
have been worn by Audrey Hepburn.

During market weeks, manufacturers may
hire models to wear the new line and walk
around temporary showrooms. Retail buyers
may wish to see how certain garments from
the line look on the human form. Models
show these garments in an informal manner,
putting on sample garments as desired by
retail buyers and showroom personnel. Market weeks are discussed later in this chapter.

Trunk Show

Trunk shows are a specific type of informal
fashion show at a retail store, featuring garments from one manufacturer or designer
(Fig. 2.7). The complete line from the designer
is shipped to a store in "trunks" or sales representative's cases.
Company represen-
tatives or the design-
er him- or herself ac-
companies the trunks
to interact with the
customers during the
in-store event. Mod-
els walk through the
retail store, empha-
sizing the garments.

Producing trunk
shows is advanta-
geous to both the
manufacturer and the retailer. Retailers rarely
buy entire collections from a particular manufacturer for their stores. Normally, retail
buyers edit from the manufacturer's offerings,
selecting only the colors, styles, and sizes they
believe will most likely sell to their customers. With a trunk show, customers are able to
see complete collections from the producer.
They are able to order any styles, sizes, or colors they like from the line. Retailers benefit by

selling merchandise without taking the risk of carrying the merchandise in the permanent stock. Designers and manufacturers benefit as well by being able to evaluate consumer reaction to the line, learning customers' preferences, and identifying best sellers.

Mannequin Modeling

Some retail stores, shopping centers, and fashion exhibits utilize this simple form of the fashion show. **Mannequin modeling** involves live models in a store window or on a display platform. These live models strike poses like the stationary display props they have been named after. This type of informal modeling requires a lot of discipline and composure by the models, who must pose in stiff positions (Fig. 2.8). Inevitably, customers try to make these models laugh and move.

In a 21st-century spin on mannequin modeling, Daphne Guinness, artist and socialite, appeared as a mannequin model in the window of the Paris department store Printemps for a display called "Visions Couture." The spin, however, was that she really wasn't there. Instead, she appeared as a virtual statue, created from a cutting-edge, scanned photographic image by Nick Knight of SHOWstudio. Also appearing in the window, next to the statue, was a short fashion film of the outfit also shot by Knight, and an interactive display by multimedia artist Danny Brown (Diderich, 2012). This is another example of new ways to create multimedia fashion show presentations. In Color Plate 3, Daphne Guiness readies herself for the Met Gala in Barney's window in front on an audience as a performance art piece.

In this section, we have introduced production, runway, and informal fashion shows as tools to sell fashion and create entertainment. In the next section, we focus on specialized fashion shows used by designers and manufacturers to introduce new lines to retail

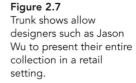
Courtesy of WWD/Donato Sardella

Figure 2.7
Trunk shows allow designers such as Jason Wu to present their entire collection in a retail setting.

Courtesy of WWD/John Aquino

Figure 2.8
Mannequin modeling gives audiences a chance to see live models pose as if they were a display prop in retail environments.

buyers, fashion media, exclusive customers, and celebrities. Most of these shows are produced as formal runway shows and may be reproduced as multimedia production shows.

[handwritten margin note: What are the market levels?]

SPECIALIZED FASHION PRESENTATIONS

Each market level of the fashion industry utilizes fashion shows to present the latest trends in fashion apparel and accessories to their potential customers. Fashion shows have developed into specialized fashion presentations aimed at specific target markets within the industry. These specialized presentations include haute couture shows, ready-to-wear shows produced at fashion weeks, trade show fashion shows produced at trade weeks, trade association shows, and consumer shows. Most of the specialized presentations are produced by manufacturers or designers to show retail buyers, the fashion media, and celebrities new trends. In the case of haute couture shows, exclusive private clients are also invited to the runway shows to view the latest designs. Trade association shows may also incorporate a broader audience and include consumers.

Location plays an important role in specialized fashion presentations. Historically, Paris, Milan, London, and New York have been the major international cities where fashion trends are presented. However, in the 21st century, many other international capitals are making a name in the fashion world. Although haute couture shows are presented only in Paris, the world is a stage for ready-to-wear shows and trade shows. Throughout this section we highlight the global nature of these specialized presentations.

Fashion is presented to the retail trade and fashion media approximately 2 to 6 months before consumers see the merchandise in stores. During the spring season, fall fashion collections are introduced, while spring collections are shown in the fall months. Shows are held far in advance of the selling season to allow manufacturers ample time to produce the merchandise previously ordered by retail buyers for upcoming selling seasons. Haute couture fashion is shown first. Most haute couture is designed for, and sold to, individual clients who handpick items from the line to be custom fit and adapted for one-of-a-kind looks. Retail buyers view the haute couture shows to identify the earliest inspirations and trends of the season. These trends will be repeated in the ready-to-wear lines from which buyers will select items for their stores.

Haute Couture Shows

Haute couture is the French word for "high fashion" and the name of the French industry that produces high fashion garments. Couture shows are the source of fashion leadership and innovation supporting the trickle-down theory of fashion. Highly detailed and sophisticated items are presented first at the highest price points to a limited audience and later are adopted at lower price points with less sophistication and detail by a larger audience. These innovations serve as inspiration for mainstream fashion houses.

Because haute couture is considered the height of fashion, it must be innovative. The innovativeness of some haute couture has often led to controversy over the appropriateness of the fashion themes. In 2000, John Galliano, designing for Christian Dior, was accused of going too far with his "wet world" couture line that was themed around tramps and hobos (Foley, 2000). Although the collection received some strong media attention, politicians and journalists felt that it trivialized a human tragedy. Critics considered it to be an example of a designer tossing out responsibility for hype. Other controversial themes of the 1990s included Alexander McQueen's Highland Rape line (showing bloodied models with slashed clothing) (Fig. 2.9) and Jean Paul Gaultier's Hasidic collection (models wearing side locks). Although not an haute couture designer, Calvin Klein has also been controversial from time to time as evidenced in his Heroin Chic theme (dark-eyed makeup and ashen skin paints to create a gaunt, burned-out look) for ready-to-wear. Haute couture designers past, present, and future will always push the edge of the envelope and use the runway show to reflect their concept of beauty and fashion.

The **Fédération Française de la Couture, du Prêt-à-Porter des Couturiers et Créateurs de Mode** (n.d.) has been France's governing body of fashion since 1973. This organization evolved from the Chambre Syndicale de la Haute Couture, which was founded in 1868. This body organizes the Paris fashion shows, including haute couture, ready-to-wear, and menswear, as well as represents the French fashion industry abroad. The organization has three divisions: the Chambre Syndicale de la Haute Couture, Chambre Syndicale du Prêt-à-Porter des Couturiers et des Créateurs de Mode, and Chambre Syndicale de la Mode Masculine.

Some of the criteria necessary to be a member of the haute couture division include having workrooms established in Paris that provide quality workmanship; a designer who creates the collection, including custom-made pieces, for clients; and fashion show presentations of collections twice annually. Many of the major couture houses take their collections to other countries after the Paris shows. Some of the most important looks are flown to New York, Tokyo, and the Middle East and shown to potential customers.

Ready-to-Wear Shows

Although haute couture is the highest, most exclusive work that a fashion house produces, the bread and butter for the fashion

© Jonathan Player

Figure 2.9
Innovation or trivializing a tragedy? These shredded garments were part of the Highland Rape line designed by Alexander McQueen.

house is **ready-to-wear**, mass-produced fashion. Ready-to-wear is produced in many countries throughout the world. The highest price point ready-to-wear is considered the designer category. This category consists of ready-to-wear from successful designers who own their own business or have a "signature collection" with their name on the label. To remain profitable, all haute couture designers also create ready-to-wear lines.

Designer collections are generally introduced immediately following the haute couture shows. Many countries, including the United States, bring together designer ready-to-wear vendors for fashion week. **Fashion Week** is designated as a time when many designer collections are assembled and shown as a series of fashion shows. Figure 2.10 is a

Advertisement appeared in Women's Wear Daily, *January 25, 2012.*

Courtesy of WWD/Robert Mitra

cooperative advertisement from Kopenhagen
Fur announcing Copenhagen Fashion Week.

During fashion weeks, fashion shows
are the primary promotion tool used by

designers to show their latest lines. During
fashion week, each designer has one opportunity to show his or her line. Fashion shows
are presented daily on the hour, scheduled
so buyers might attend as many as six or
eight shows each day. Although designers are allowed only one showing of their
lines, they may digitally reproduce their
show for later viewing on the Internet. In
Figure 2.11, notice that no props or staging
elements other than lighting are used, and
the only signage is the designer or brand
name presented on the back wall, because
many different designers will use the same
stage with limited time between shows to
setup and strike. Typically 75 to 100 garments are presented in 30 minutes or less,
leaving audience members little time to
move onto their next appointment. Often,
more than one show will be scheduled for
the same time so retailers and journalists
must decide which show they will attend.
As an example, by the second decade of the
21st century, 322 fashion shows and presentations were spread over 9 days, causing
editors and buyers to pick and choose which
shows were most important to attend during New York Fashion Week (Lipke, 2012).

In a move to establish a viable alternative to live runway shows and allow fashion
week attendees to experience fashion shows
in a new way, KCD, a production and public relations firm, launched a digital platform
for runway shows during New York Fashion
Week. The site, Digitalfashionshows.com,
provides designers a central hub to stage
online shows as pretaped segments. Like
traditional fashion week shows, the site is
by invitation only and viewers must log in
with a password. The site allows viewers to
watch the segments on a computer, tablet, or
mobile phone. While viewing the site, editors and buyers can also view notes scrolled

along the bottom of the video, view still images of each look from a variety of angles, and tag their favorites. Ed Filipowski, the creator of this innovative platform, emphasized that digital runway shows are not meant to replace or replicate the experience, pizzazz, and glamour of live runways shows; it merely provides a time-efficient tool for buyers and journalists who are caught in an increasingly demanding and cluttered show season (Lipke, 2012).

The digital fashion shows highlighted above are examples of media shows aimed at buyers and the media. **Media shows**, also previously known as *press shows*, are specifically held for members of the media prior to presenting the fashion story to the public. Members of the media represent print, broadcast, Internet, and wire services. Media representatives are routinely provided information about the merchandise, designer, or event through media kits, media releases, and photographs. Some journalists will bring their own photographers for exclusive pictures. In reality, fashion weeks serve as one gigantic media event, hosting hundreds of media shows in a short period of time.

> "Our goal is to establish a significant viable alternative to live runway shows and a way for editors and buyers to experience fashion shows in a new way."
> —Ed Filipowski, co-president, KDC Worldwide

New York

Each year the schedule is tenuous as countries jockey for the first position to introduce the latest ready-to-wear lines. Historically, the ready-to-wear shows began in Europe and concluded in New York. However, in 1999, in an attempt to gain stature as a fashion capitol, New York scheduled the American shows before the European shows.

American designers wanted to stake claim on trends at the beginning of the season. However, this was in direct conflict with retailers who wanted to see the New York shows last for the sake of convenience and their ability to sum up the trends. Into the second decade of the 21st century, organizations including the Council of Fashion Designers of America, the British Fashion Council, Camera Nazionale della Moda Italiana in Milan, and the French Federation de la Prêt-à-Porter Feminin continue to negotiate over fashion week show dates, but the order has remained unchanged with collections showing first in New York, followed by London, Milan, and concluding in Paris.

Mercedes-Benz Fashion Week is the most important fashion event held in the United States. The multiple-day event, held each spring and fall, is a marathon of fashion shows with many designers showing their latest lines to retailers and journalists. Mercedes-Benz Fashion Week was originally created as **7th on Sixth,** a nonprofit organization established by the **Council of Fashion Designers of America (CFDA)**, which is a nonprofit trade organization for North American designers of fashion and fashion accessories. In 1993, 7th on Sixth organized, centralized, and modernized the American runway shows and provided a platform for American designers to present their collections to a worldwide audience of media and buyers.

In 2001, CFDA sold 7th on Sixth to IMG, a sports management and marketing company. IMG purchased the fashion shows because of its ability to generate sponsorship and provide more televised fashion events. Historically, New York Fashion Week was held in tents at Bryant Park; however, in 2009, Mercedes-Benz Fashion Week in New York City moved to Lincoln Center (Color Plate 4). The relocation of the shows to Lincoln Center was supervised by Stephanie Winston Wolkoff who became the founding Fashion Director of Lincoln Center.

London

London, the city associated with the 1960s fashion revolution of Mary Quant, Carnaby Street, and the Mod Look, remains the center of innovation and classic British fashion. Twice a year, London hosts London Fashion Week, organized by the **British Fashion Council**. London designers have a reputation for creating cutting-edge, wearable collections. Among the most talented British designers are Zandra Rhodes, Stella McCartney, Caroline Charles, and Vivienne Westwood. Young, experimental designers continue to keep London a fashion center.

Milan

The **Camera Nazionale della Moda Italiana** (the National Chamber for Italian Fashion) is the nonprofit association that coordinates and promotes the development of Italian fashion (Camera, 2012). The organization oversees activities of the couture designers and ready-to-wear, shoe, and accessory manufacturers. The Camera organizes group events, including the ready-to-wear shows in Milan. The Italian ready-to-wear industry has been gaining international significance because much of the high fashion industry and design activities take place in Rome. However, due to the aggressive nature of Paris couture and the confusion over show dates, many Italian designers show their couture collections in Paris.

The semi-annual fashion shows featuring Italian ready-to-wear are held in Milan just prior to the designer shows in Paris. Italy is primarily known for knitwear, sportswear, and accessories by such designers as Giorgio Armani, Missoni, Fendi, and Valentino. The fast-paced Milan ready-to-wear shows are presented at the Fiera, a three-story convention center on the outskirts of Milan.

Paris

Prêt-à-porter is the ready-to-wear fashion industry in Paris. The **defiles des createurs** are the designer runway shows featuring the newest creations from France as well as other international designers. The ready-to-wear shows are scheduled by the Prêt-à-Porter des Couturiers et des Créateurs de Mode, as we learned earlier in this chapter. Paris fashion shows have been presented at a variety of venues such as tents, the Tuileries, the Bois de Boulogne, the Palais de Congres, and the Louvre.

Newcomers

Newcomers continue to enter the fashion week frenzy with formal runway shows. One country to show off its fashion forwardness is Germany, which hosted its first Mercedes-Benz Fashion Week Berlin in 2007 and continues to have a strong showing with over 100,000 visitors each year. The 4-day affair includes approximately 50 fashion shows and presentations in at tent at Brandenburg Gate and other off-site venues (Drier, 2012). Mercedes-Benz Fashion Week Berlin is Germany's most important stage for emerging talent as well as established brands. The work of Berlin-based designer Yujia Zhai-Petrow is shown in Color Plates 5a and 5b,

Toronto Fashion Week is Canada's biggest fashion event with exciting, cutting-edge designs (Walji, 2012). As part of IMG Canada, the World MasterCard Fashion Week, as it is formally known, premiered in 1999 and has struck a good balance between showcasing Canada's top established designers and featuring new talent that has put Canada on the global fashion map (Fig. 2.12). The week-long event features over 60 runway show and presentations (Karimzadeh, 2012). Ben Barry is the CEO of the Ben Barry Agency, a model agency headquartered in Toronto, Canada. His company scouts and sources models of all ages, sizes, backgrounds, and

> "Toronto is a regional fashion week. With increase in public interest has come this explosion of fashion weeks in every nook and cranny of the Earth that has a consumer base to support it. So, you have Mumbai, Sao Paulo, Kiev, and Toronto is on that level. . . . It doesn't have to be a global appeal. But that doesn't mean it isn't meaningful."
>
> —Bernadette Morra, editor-in-chief, *FASHION* magazine

abilities for fashion and beauty brands. His perspective on model casting diversity is profiled in Notes from the Runway: Model Diversity in Fashion Shows.

A sampling of other fashion weeks include Karachi Fashion Week in Islamabad, Pakistan; Fashion Rio in Rio De Janeiro, Brazil; Hong Kong Fashion Week; Vancouver Fashion Week, Canada; Amsterdam International Fashion Week, the Netherlands; Copenhagen Fashion Week, Denmark; Kobe Fashion Week, Japan; Vibrant Fashion Week in Ahmedabad, India; Audi Joburg Fashion Week in Johannesburg, South Africa; and Istanbul Fashion Week,

Figure 2.12
Models on runway at Toronto Fashion Week.

WireImage

Turkey. A complete listing of international fashion weeks is available at http://www.fashion.org.

Mercedes-Benz Fashion Week, as a division of IMG Fashion, has multiplied, producing a number of leading fashion events around the globe to create international platforms for fashion. Besides producing New York and Berlin Fashion Weeks, Mercedes-Benz Fashion Week is also the sponsor for Mercedes-Benz Fashion Mexico, Mexico City; Mercedes-Benz Fashion Week in Stockholm, Sweden; Mercedes-Benz Madrid Fashion Week, Spain; and Mercedes-Benz Tokyo Fashion Week, among other fashion events.

Trade Shows

The term **trade** refers to any activity aimed at distribution of fashion and related products within the industry. National and global **trade shows** are groups of temporary exhibits of vendors' offerings for a single merchandise category or group of related categories. Trade shows are produced to sell raw materials to manufacturers, or manufactured goods to retailers. Trade shows differ from fashion weeks. At a fashion week, much of the viewing of lines takes place at orchestrated fashion shows. At a trade show, much of the viewing of lines takes place at temporary booths with a limited number of fashion shows presented during a day or week. The advantage to a trade show is the ability for buyers and journalists to view many different vendors' offerings in one location.

Trade shows may be held once or several times during the year. WWDMAGIC (Fig. 2.13) is a biannual trade show held in Las Vegas each February and August. Originally conceived as a market for the upcoming menswear season, vendors at MAGIC also provide fill-in merchandise for the current season. Buyers from regional chains and specialty stores work the show to get a sense of what trends are likely to be important for the next season. **Market calendars** publicize the dates for trade shows. These dates are generally termed **market weeks** and correspond with manufacturers' seasonal delivery dates. For example, in addition to fashion weeks, New York City hosts over 75 major fashion trade shows and market weeks annually (Karimzadeh, 2011).

Trade shows are not limited to the United States. Many international cities host trade shows showcasing international designers for American and international media. This may be attributed to the growing global economy, ease of travel, and the Internet. In the United States, we commonly use the term *trade show*; however, in other countries the term **trade fair** is more common. Canada, France, England, Italy, Germany, Russia, China, Japan, and Brazil are just a few of the countries that host trade shows. The Profile Show held in

Figure 2.13
Daily fashion shows feature current trends at WWDMAGIC in Las Vegas.

Courtesy of WWD

Toronto, Ontario, Canada, is an example of an international trade show featuring apparel and accessories for men's, women's, young contemporary and junior labels, children's, and lifestyle brands. Interstoff is a renowned international fabric trade show held in Germany and, more recently, Asia. The trade show produces fashion shows to highlight the textiles offered by various vendors (Fig. 2.14).

Trade shows and apparel marts have a close working relationship. Trade shows are often produced at **apparel marts**. Regional apparel marts are wholesale centers located in major cities throughout the United States. Marts lease space to manufacturers who are able to offer their lines closer to the retailer's geographic location so retail buyers do not have to travel to New York City to purchase merchandise. These fashion centers offer the convenience of many manufacturers in one location. Many small store buyers have found the regional centers to be very responsive to their needs. In addition to the convenience and reduced expenses, the regional marts sponsor retailing seminars and fashion shows for participants.

At apparel mart fashion shows, fashion buyers are given an opportunity to determine trend themes presented by the manufacturers prior to visiting individual showrooms. These fashion trend shows help the retailers pinpoint the merchandise and trends that would meet the needs of their particular customers. These shows are an entertaining and uplifting start to the chaotic buying process.

The major U.S. apparel marts are located in Los Angeles, Dallas, Chicago (Fig. 2.15), and Atlanta with smaller regional marts located throughout the country. These centers make vendors accessible for many small retailers who find it difficult to visit major market centers. The convenience and generally lower cost associated with visiting a regional center add to their popularity.

The Dallas Market Center is the largest apparel mart in the Southwest. For over 40 years, the Kim Dawson Agency and the Dallas Market Center have had a strong partnership. Kim Dawson, a former model in Paris and New York, returned to her Texas home in the mid-1950s at the cusp of the emerging fashion industry in Dallas and opened her agency in 1959. She was named the fashion director of the Dallas Apparel Mart in 1964, and her agency was well placed as the Dallas fashion scene emerged as a major market center in the United States. Interestingly, the agency began by representing women who were hired primarily for tea-room modeling. However, in the 21st century the Kim Dawson Agency, now run by her daughter, has a worldwide reputation for developing internationally recognized models and talent for runway, commercial, and print ("Kim Dawson," 2009). The Kim Dawson Runway Café, within the Dallas Market Center, hosts lunchtime fashion shows during trade shows, such as the Dallas Apparel and Accessories Market.

The California Market Center houses fashion showrooms for the contemporary market and organizes fashion fairs such as the Los Angeles Textile Show. In addition to traditional media, the market center uses its blog, as well as Twitter and Facebook accounts, to promote new exhibitors, special events, and brand information. The market center also hosts buyers at an annual fashion show in October, highlighting brands that have showrooms in the building (Tran, 2011).

Regional apparel marts introduce the new lines of merchandise through fashion trend shows held for the retail buyers at the start of a market week. According to Yvette Crosby, former fashion director for the California Apparel Mart, she had approximately 48 hours to pull together a fashion show for the

Figure 2.14
Model on the runway at
the Interstoff trade show.

Courtesy of WWD/Alex Lee

Courtesy of WWD

Figure 2.15
Models on the runway at a Chicago trade show held at the apparel mart.

center. This involved selecting merchandise to be shown from the various showrooms, coordinating into scenes the diverse themes of goods being presented, hiring and training the models, and staging the show in the apparel mart theater. Although it was hectic, the show was pulled together at the last minute. Commentary was not used. Music was selected to coordinate with the looks being featured. Dramatic lighting emphasized the changes in groups or themes.

Trade Association Shows

Trade associations are groups of individuals and businesses acting as a professional, nonprofit collective in meeting their common interests. Membership in trade associations provides a means for information exchange and political action to benefit the public opinion and legislative concerns. Trade associations represent almost every division of the fashion industry. These associations may be very specialized, such as the Jewelry Industry Council, Cotton Incorporated, or the Cosmetic, Toiletry and Fragrance Association. Other associations focus on a broad or more generalized representation, such as the American Apparel and Footwear Association and the National Retail Federation. Fashion shows are a way to provide information and entertainment to association members. Cotton Incorporated used the fashion show in an innovative way to capture consumers' attention with its world premiere, 24-Hour Runway Show in 2011 (Fig. 2.16). The show featured 1,440 looks and was streamed live on MTV.

Consumer Shows

As the name implies, **consumer shows** are directed toward consumers. These shows may be sponsored by a retailer to introduce customers to the latest fashions, or they may be sponsored by a charitable or school organization as an entertainment and/or fundraising special event. Many consumer shows are presented for a specific target market.

Figure 2.16
Advertisement for
Cotton's 24-Hour Runway
Show.

Advertisement appeared in Women's Wear Daily,
November 16, 2011

Niche markets that might benefit from the promotion of a fashion show are endless. **Specialty market shows** highlight trends from a specific product category or a certain body type. **Special interest shows** are presented to consumers that have a special affinity with each other or a unique vocation that can be represented through fashion.

Retail department stores in Paris have a reputation for presenting consumer fashion shows to international guests. The two large department stores in Paris, Printemps and Galeries Lafayette, both produce weekly fashion shows for their international clients. At Galeries Lafayette weekly Friday fashion shows are presented by a team of six professional models who show off the latest trends from the most famous designer and couturier collections. This 30-minute presentation requires reservations and includes a commentary conducted in English. Printemps presents a more informal fashion show on Tuesday mornings. Retailers in your community too, may host occasional fashion shows to highlight seasonal trends or promote community goodwill.

The show at Galeries Lafayette is an example of a fashion trend show. **Fashion trend shows** are produced to introduce consumers to the latest trends in silhouettes, fabrics, colors, and themes for new seasonal merchandise. Fashion trend shows are presented to consumers at the beginning of the season and each show segment features a major trend. Fashion directors and buyers identify trends by attending haute couture shows, ready-to-wear shows, and trade shows. Upon returning home these professionals identify the specific trends that will be represented in the merchandise buys for their company. Finally, the identified trends are shown to consumers to get them excited and want to buy the new merchandise.

Model Diversity in Fashion Shows
Dr. Ben Barry

Courtesy of Ben Barry

A change is underway in the fashion industry. Emerging designers and mass brands are rejecting the traditional practice of exclusively casting models who are thin, young, Caucasian, and tall in their fashion shows; instead, they are selecting models who reflect a variety of sizes, ages, races, and heights. Examples of brands that have recently featured diverse models on their runways include emerging labels Mark Fast and Vawk, and established houses Tom Ford and Jean Paul Gaultier. According to Louis Vuitton designer Marc Jacobs, in reference to a fall Paris Fashion Week show, the decision to cast diversity is deliberate: "I set out to cast a variety of sexy women—younger, older, thin, voluptuous, from every ethnic background" (Odell, 2010, p.1).

Why Cast Diversity?

Designers and brands cast diverse models because of the positive impact doing so will have on their bottom line. Because models are the bridge between consumers and clothing, showing retailers and consumers how clothes fit and flatter a range of shapes and sizes is an effective marketing strategy. Recent empirical research (Barry, 2012) based on a sample of over 2,500 North Americans—found that consumers increased purchase intentions for clothing when it was showcased on models who reflected their sizes, ages, and races versus models who did not. No wonder Mark Fast became his retailers' best-selling brand after he featured model diversity in a recent spring London Fashion Week show. The buyer for London retailer Browns Focus remarked, "The show has opened up [Mark Fast's] customer base. After the show, we had a host of customers from sizes 6 to 16 coming in" (Bumpus, 2009, ¶ 13).

How to Cast Diversity?

Model Mix. Casting diversity does not mean replacing thin models with curvy ones, or young models with mature ones. Instead, there is a clear strategy to follow when selecting diverse models for fashion shows. Begin by analyzing the featured brand's target market—the size, age, height, and race ranges of the intended consumers. You'll then select models who reflect the physical and demographic diversity of this population. For example, if a women's wear label sells sizes 2 through 16 and the age of its target consumers is 18 to 35, select female models who represent these same size and age ranges.

The Agency. Right now only a few modeling agencies represent models of all sizes, ages, and heights. You'll need to find agencies with "plus size" (i.e., models size 6–18), "classic" (i.e., models over 30 years old), and "petite" (i.e., models under 5 feet 6 inches) boards. Most cities will have agencies that include them. You might find, however, that no agency in your city represents models outside of the traditional ideal—especially if you're looking for diverse male models. No problem. You can find "real people" (i.e., nonprofessional models) who meet the diverse demographic criteria to participate in your show. Post casting notices via social networking, and hold open calls to meet the applicants. No experience is needed. You'll train your new recruits during rehearsals (see later section) to ensure they're confident and polished.

Sample Size. If you're producing a show for one of the many fashion weeks around the world, you'll likely encounter a challenge when casting models of different sizes. Labels showing during these weeks will provide you with a prototype—a sample—of each garment in their collection because the show takes place months ahead of their retail production. The standard women's sample is a size 2, which means the female models you'll have to hire will be a size 2. Your chance to cast diversity is not doomed; you'll just need to plan ahead. Work with the label to create samples in three different sizes to best reflect the size diversity of their consumers. They do not need to make each sample in each size, but rather create different samples in different sizes. You can then cast models according to the number of samples in each size.

Runway Rehearsal. Unprofessional and inconsistent runway walks destroy fashion shows by taking the audience's attention away from the clothes. Because curvy, mature. and petite models often have less runway experience than models who reflect the traditional ideal, you'll need to organize a few practice runway sessions to ensure their walks convey the attitude and style you envision. Invite all the models to attend these rehearsals to develop a consistent strut and look and also build model comradery. Pay particular attention to the models' "pose" and "face" at the end of the runway, ensuring that they all pose at the same spot and hold their pose for the same amount of time.

Styling. Hair and makeup artists as well as wardrobe stylists have a tendency to forget the fashion when they're working on curvy and mature models. The result is a drab and dull aesthetic that more closely resembles a passport mug shot than an inspiring fashion look. As show producers, one of your tasks is to oversee the creative direction of the styling and aesthetic. You'll first work with the creative team to determine the look for the show, and then you'll make sure that each model is styled in a manner that represents this vision. Your guiding principle is that all models, regardless of their sizes or ages, convey fashion's artistry, creativity, and glamour. After all, no retailer or consumer will be inspired to buy the fashions you're showing if the models look unfashionable.

Industry Attitudes. Despite the movement toward diversity in fashion, selecting models of different sizes, ages, races, and heights goes against the industry's current casting norm of exclusively hiring one ideal of beauty. You'll likely encounter resistance from members of your own fashion show production team, including the labels themselves, when you first suggest the idea of diversity. Don't let this obstacle deter you. Make your case for showcasing diverse models on the runway by explaining why it makes good business sense, and outlining your strategy (i.e., model mix) and plan (i.e., runway rehearsal, styling) to effectively execute it. Creating a fashion industry that celebrates and inspires everyone starts with you—and your fashion show.

Dr. Ben Barry is an Assistant Professor of Equity, Diversity and Inclusion at the School of Fashion, Ryerson University, in Toronto, Ontario, Canada. He previously founded the first modeling agency in the world dedicated to representing fashion models of all sizes, ages, heights, backgrounds, and abilities. Dr. Barry holds a B.A. in Women's Studies from the University of Toronto and a Ph.D. in Marketing from the University of Cambridge.

THE BACKGROUND—A RECAP

- Fashion shows are big business within the fashion industry and a major form of fashion promotion.
- The most important reason that fashion shows are produced is to sell merchandise; however, other reasons for producing fashion shows include sharing information, attracting customers, fund-raising, and training.
- Fashion shows can be produced as grand extravagant production shows, formal runway shows, or minimal informal shows. All show categories can also be reproduced as multimedia production shows.
- The most common type of fashion show is the runway show where models parade merchandise down a runway.
- Fashion shows have developed into specialized fashion presentations aimed at specific target markets and include haute couture shows, ready-to-wear shows, trade show fashion shows, and consumer shows.
- Haute couture fashion is shown first each season. Retail buyers, celebrities, and private customers view haute couture shows to identify the earliest trends of the season.
- Ready-to-wear fashion is presented at fashion weeks when many designer collections are brought together and shown as a series of fashion shows. Fashion weeks are produced in many international cities.
- Trade shows are groups of temporary exhibits of vendors' offerings for a single merchandise category or group of related categories and present fashion shows on a more limited basis, identifying major trends for the season.
- Consumer shows are directed toward customers and introduce the latest fashions, or provide fund-raising opportunities.

KEY FASHION SHOW TERMS

7th on Sixth	☐ formal runway show *dramatized, or spectacular*
apparel marts	haute couture
British Fashion Council	☐ informal fashion show
Camera Nazionale della Moda Italiana	in-store training fashion show
consumer show	instructional video
cooperative fashion show	magazine tie-in show
cooperative promotion (co-op)	mannequin modeling
Council of Fashion Designers of	market calendar
America (CFDA)	market week
defiles des createurs	media show
documentary video	☐ multimedia production show
fashion trend show	national promotion
fashion week	point-of-purchase video
Fédération Française de la Couture, du	prêt-à-porter
Prêt-à-Porter Couturiers et	primary resources
Créateurs de Mode	production show

promotion	trade
ready-to-wear	trade association
retail promotion	trade fair
secondary resources	trade promotion
special interest show	trade show
specialty market show	trunk show
tertiary resources	

QUESTIONS FOR DISCUSSION

1. Have you attended a live fashion show? How did it make you feel? What do you remember most about that show?
2. Have you watched a fashion show on a website? What was different about watching this type of fashion show from watching a live fashion show?
3. What is the difference between haute couture and ready-to-wear? Explain why one is more profitable for fashion designers than the other.
4. Who is the target market for a trade show? What makes trade shows different from fashion weeks?
5. What are some issues that newcomer countries face in trying to establish their own fashion weeks?

FASHION SHOW ACTIVITIES

1. Identify one or more websites that feature fashion shows from the four major fashion capitals (New York, London, Paris, Milan). Write down distinguishable differences in the fashion presented in each country. Do the same for one or more newcomer countries. Be ready to discuss this in class.
2. Research the area where you live to determine where the closest regional apparel mart is located. Research what trade shows are regularly held at the apparel mart. Identify a trade show and arrange a field trip to visit showrooms, talk with mart staff, and attend a fashion show.

THE CAPSTONE PROJECT

In the next step in planning your fashion show, it is important for you to decide which type of show will work best based on your group's goals for the event. For fashion show teams, each member should develop a list identifying the pros and cons for producing a production show, a formal runway show, or an informal show at your school or in your community. After each member has created a list (which might take several days), the fashion show team should come together and discuss all three production types, combining positive and negative aspects of each show type into a master list. From the master list, the fashion show team should be able to create consensus on which show type is the best choice for your show. Discuss the challenges ahead of you as you plan your upcoming show.

REFERENCES

Alpha male. (2012, January 17). *Women's Wear Daily*, pp. 6–8.

Barry, B. (2012, June). New business model: Are fashion companies missing out on the bottom line when they only use one type of model. *Elle Canada*, 108–114.

Bumpus, J. (2009, October 12). Fast fashion. Retrieved from http://www.vogue.co.uk

Camera Nazionale della Moda Italiana (2012). Retrieved from http://www.cameramoda.it/en/associazione/cosa-e-la-cnmi/

Corinth, K. (1970). *Fashion showmanship*. New York, NY: Wiley.

Diderich, J. (2012, January 20). Mannequin two. *Women's Wear Daily*, p. 11.

Drier, M. (2012, January 10). Starting healthy. *Women's Wear Daily*, p. 4.

Fédération Française de la Couture, du Prêt-à-Porter des Couturiers et des Créateurs de Mode. (n.d.). *Federation*. Retrieved from http://www.modeaparis.com/en/federation/

Foley, B. (2000, January 26). Dior: The saga continues. *Women's Wear Daily*, pp. 8–9.

Kim Dawson Agency models. (2009). Retrieved from http://www.kimdawsonagency.com/

Karimzadeh, M. (2011, June 22). N.Y. shows look to add value. *Women's Wear Daily*, p. 2.

Karimzadeh, M. (2012, January 30). Fresh title. *Women's Wear Daily*, p. 11.

Lipke, D. (2012, January 23). KCD readies for digital platform for runway. *Women's Wear Daily*, p. 2.

Lockwood, L. (2012, January 13). Moms to strut their stuff during Fashion Week. *Women's Wear Daily*, p. 12.

Odell, A. (2010, March). Curvy, adult, diverse models walk Louis Vuitton. Retrieved from http://nymag.com

Swanson, K. K., & Everett, J. C. (2007). *Promotion in the merchandising environment* (2nd ed.) New York, NY: Fairchild Books.

Tran, K. T. L. (2011, June 22). Los Angeles fairs cast wide net. *Women's Wear Daily*, p. 5.

Walji, N. (2012, March 16). Toronto Fashion Week launches Canadian designers onto world stage. Retrieved from http://www.cbc.ca

1. Explain in your own words the definition of "Promotion"

2. What is the difference between primary and secondary resources?

3. What are the reasons for producing fashion shows?

4

CHAPTER THREE
The Plan

AFTER READING THIS CHAPTER, YOU SHOULD BE ABLE TO DISCUSS:

- The definition of *fashion show planning*

- Different fashion show leadership types

- Audience formation and demographic characteristics

- Establishing date, time, and the fashion show venue

- The definition and use of a *fashion show theme* and *scene themes*

- How to establish a fashion show planning budget

- Why it is necessary to create a fashion show calendar and timeline

- How to protect people, merchandise, and the venue

When the Marc Jacobs show starts on Monday of New York Fashion Week at 8 p.m., approximately 500 invited guests will watch the show that will display 63 outfits worn by as many different models, each one scheduled to be on stage for 45 seconds (Trebay, 2011). With a show budget of at least $1 million, how does the show come together? Planning!

The planning process for the Marc Jacobs show begins with the designer's inspiration for the collection. Then it takes an army of professionals with military-like scheduling to bring this event from planning to reality. Joseph Carter, the head designer, begins draping fabric on his fit model, Jamie Bochert. Then, Julie Mannion, the co-president of KCD, the fashion production and public relations firm, starts scheduling all of the people and logistics to bring the show from the designer's concept to the dramatically designed stage at the 69th Regiment Armory on Lexington Avenue.

To bring this show to life, stylist Venetia Scott, milliner Stephen Jones, manicurist Elisa Ferri with her team of 4 assistants, D. J. Frederic Sanchez with 4 sound engineers, 50 hairdressers, 35 makeup artists, and 70 dressers work on a frantic time schedule. Other essentials that are considered in the planning stage include model casting; sample fabrication; and creating shoes, handbags, and other goods offshore to be shipped back to New York at the last minute. Before heading onto the runway, the models are presented in groups of 10 to Marc Jacobs for final adjustments. All of these efforts go into creating a spectacle that looks inspirational and effortless to the anxiously awaiting audience. The show lasts 9½ minutes. Figure 3.1 illustrates a Marc Jacobs fashion show that keeps people talking.

Planning involves all aspects of preliminary preparation necessary to present a well-executed show. Planning must be appropriate to the purpose of the show and the abilities of the group producing the show.

Figure 3.1
Season after season, Marc Jacobs delivers another dramatic show that keeps people talking.

Courtesy of WWD/John Aquino

A back-to-school fashion show should focus on fall school clothes, using children as models and attracting parents and children as the audience. Planners for charity shows should keep in mind the purpose of raising money when planning an event, but should not overprice the show tickets for the intended audience.

Planning a fashion show is similar to how a journalist plans an article. The lead paragraph in a news article starts with the five Ws—who, what, where, when, and why—of the story, whereas the person or group putting on the fashion show must consider the same five Ws for the fashion show. Without appropriate planning, unexpected problems, which could have easily been avoided, occur.

> "A runway show is a production that requires the participation of different teams and demands painstaking planning. For this reason, a detailed production plan is a must, and work must begin months before the big day."
> —Estel Vilaseca, author of Runway Uncovered

DEVELOPING LEADERSHIP

Professional designer runway shows, which are produced for such events as fashion week in New York, London, or Milan, or the prêt-à-porter and haute couture shows in Paris, typically rely on the designer's public relations officer to assist the designer in hiring a show producer. Retailers, fashion schools, and charitable organizations more typically use the skills of a staff member, faculty member, or community volunteer to serve as fashion show director to produce the show. Both types of shows require leaders with strong organizational and managerial skills. We will look at both types of leadership styles.

Leadership for Industry Shows

According to Lee Widdows and Jo McGuiness (1997), the public relations representative from the designer's company, depending upon the wishes of the designer, may put together or make recommendations on the composition of the show production team. This team includes the show producer, stylist, makeup artists, hairdressers, models, and behind-the-scenes stage crew.

Show Producer

The **show producer** is the individual or firm hired to bring all of the fashion show elements together, translating the designer's vision into a three-dimensional live show. These responsibilities include, but are not limited to, casting the models, overseeing the design and construction of the set, supervising hair and makeup artists, and directing the lighting and music crews. The show producer is in charge of a large staff that takes the initial plans and translates these ideas into the actual show.

In addition to organizational and communication skills, the show producer must be creative. The show producer sets ideas—which enhance the designer's image through set design, choreography, music, and lighting—in motion. With good industry contacts and positive working relationships with model, hair, and makeup agencies, staging firms, and media representatives, the show producer can hire the best team for the job.

The show producer works with the designer and stylist to decide which models will wear which outfits. By choosing the best models to wear the most significant outfits, the interest from the major fashion editors can almost be guaranteed. Understanding what helps or hinders the fashion media is also part of the show producer's responsibilities. Figure 3.2 shows Kelly Cutrone getting ready for an upcoming show.

Stylist

"Since the turn of the millennium, the term 'stylist' has shot from obscurity to everyday pop-usage without, so far, being pinned down precisely in any dictionary," according to Sarah Mower in *Stylist: The Interpreters of Fashion* (2007, p. vii). There are at least two types of stylists, focusing on editorial or celebrities, working today.

The first type is the **editorial stylist**, who works for designers and for print and multimedia publications. Editorial stylists may work freelance for a number of different designers and publications or as employees of publications, such as *Elle*, *Harper's Bazaar*, or *T: The New York Times Style Magazine*. It is the responsibility of the editorial stylist to provide creative input to the fashion designer and show producer, and to present the clothes with an eye for upcoming trends. The stylist is responsible for planning how to highlight key pieces of the collection through editing and accessorizing and supervises the merchandise and dressers for a fashion designer. Editorial stylists working for fashion magazines, such as Grace Coddington for *Vogue* or Joe Zee for *Elle*, turn fashion into visual stories. Editorial work is also part of the digital

> "The five key points are: the selection of garments that are going to be presented, the right number of looks, between twenty-four and thirty-six, the organization at the start of the runway show, a balanced pace in the presentation of the clothes, and of course, the lighting."
>
> —Laird Borelli,
> Fashion editor, Style.com

Figure 3.2
Kelly Cutrone is the founder of the fashion public relations, branding, and marketing firm People's Revolution.

Courtesy of WWD/Talaya Centeno

revolution, including filming fashion shoots or model castings and broadcasting these programs on television or online, or featuring them via social media.

The second type is the **celebrity stylist**, who focuses on dressing his or her clients for special events. For example, Rachel Zoe has become known for her work dressing such clients as Anne Hathaway for the Academy Awards. Her reality television show, The Rachel Zoe Project, makes the audience aware of her job. She has expanded her styling work into designing apparel and accessories. Although the celebrity stylist is an important figure in current fashion, this chapter will focus primarily on the role of the editorial stylist.

Journalist Teri Agins (2006) profiled fashion stylist Lori Goldstein as she worked with designer Vera Wang to develop her collection. Ms. Goldstein works as a freelance consultant to Ms. Wang in addition to other designers, such as Nina Ricci in Paris. As Ms. Wang began working on her collection, Ms. Goldstein suggested fabrics that would emphasize the inspiration for the collection. Later she helped edit the number of runway looks from 70 to about 45, helped select the 20 models that would walk the runway, and helped create the models' "look" with just the right shade of lipstick and a soft hairstyle to complement the fashion era and the theme. Ms. Goldstein also helped determine the order in which the garments were presented and the timing of the show.

A big part of the stylist's job is to anticipate the way the fashion winds are blowing and advise the designer about emerging trends. The best stylists, who can earn $8,000 or more a day, help designers create the image for the designer's product lines, which in many cases have extended beyond garments into accessories, handbags, home furnishings, fine jewelry, and other merchandise categories (Agins, 2006). The stylist must understand the designer's target audience and help to interpret the look with attention to detail, appropriate model fit, and use of suitable accessories. Stylists also work on the garment order and which individual garments are coordinated to form an outfit, strongly influencing the overall impact of the merchandise. These fine details give the collection its feel, from classy to sexy or formal to casual. Reah Norman, a well-known fashion stylist working in Los Angeles and New York, transports us into her world in Notes from the Runway: So, You Want to Be a Fashion Stylist? . . .

Leadership for Consumer and Education Shows

Retail stores, fashion schools, and charitable organizations may be able to hire a fashion show producer, but more frequently they use their own personnel. A retail store has an in-house fashion, special events, or public relations director. A school typically utilizes a faculty member, who teaches a fashion show production course, whereas a charitable organization may select its fashion show director from the group's membership.

A retail store **fashion director**, *public relations director*, or *special events director* is an individual responsible for creating the fashion image for that particular retailer. The fashion director, in cooperation with the store's buyers, is responsible for selecting silhouettes, colors, and fabrics for the upcoming season and establishing a sense of fashion leadership for the store to present to the public. Fashion show and special event production plays a major role in the job of a fashion director.

A school production or charitable organization may have a fashion show director or co-directors, especially if the show is produced by volunteers. A **fashion show director** is the individual charged with the responsibility of producing the school or charitable organization fashion show, planning all arrangements, delegating responsibilities, and accepting accountability for all details. In school or charitable organization productions, the fashion show director may be a faculty member or a person selected or appointed by the group members. Figure 3.3 is an organization chart that represents fashion show leadership for a school show.

A fashion show director must have several traits. The director must be able to communicate with all parties involved, both verbally and in writing. Verbal communication must usually be accompanied by written communication. Information should be put in writing so that all individuals are aware of details. People often give directions verbally in a hurried manner, only to have the hearers forget later what was said exactly; written communication allows both parties to refer

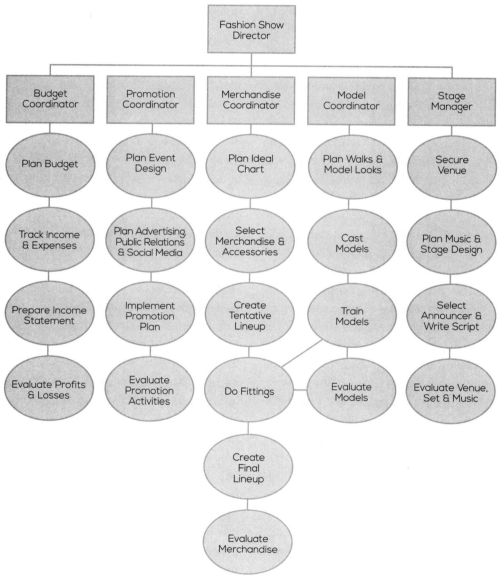

Figure 3.3
An organization chart illustrates fashion show leadership and responsibilities of each team. *Key:* Boxes are used to designate the people involved with a fashion show activity; ovals represent an action executed with written evidence.

Illustration by Carly Grafstein

back to what details were assigned. E-mail and texting are great tools for keeping everyone informed in an instant. In addition, the director must keep a written **diary** or record of all plans for the show. This diary serves as a reminder to the director of tasks to be completed, follow-up dates, and future needs of the show. The diary may also be a helpful tool if an organization decides to produce another show in the future.

The show director must communicate planning activities to all concerned individuals. A retail fashion show director should keep all salespeople informed far enough in advance about the details of the show so that they may promote the event to their customers. A school group or civic organization must pass information to all members so that they may invite their friends, families, or other people who might be interested in attending the show.

A fashion show director must be able to foresee show problems and be flexible to work around these problems and/or inconveniences. Many problems occur during critical moments of the show and must be dealt with in a professional and timely manner. Common problems include models not showing up or merchandise exchanges right before the show, causing changes in the lineup.

The fashion show director must continually review the progress of the show, making sure the show is running smoothly and deadlines are met. Many people are involved in the show and it is important for the show director to know everything that the others are doing.

The show director must also delegate tasks to other coordinators. Each fashion show director will divide responsibilities differently depending on the size and complexity of the show. Production shows may require many area coordinators with specialized responsibilities, whereas a trunk show may require only one or two area coordinators with many different responsibilities.

Model Coordinator

A **model coordinator** is responsible for selecting and training the models, and coordinating activities that involve the models. Additional areas of responsibilities for the model coordinator may include supervising a female and a male model coordinator; a model training workshop coordinator for inexperienced models; and makeup, hair, or other beauty technicians.

Stage Manager

Most shows require the services of a **stage manager** who oversees use of the venue. The venue includes the front of the house, which involves the stage, runway, and seating. The stage manager also organizes equipment and supervises people providing services behind the scenes, such as the properties manager, stagehands, and audio and lighting technicians. The stage manager also supervises any announcers and verbal communication presented at the show. Some facilities, such as city auditoriums, have a stage manager on their staff and may require that they be hired by the group when the venue is rented.

Promotion Coordinator

Although a retail store may delegate the promotion responsibilities to the advertising or marketing department, a show produced by a school or a charitable organization selects a promotion coordinator and a program editor from its staff or students. The **promotion coordinator** is accountable for the creation and distribution of all promotional materials for the show, including news releases, photographs, posters, invitations, tickets, advertisements, signage, table decorations, and other forms of promotion. The promotion coordinator will also perform all public relations activities. This coordinator may hire photographers and a video crew for services before and during the show.

If a program is used, a program editor should be assigned. The **program editor** is responsible for all activities related to creating a program. This includes designing and printing the program, soliciting advertisements, and distributing the program at the event. Advertising is sometimes used to pay for fashion show production expenses or to benefit the charitable organization producing the show.

Merchandise Coordinator

The **merchandise coordinator** is in charge of the selection of merchandise for each scene and the entire show. As we learned earlier, this is the responsibility of the designer with the assistance of the show producer and stylist, if the show launches the designer's collection. Consumer-oriented fashion shows mounted by retail stores, schools, or charitable organizations allow the merchandise coordinator to pick clothing, accessories, and props to pull each segment of the show into a harmonized whole. The merchandise coordinator may delegate merchandise selection responsibilities for specific scenes to committee members. The merchandise coordinator also works very closely with the model coordinator to facilitate fittings prior to the rehearsal.

Budget Coordinator

The **budget coordinator** is responsible for keeping track of all the income (revenues) and costs (expenses). This coordinator helps plan the estimated budget, keeps the fashion show producer and director informed about expenses as they occur, and puts together the final budget once the show is over.

Although some fashion shows involve substantial expenses (as we learned in the opening of this chapter), not all fashion shows have million dollar budgets. However, even small shows can have substantial expenses. Cynthia Tripathi, the budget coordinator for *Get Your Fashion Fix on Route 66*, tells about her responsibilities in Notes from the Runway: Budgeting Is Vital for a Successful Fashion Show. We will discuss budget planning in more detail later in this chapter.

When delegating responsibilities, all available resources, personnel, and services should be considered. A show director must have a sense about people to determine how well they will follow through with assigned work. Sometimes the best available people are volunteers rather than individuals paid to perform a task. However, there will be those volunteers who will not take their responsibilities seriously. Enthusiasm must be proved in actions, not words. The fashion show staff should meet regularly (Fig. 3.4) to make sure all elements come together.

Responsibility Documentation

A **responsibility sheet** is a helpful tool in planning a show and delegating responsibilities and deadlines to all participants (Fig. 3.5). The show director records each delegated task on the responsibility sheet, and then distributes copies of this form to coordinators so that all individuals may know who is accountable for each task and when each task needs to be completed.

Once the leadership team is established, the fashion show executive team can start defining the show. The type and size of the target audience is determined. The team sets the date, time, and location of the show and secures the venue. The theme of the show is created, which will guide the type and quantity of merchandise to be presented.

Figure 3.4
Lynn Tesoro, cofounder and partner of the PR firm HL Group, meets with her staff as they plan 15 shows and presentations that will take place during New York Fashion Week.

Courtesy of WWD/John Aquino, Kyle Ericksen and Jenna Greene

TARGETING THE AUDIENCE

Planning a fashion show must include determining who the audience will be. For the various fashion weeks, the target audience includes the traditional and digital media representatives, influential customers, friends of the designer, and celebrities, as we learned in Chapter 1. Figure 3.6 shows the audience at a Chanel couture show. The stage was designed so the audience members felt as though they were sitting on an airplane as they watched the models walk down the aisle. For consumer shows, audience characteristics will shape all aspects of the event. The audience may consist of fashion-forward trendsetters, working women searching for new career-oriented looks, or individuals on holiday wanting souvenir apparel to show friends where they went on vacation. The merchandise selected for the show must match the audience in order to promote appropriate trends.

Audience Formation

The audience may take two different forms—guaranteed or created. An audience that is established before the show is organized is considered a **guaranteed audience**, individuals who will attend the show regardless of the fashions displayed. A show that is presented at an annual meeting of an organization with an existing membership list is considered a guaranteed audience.

An audience that is established after the show is planned, as a result of promotional activities, is considered a **created audience**. A retailer may use a fashion show to attract an audience for the premiere of a new department. The retailer is creating a new audience by producing a show that meets the needs of the audience. This audience is very concerned with the type of fashions displayed.

An audience may be gathered from many different sources. Department stores may use customer mailing lists. Communities with

RESPONSIBILITY SHEET

Show Theme _____

Show Date _____

SHOW DIRECTOR

Name_____ Phone _____ Email _____

STUDENT OR ORGANIZATION DIRECTOR

Name_____ Phone _____ Email _____

BUDGET COMMITTEE

Coordinator_____ Phone _____ Email _____

Planned budget due_____ Date completed_____

Income Statement due _____ Date completed_____

MERCHANDISE COMMITTEE

Coordinator_____ Phone _____ Email _____

Scene Themes

1. _____
2. _____
3. _____
4. _____
5. _____
6. _____

MODEL COMMITTEE

Coordinator_____ Phone _____ Email _____

Model Agency _____

Agency Contact _____ Phone _____ Email _____

PROMOTION COMMITTEE

Coordinator_____ Phone _____ Email _____

Graphic Designer_____ Phone _____ Email _____

Printer _____ Phone _____ Email _____

Type of Promotion	Contact Person	Date completed
1.		
2.		
3.		
4.		
5.		
6.		

STAGE COMMITTEE

Manager_____ Phone _____ Email _____

Date_____ Time _____

Venue Name _____

Venue Address _____

Venue Contact_____ Phone _____ Email _____

Announcer_____ Phone _____ Email _____

Figure 3.5
The responsibility sheet is a documentation of each coordinator's task and contacts, which also serves as a report about task completion.

Illustration by Carly Grafstein

Courtesy of WWD/Giovanni Giannoni

Figure 3.6
Audience members, such as the ones at this Chanel Couture show, attend fashion shows for a variety of reasons, including finding new fashion inspiration, supporting a charitable cause, or purely for entertainment.

local business or social organizations may share their membership lists. Fashion students from universities, colleges, and high schools are always an eager audience. Fashion shows are generally more successful when they are promoted to a specific audience, rather than to the general public. The size, age, gender, income, and occupation of the targeted audience must be appraised. Other considerations are the interests and lifestyles of the audience, and the occasion and/or season for which the show is being held.

The size of the audience often determines the type of show, although sometimes the type of show can determine the size of the audience. All members of the audience need to be able to easily view the fashions from a comfortable location. A production or runway show may be required if the audience is large, filling a grand ballroom or an auditorium. Small audiences allow a more intimate environment between the models and the audience; therefore, an informal show setting within a

retail store or restaurant may be appropriate. If it is necessary to limit the number of people attending a fashion show, reserved tickets or RSVPs may be required.

Audience Demographics and Psychographics

Demographics are the statistics (including age, gender, education, income, occupation, race and ethnicity, and family size) used to study a population (Swanson & Everett, 2007). **Psychographics** profiles the lifestyle of consumers based upon activities, interests, and opinions. Measurable audience demographic characteristics and psychographic interests should be considered when planning a show. Young audiences need to be entertained with plenty of action. It is also necessary to have louder, more contemporary music with a faster beat for a younger crowd. A mature crowd is usually more interested in the specific merchandise presented, with music targeted to the taste of the audience. If the audience is mixed, the show theme and music should appeal to many age groups.

If selling merchandise is the primary reason for producing a show, then it is important to be aware of the income of the audience. Through database management, retailers know the approximate spending habits of their customers, and this should be reviewed before selecting the merchandise. Merchandise that is too expensive, or has the appearance of being too expensive, will intimidate customers, and they will feel embarrassed that they cannot afford to purchase anything. Conversely, merchandise that is too inexpensive in the eyes of the audience will be overlooked as nonstatus items. Fashions ill matched to the audience will lose both immediate sales and future sales because the audience will not return to the store.

Consider whether the members of the audience will purchase the featured masculine or feminine merchandise for themselves or for someone of the opposite gender. Intimate apparel specialty stores may present a fashion show for its male customers just before Christmas or Valentine's Day. These fashion shows can be very successful promotional tools. Men, who may be uncomfortable entering a lingerie store, might welcome an invitation to a preholiday intimate apparel fashion show. For example, the first Victoria's Secret fashion show was a traditional runway show held at a New York hotel before Valentine's Day to promote the brand.

Fashion show planners should also review the occupations and interests of the audience members. Are members of the audience looking for career clothing or recreational clothing? Some customers may feel they can spend more money if the garments will be used for business instead of pleasure, although others might be looking for apparel to wear on skiing or surfing vacations, or for a special occasion, such as a formal dance or wedding.

Considering the age, income level, gender, occupation, interests, and lifestyle of the audience when planning a show helps the show producers meet the expectations of the audience. Forgetting one element can change the atmosphere of the show and decrease the opportunity for ticket and merchandise sales.

TIMING THE SHOW

While planning a fashion show, timing certain activities of the show is crucial. The schedules for fashion week shows are planned years in advance and the timing of these shows has created many conflicts between the organizers of the New York, London, Paris, and Milan shows, as discussed in Chapter 2. Poor scheduling and timing will cause stress and create havoc as the show time draws near. What can go wrong often does. Having a contingency plan alleviates some of the chaos.

Show Schedule

First, the day, date, and time of the show must be set. This must be established at the same time that the venue is being booked so all efforts can be coordinated and the planners will not be disappointed if the venue is not available. Time of the show must be set so that all participants and audience members can allocate travel time to and from the show. Check for possible conflicts with other events. Avoid selecting a day that is already filled with other community activities.

Some shows are developed 6 months to a year in advance, although others, such as trade show presentations, are pulled together just a few days in advance. Establishing a *timeline*, a way of displaying a list of tasks in chronological order, helps bring order to the process. Timelines are frequently recorded on planning calendars (Fig. 3.7) to help fashion show directors, coordinators, and staff to

FASHION SHOW TIMELINE

Responsibility	Earliest Planning	Latest Planning
Select Show Director and Coordinators	6-12 months	5 weeks
Decide Show Date, Theme, Venue, Audience	6-12 months	5 weeks
Strike Show	day of show	
Evaluation	1 day after show	1 week after show
Budget Committee		
Plan Budget	5 months	5 weeks
Keep Records	continuous	
Prepare Income Statement	1 day after show	1 week after show
Model Committee		
Select Models	3 months	3 weeks
Prepare Tentative Lineup	1 month	2 weeks
Set Choreography	1 month	week of show
Merchandise Committee		
Plan Merchandise Scenes	4 months	3 weeks
Review Merchandise	3 months	2 weeks
Prepare Tentative Lineup	1 month	2 weeks
Schedule Fittings	2 weeks	week of show
Pull Merchandise	week of show	
Prepare Final Lineup	week of show	
Transfer Merchandise	1 week	day of show
Return Merchandise	day of show	1 day after show
Stage Committee		
Reserve Venue	6-12 months	5 weeks
Begin Music Selection	3 months	2 weeks
Plan Set 3 months	2 weeks	
Write Script	1 month	week of show
Plan Seating Arrangement	1 month	week of show
Technical Run-Through	1 week	1 day
Dress Rehearsal	1 week	day of show
Promotion Committee		
Plan Design	6 months	5 weeks
Send to Printer: Poster, Invitation, Tickets	6 weeks	3 weeks
Plan Advertising	3 months	2 weeks
Plan PR	3 months	2 weeks
Write Press Release	2 months	3 weeks
Distribute Press Release	6 weeks	2 weeks
Distribute Posters	6 weeks	2 weeks
Run In-Store Advertising	6 weeks	week of show
Send to Printer: Program	1 month	10 days
Mail Invitations	1 month	2 weeks
Run Print Advertising	1 month	week of show
Start Social Media Campaign	1 month	week of show
Send Thank You Notes	1 day after show	1 week after show

Figure 3.7
The timeline of responsibilities helps the fashion show director, coordinators and staff members stay on schedule with their various jobs.

Illustration by Carly Grafstein

Figure 3.8
The Fashion Calendar lets fashion insiders know when fashion events are scheduled to take place.

Courtesy of FashionCalendar.com

know which milestones need to be achieved at specific predetermined times.

Individuals within the fashion industry are familiar with the **Fashion Calendar** (Fig. 3.8), updated daily online with hard copy issues mailed every other week, which lists American and international fashion events. It serves as a guide for retailers, manufacturers, and the media to keep industry insiders aware of market weeks. It provides a clearinghouse for dates and relevant information regarding key fashion events, helping to avoid potential conflicts.

Length of the Fashion Show

The length of the fashion show should also be established early in the planning process. Usually this helps to determine the number of outfits featured in the show. A show within a retail store should last no longer than 30 to 45 minutes to keep the audience interested in the show. If the audience is more fashion forward, then they may be able to view more clothes in a shorter period of time, and absorb more fashion trends. A younger audience dictates a faster-paced and shorter show. As we learned at the beginning of this chapter, some fashion week shows last less than 10 minutes.

FINDING A VENUE

Once the date is established, where to hold the show is considered. This is called the **venue**, or the location where the show will take place There are many options to consider. Will you hold the show in a hotel, restaurant, or school auditorium? On the retail sales floor? In the manufacturer's showroom? Is your choice available? The stage manager and members of the stage committee are responsible for determining the location of the show if it is not already set by the sponsor of the show, by a school, or by the charitable organization.

Working with a Hotel

The stage manager or someone delegated by the fashion show director should make an appointment to speak with the hotel representative as soon as the date is set. The individual in charge of hotel sales may have such titles as Sales, Marketing, or Event Manager. Depending upon the size and type of hotel there may be one or more people directly involved in the services relating to banquets and catering or sales and marketing.

It is best to have some simple qualifying questions ready prior to the first meeting. Some qualifying questions include the following:

"But having a runway show inside the Louvre has a meaning that goes beyond the simple concept of fashion. . . . It is a statement, a continuation of a long tradition of beauty and sensibility, of passion and a love of art. It's a very positive message. A way to reaffirm our Italian spirit and our culture."
—Massimiliano Giornetti, creative director, Salvatore Ferragamo

1. Is there a specific date when the show is to be held or is the date somewhat flexible?
2. What is the size of the audience?
3. What type of seating arrangements will be needed?
4. Will food service take place in the same location as the fashion show?
5. What sound and lighting systems, staging, and dressing area facilities are available?

The sales director will assist fashion show producers in every aspect of planning as it relates to room rental and food and beverage service. Other services may include setting up, serving, and cleaning up.

There are additional concerns in relation to the physical facilities. The number of people that are able to attend may be limited by the size of the room. However, show planners should work with the type of hotel that can offer the services desired by the group. If a room for an audience of 250 is needed, but the hotel can handle only 100 people, it does not make sense to waste the time of the hotel personnel. The hotel should be able to provide tables, tablecloths, serving dishes, plates, glasses, flatware, and napkins. Some hotels, particularly in larger cities, may be able to provide various seating arrangements from theater style to luncheon style. Extra amenities might include runways and skirting, stages, public address systems, audio-visual projection systems, and technicians to run the media. The show planners should get a list of expenses for using the facility, hospitality, and personnel.

Hotels rarely permit people to use outside caterers or to "self-cater" events. Outside food service preparation has generally been a hassle for hotel personnel and health regulations or state laws may prohibit this type of activity.

Depending upon the target audience, alcoholic beverages may be served to a fashion show audience. If the hotel has a liquor license, the hotel can set up a cash or hosted bar. Show planners should investigate local rules about food and beverage service. For example, some schools do not allow alcoholic beverages to be served at school functions.

When the arrangements are finalized, a contract should be written and signed by both parties. Fashion show planners should be suspicious if a contract is not required as it protects both the hotel and the organization using their services.

Working with a Restaurant

Many of the concerns relevant to working with a restaurant are similar to those discussed when working with a hotel. Restaurants or cocktail lounges may allow fashion show producers to use their facilities as long as the show does not interrupt normal business activities. Owners and managers of such establishments recognize that a fashion show may increase traffic to their site.

A common use for a restaurant is for informal modeling provided by a local retailer during the lunch hour. This would not require the use of specialized music or a large technical staff.

Problems to consider before using a restaurant or lounge for a fashion show might include health regulations and the age of the participants. Dressing rooms cannot be placed in or near kitchen areas, as required by state health officials. Fashion show staff under legal drinking age may not be allowed at the facility during certain business hours.

Working with a Campus Venue

Many high school or college campuses have ballrooms and/or auditoriums that can be used for staging fashion shows. Arrangements to use these venues should be made well in advance, particularly when the popular locations are scheduled for many different school activities. Campus ballrooms and auditoriums are generally booked every night of the week,

especially near the end of the fall semester with Thanksgiving and Christmas holiday events. Such locations may require reserving the space 6 to 12 months, or even more, in advance of the planned show.

Fashion show planners can expect school venues to have strict guidelines and restrictions for use. These guidelines can regulate and limit hours of room availability, the type of food and beverage service, a minor's participation, and participants' willingness to sign liability waivers. Planners can also anticipate regulations regarding ticket sales. In some places, tickets may be sold only through a campus ticket office or through a company such as Ticketmaster, increasing expenses due to setup fees.

Despite some of the limitations and regulations, there are many benefits to using campus facilities. Benefits include a built-in sound system and stage lighting, a portable runway, campus liability insurance, licensed food service, and an experienced staff to set up and take down the seats and runway. The venue might also have the capability of advertising and promoting the event through on-site video screens and signs.

A contract established between the manager of the school venue and the fashion show's director and stage manager clearly states the expectations and expenses for both parties in the rental agreement. The contract approval process can also provide an outline of the steps required for student organizations in their event planning.

Serving Food and Beverages

Food served to the audience depends upon a number of conditions, including the type of show being presented and the budget. Service may be as simple as providing beverages or as elaborate as a multiple course meal (Fig. 3.9).

Courtesy of WWD/Steve Eichner

Figure 3.9
The audience members invited to the 40th anniversary fashion show by Ralph Lauren were treated to a luxurious dinner at the Conservatory Garden in Central Park, which made the event more social.

Retail organizations trying to attract the customer interested in business apparel have presented breakfast and lunch shows. These shows feature a simple and attractive breakfast or lunch during the time this customer traditionally shops or prior to going to the office. Tying mealtime to the entertainment of the fashion show has proved to be a popular approach to attracting this type of client.

Charitable organizations like to include a social element with the formal fashion presentation. A cocktail hour before and/or a meal after the presentations are typical methods of combining food and fashion.

Most restaurants, hotels, or other facilities require using their food and beverage services. This limitation should be discussed when selecting the fashion show location. If there are no such restraints from the location management, it may be appropriate to work with any caterer.

Working with Catering Services

A retail store or a vendor presenting a fashion show at its own location is more likely to work directly with a caterer. A runway may be set up on the retail sales floor where the merchandise is located or in a special room reserved for fashion shows. A vendor may show the collection right in the showroom. A caterer should be able to provide the fashion show planners with samples of their work and information about the type of clients and food served in the past. Photographs of prior parties or events should be able to give the fashion show planners an idea of how previous events were handled. Generally, caterers will provide the names of patrons who have used their services. It is a good idea to check some of the references or check with other people who have used a particular caterer.

A contract should be prepared to protect both the caterer and the fashion show producers. It should explain what will be served, the costs, and any other obligations

of the caterer. Now that the date, time, and place are set, the show planners are ready to consider the theme of the show.

CREATING FASHION SHOW THEMES

Fashion shows should have a **theme** with a creative title, which will tell the audience the nature of the fashion show. These should be selected during the planning stages. The theme can be developed around the targeted audience, about the merchandise designed or selected, or based upon current events. It allows the promotion plan, merchandise selection, and other planning elements to be joined to provide show continuity.

Show Themes

As we learned at the beginning of the chapter, the creative director or designer sets the vision for fashion week or other industry fashion shows. For a retail store, the theme may be established by a fashion trend story that the retail store's public relations or promotion director expects will be attractive to the store's target customers. A fashion school's faculty members, students enrolled in a class, or students involved in a fashion club will select the theme for their show.

Probably the easiest show theme will come from a season or a holiday. Lingerie shows are always popular around Valentine's Day, just as back-to-school shows are expected in August and September. Special occasion, holiday, and resort wear shows are common in October, November, and December. Changing seasons always bring about fashion show ideas, prompting show titles such as *A Holiday Affair*, *Springsational*, or *Summer Fashion Countdown*.

If a holiday theme has been overdone, then current events can be used to create a theme. Current music or art trends may lend themselves to a theme, particularly if the music or art is popular with the selected audience. For example, *Rock the Runway* incorporates music trends as well as clothing themes, whereas *Lights, Camera, Fashion!* involves the excitement of the entertainment industry with that of fashion.

A special interest of the audience may also be an easy theme to develop. Travel inspires such theme ideas as *Wear to Go* and *Get Your Fashion Fix on Route 66*. The outdoor atmosphere may be perfect for a sporting goods fashion show, such as *Safari in Style*, attracting an outdoor audience to the event. *The Professional You!* is a theme appropriate for a career clothing fashion show. *Runway to Wonderland* and *Model Behavior* are examples of fashion shows with popular entertainment themes.

Fashion show themes relating to the type of merchandise or sponsor being presented might include *Bridal Gala*, *Symphony Fashion Jubilee*, or the *Junior League Soiree*. Themes could also be related to the designer presenting the fashions. The *Oscar de la Renta Collections*, *The World of Ralph Lauren*, or *Breakfast with Donna Karan* reflect designer themes. When a fashion show is sponsored by a vendor, publication, or organization, it is often a given that the sponsor's name will be included in the theme. It not only promotes the vendor but can also pull in a larger audience if the vendor is well known. The cover headlines from *Women's Wear Daily* are always creative, often a play on words, and may provide inspiration for your fashion show theme.

Scene Themes

Production fashion shows are divided into scenes or segments depending on the type of merchandise selected. After a show theme has been developed, each scene can be created to coordinate with the chosen title.

The Victoria's Secret production fashion shows are typically divided into several different scenes. Kristin Dian Mariano (2011) reported the scene themes for a Victoria's

Secret fashion show, which opened with *Ballet*, showing dancers performing in red costumes followed by models wearing ballet-influenced lingerie. Another theme, *SuperAngels*, featured models with superhero costumes complete with flowing capes. The show also included lace and jewel-encrusted garments with a Latin inspiration in a scene called *Passion*, a turn-of-the-century New Orleans scene called *I Put a Spell on You*, and an underwater effect identified as *Angels Aquatic* and it ended with a sparkly homage to the brand's loungewear line, titled *Club Pink*.

Runway to Wonderland, a fashion show produced by merchandising students at Northern Arizona University, featured the fusion of fashion trends with images based upon *Alice in Wonderland*. The show was divided into six scenes, each with a distinctive apparel category and complementary theme. The show opened with *Stuck in a Dream*—sleepwear was featured. The second scene, *Chasing the White Rabbit*, highlighted active-and outdoor wear, while casual clothing was presented in *Afternoon with the Caterpillar*, the third scene. A *Mad Tea Party* offered a look at clothing worn after five or on dates, and business apparel was shown in the fifth scene, *Meeting the Queen of Hearts*. The final scene, *A Twisted Fantasy*, featured original designs from collegiate fashion designers from the university and nearby community colleges. Musical selections, dance routines, and skits helped emphasize the various merchandise and Wonderland themes. A discussion of the stage design and music selected to coordinate with the fashion show theme and scene themes is found in Chapter 7.

ESTIMATING THE BUDGET

Many inexperienced fashion show producers think fashion shows cost little or nothing to produce. Even informal shows can involve some substantial costs. As the show becomes more elaborate and complex, the costs increase. The **budget** is an estimate of the revenues and expenses necessary to produce the fashion show. It is the best guess of what the income will be from ticket sales, silent auctions, donations, sponsorship, or vendor cooperative financial support. The costs include everything from model fees to set design and venue rental. The budget must remain flexible, an essential part of the forecasting and planning process, because there may be some unexpected or hidden costs. Budget revisions need to take place as circumstances change.

The type of show being produced, its audience, location, and special features are directly dependent upon the amount of funds available in the budget. The least expensive type of show to produce is an informal show presented right at the point of sale, in the manufacturer's showroom or on the retail sales floor. The most expensive shows are large benefit programs or specialized couture shows for private customers and the fashion trade. These shows require large numbers of support staff as well as hotel and equipment rentals. Some of the top designer fashion shows have been reported to cost over a million dollars. The Victoria's Secret fashion show discussed earlier was estimated to cost $12 million, making it one of the most expensive shows ever produced (Fernandez, 2011). The diamond-encrusted fantasy bra worn by Miranda Kerr, the event's iconic symbol, was priced at $2.5 million.

Regardless of a show's extravagance, fashion show planners must evaluate all of the various expenses involved in producing the show during the initial stages of planning. To achieve the goals set for the production, the budget process must be approached in a methodical manner.

The Fashion Show Planning Budget

The fashion show planning budget is a projection of all of the anticipated revenues and expenses for each fashion show. Some shows, which are staged to raise money for charity or scholarships, keep a close eye on both sides of the budget sheet. Other shows, staged primarily for public relations or fashion image, may not plan to make a profit. Whatever the reason for the show, an accurate accounting of expenses and revenues is necessary.

Betsey Johnson started staging her fashion shows at 7th on Sixth in 1993, when the New York Fashion Week shows began at Bryant Park (Wilson, McCants, Fung, & Kletter, 2000). Johnson spent anywhere from $80,000 to $400,000 each season, depending upon the theme of her collection and her budget. She felt one of the best things about showing at 7th on Sixth was her ability to stick to her budget.

The first step in planning the budget for a fashion show is to consider all of the possible expenditures. Figure 3.10 is a fashion show planning tool that identifies all of the possible fashion show expenses. The fashion show budget coordinator, in cooperation with the fashion show director and coordinators, should get estimates for the various costs. Written estimates should be provided for large expenses, such as venue rental fees and catering. Each show will incur a specific set of expenses. For example, there is generally no venue fee if the show is held in the retail store or vendor's showroom. The plan for expenditures should be updated as the actual expenses are incurred. These records should be kept for a final assessment of the current show, and they should be available for evaluation and reference when planning for future shows. Figure 3.11 is an example of a fashion show planning budget, which is formatted as

POSSIBLE EXPENSES

Venue Rental
Chairs
Decorations
Lighting
Public address system
Runway
Stage design
Tables

Food or Catering
Entertainment
Food service
Hospitality for celebrities and guest designers
Hotel rooms
Transportation

Show Personnel
Cue personnel
Dressers
Hair stylists
Hosts/ushers
Makeup artists
Models
Transportation staff

Promotion
Advertising production
Advertising time and space
Brand image
Invitations
News releases/media kit
Posters
Programs
Publicity materials
Social media
Tickets

Photography, video, and technology
Bloggers
Photographers
Video crew
Website designer

Technical and support staff
Electrician
Sound designer

Miscellaneous or general expenses
Alterations, damages, or replacement of merchandise
Emergency reserve
Gratuities
Insurance
Security
Taxes
Transportation

Illustration by Carly Grafstein

Figure 3.10
Identifying possible fashion show expenses is one of the first steps in creating a fashion show planning budget.

Fashion Show Planning and Final Budget

PLANNED REVENUE	**ACTUAL REVENUE**
Ticket Sales	Ticket Sales
Donations	Donations
Auction Sales	Auction Sales
Sponsorships	Sponsorships
_____	_____
Total Planned Revenue	Total Revenue

PLANNED EXPENDITURES	**ACTUAL EXPENDITURES**
Budget Committee	**Budget Committee**
Ticket Printing	Ticket Printing
Food	Food
Miscellaneous	Miscellaneous
Total	Total
Merchandise Committee	**Merchandise Committee**
Garment Damages	Garment Damages
Garment Bags/Tags	Garment Bags/Tags
Supplies	Supplies
Thank You Cards	Thank You Cards
Miscellaneous	Miscellaneous
Total	Total
Model Committee	**Model Committee**
Food	Food
Hair	Hair
Make-up	Make-up
Model Gifts	Model Gifts
Miscellaneous	Miscellaneous
Total	Total
Promotion Committee	**Promotion Committee**
Advertising	Advertising
News Releases	News Releases
Media Kits	Media Kits
Silent Auction	Silent Auction
Design Services	Design Services
Programs (Printing)	Programs (Printing)
Posters (Printing)	Posters (Printing)
Invitations (Printing)	Invitations (Printing)
Total	Total
Stage Committee	**Stage Committee**
Venue Rental	Venue Rental
Sound Designer	Sound Designer
Custom Lighting	Custom Lighting
Concessions	Concessions
Projector	Projector
Props	Props
Plywood/Craft Supplies	Plywood/Craft Supplies
Miscellaneous	Miscellaneous
Total	Total

Total Planned Expenditures $0.00   **Total Actual Expenditures $0.00**

PLANNED PROFIT/LOSS	**ACTUAL PROFIT/LOSS**
Planned Revenue	Total Revenue
Planned Expenses	Total Expenses
Planned	**Actual**
Profit/Loss _____	**Profit/Loss** _____

Figure 3.11
The fashion show planning budget shows the planned revenues and expenses as well as space for the final actual financial results after the event is completed.

Illustration by Carly Grafstein

an accounting statement with space for the planned revenues and expenses as well as space for the final financial figures after the event has been completed. It is a living document, updated as new information is available.

The fashion show director and staff should be aware of the following categories of anticipated expenses:

Venue rental
Food or catering
Models
Hair stylists and makeup artists
Promotion, including advertising, public relations, and social media development
Photography, video, and technology
Technical and support staff
Miscellaneous expenses such as decorations, transportation, hospitality, depreciation of merchandise, insurance, and taxes

Venue Rental

One of the largest expenses associated with the cost of presenting a fashion show is renting the venue. A charitable organization may ask for reduced or waived rental rates, but members of such groups must realize that hotels, restaurants, and caterers are often asked for such gratuities. These companies are in business to make a profit, but some may be willing to throw in amenities to benefit the cause or charity.

Realistically, most groups, whether they are nonprofit or profit making, will have to lease the space for the event. A **nonprofit organization** has 501(c)(3) status as designated by the Internal Revenue Service. The organization has published articles of incorporation and a board of directors. All profits earned by the organization are returned to the organization. A nonprofit organization may sell tickets and/or ask for donations, using money raised for operational expenses and/or charitable causes.

Costs for the site rental should include the time to set up the facility, rehearse, present the fashion show, serve refreshments, and clean up. Some of the activities, such as room setup and cleanup, may be handled by the employees at the venue. Depending upon the room and facilities, these activities may require outside help.

If a rehearsal is required, the estimated cost of using a rehearsal room or renting the site of the actual fashion show must be included in the expenses. If it is not possible to use the contracted space for a rehearsal, another room may be needed for planning choreography and practicing the show. Costs for renting all rehearsal rooms must be added to the budget.

One of the first questions the hotel's sales or marketing director will ask about is the date of the show. The season, day of week, and time of day will affect the price for the room. During the busy seasons, especially Thanksgiving through New Year's Eve and the traditional wedding period, hotel banquet rooms are solidly booked, as much as a year in advance. Saturday nights are more expensive than weeknights. Evenings are more costly than times during the day. The show planners should keep in mind that a hotel sales director may not be able to accommodate you if an event on the date you want for your show is already reserved. It is best to reserve the venue you want to use as early as possible.

If a meal is served in one room while the show is presented in another, there will be additional charges for the use of two rooms. The hotel representative and show producers must consider where the models will change. One possibility is to use an adjacent meeting room. Another prospect is to use nearby hotel rooms. Costs for these spaces must be factored into the budget. Some hotels may be willing to waive or negotiate reduced rates for the rental of the rooms if specified food and beverage expenditures are met. The fashion show planners should expect to pay a deposit for the hotel services.

Food or Catering Expenses

There are two factors to be evaluated in relationship to food service budgets. Food and beverages to be served to the audience must be a foremost concern. However, it may also be necessary to provide refreshments to the crew during rehearsal, setup, and stage strike. Feeding the behind-the-scenes crew and models is an appropriate gesture. Union rules may require serving food to union members dependent upon the amount of time involved.

Although an actual contract most likely will be negotiated, at minimum the fashion show staff should expect a written estimate regarding food and catering services. Most likely a deposit or prepayment may be required.

Model Expenses

The expense of hiring professional models varies from one city to another. Customarily, models are paid on an hourly basis, and this fee will include their time at fittings, rehearsals, and the show. Top international models may demand very high salaries.

Each year *Women's Wear Daily*, *Vogue*, and the *New York Times* report the astronomical salaries paid to supermodels. Readers are dazzled to hear that a model is paid $5 million to pose for an advertising campaign or $25,000 per day to walk the catwalk shows. Although the world's highest paid model, Gisele Bündchen, earned $45 million in a year (Blankfeld &

Bertoni, 2011), other models may earn as little as $75 per hour or nothing.

Designer shows have the potential to pay the highest runway rates. For name models at the top of their career, agencies negotiate the highest possible rates. Modeling fees for top models at designer shows may run as high as $1,000 to $5,000 or more, whereas new models are paid in dresses (Mears, 2011). Hundreds of new young models, such as the girls glamorized on television reality shows, work freelance, without benefits, and are often indebted to their agencies for apartment rentals, plane tickets, and various other expenses.

Because amateur models are often used for retail or charity shows, it may be appropriate to offer them a gift, such as a discount or a gift certificate. The discount will be included as part of the store's markdown allocation and is not considered part of the fashion show budget. Costs for any gifts or flowers presented to amateur models, however, should be considered a part of the fashion show budget.

Hair Stylists and Makeup Artists

If professional hair and makeup personnel are used to create the "look" for models, their fees must be included as expenses. Even if members of the model committee take on the task of doing hair and makeup as part of their committee responsibilities, the cost of supplies, such as hairspray and makeup, is part of the budget.

Promotion Expenses

Activities relating to advertising and public relations should also be included in the budget, including all duties from designing and producing to distributing the materials that are created. Invitations, posters, programs, and tickets need to be designed and printed; invitations need to be mailed, printed in a newspaper or magazine, or posted on the

Internet. If tickets are used, there is a cost for buying printed coupons or designing special personalized tickets. The costs for all of these materials must be included in the budget.

To project a consistent look and prevent duplication of the printer's setup costs, one printer can print invitations, posters, programs, and tickets. Also, a printer may prefer to bid on a package rather than individual items. Printing costs are determined by the types of services required. Each service increases the cost. There is a cost involved if the size of any artwork needs to be enlarged or reduced to fit on the different sized products. Basic black ink is the least expensive color to reproduce. Colored inks and the use of multiple colors are more costly. The type, weight, and color of paper will also affect the overall printing cost.

Promotional expenses must include the cost of creative production, which involves any artwork, graphic design, or layout for print or digital materials. It also involves any photography, models, filming or video recording, or studio rental. The creation of media releases and media kits may be the responsibility of someone working for the firm producing the show, an outside media agent, or a student on the promotion committee. Those costs of developing media releases, photographs used in the media materials, and any additional materials used to publicize the event must be incorporated into the budget.

If advertising plans include buying spots on radio or television, the cost of producing the commercial becomes a budget item. Buying space in the newspaper or magazine must also be added to costs.

Photography and Video Expenses

Photography expenses will need to be considered as part of the budget. The fashion show staff will need to determine the type of photography required. The staff may wish to include a photograph rather than artwork for invitations and advertising purposes. This would require hiring a photographer and model far in advance of the show to allow time for printing or posting to the Internet.

A photographic record of the show may also be desired. Expenses relating to hiring the photographer and his or her supplies will need to be figured into the budget. Media photographers from a newspaper or magazine are sent by their employers to record the event for their medium. Because media photographers are guests and often are the target for fashion show publicity, their expenses are not included in the budget.

A DVD of the show is frequently desired and commonly recorded. The production may be a simple start-to-finish documentary of the event or an elaborately edited production. Manufacturers regularly record their fashion shows to use as an employee training tool, teaching sales personnel about the items in the latest line, or as a promotional strategy, playing a recording of the show in the retail sales area to educate customers about the styles being offered. Educational institutions use fashion show videos as recruiting materials to attract new students to the school where the show is produced, or as a historical record. Students enrolled in fashion show production classes like to view the shows produced by previous classes and to use them as a guide for creating their own assignments. Students also like to keep a DVD as part of their portfolio for future employment.

Technical Staff and Support Staff Expenses

Salaries for any people hired to perform technical aspects of the show are also part of the budget. Examples of such technical staff include the carpenters hired to build, set up, and paint the stage, runway, backdrops, or props. The services of electricians who work on the lighting and public address system may be needed. Musicians, recording personnel, or D.J.s may be hired to provide the essential musical mood.

The support staff includes all behind-the-scenes personnel who facilitate the smooth and professional appearance of the show. These people are typically the unsung heroes of the show. The budget must cover the expenses for the dressers, alterations and pressing people, and security. For charity shows, many of these indispensable participants may be volunteers.

The need for **hosts** and **ushers**, people in charge of greeting people, handing out programs, and directing the audience members to their seats, increases as the show gets larger and more complex. Members of professional or charitable organizations may serve as volunteer hosts for charity shows. Commercial events may need to hire people or use company employees or interns, as we learned in Chapter 1, to help seat the audience.

Members of the audience will be impressed with the organization presenting the show when guests are handled courteously and professionally. Hosts or ushers may act as greeters. The hosts should have a detailed list of guests for shows that require reservations and/or special seating. Hosts and ushers then direct guests to their seats. Having prearranged seating charts makes the job easier for the hosts and ushers and makes the guests feel welcome.

Gratuities are the cash tips given to service people such as wait staff and attendants in the coat check area and restrooms. Tips may be included in the cost to the hotel, restaurant, or caterer and are negotiated at the time the location and services are reserved.

Miscellaneous Expenses
Any expenses not previously discussed are considered miscellaneous expenses. Decorations and transportation are two examples. Decorations for the physical facilities may be limited to the stage and runway setup. More elaborate scenes may include floral arrangements or special table settings. Adornment of the room is determined by the type of show, location, audience, and budget allocation. A fashion show with a nautical theme could include miniature ships and red, white, and blue table accessories. A southwestern theme could be decorated with coyotes, cactuses, conchas, and brightly colored textiles.

Ideas for ornamentation are limitless. The theme of the show can be greatly enhanced by using decorative elements. Charitable organizations may use table centerpieces as additional fund-raisers by holding a raffle for these elements. The only constraint for decorating is budgetary limitations.

Transportation costs must be considered. Clothing may have to be moved from the store or vendor's showroom to the location of the show. Equipment such as runways, rolling racks, steamers, and furniture may have to be moved. Transportation of celebrities from another city or within the city may also have to be considered, so hiring a limousine for ground transportation may be necessary.

Hospitality includes arrangements for housing, food, or entertainment for special guests. A celebrity designer may be brought to a city to meet potential customers at a retail store or for a benefit show. The designer may request the participation of his or her favorite models. Additional personnel, such as a fashion show coordinator or stylist from the designer's staff, may travel with the designer to coordinate activities with the local retail store promoting the designer's appearance. Senior executives of the retail company may arrive from other parts of the country. Hotel rooms, meals, and transit must be provided for out-of-town participants. Any special activities before or after the fashion show for patrons of an organization must be included in the budget.

Merchandise can become damaged or lost even though great care is taken in preserving the condition of the garments and accessories. Sometimes items break, seams fail, or merchandise is missing after the show. The cost of replacing or reconditioning merchandise to its original condition is another item that should be added into the budget.

The value of the merchandise may require purchasing special insurance to guarantee the product in case of theft or damage. Insurance may be needed for such high-cost items as fine jewelry, furs, or designer clothes. The cost of the insurance or security becomes part of the budget.

Depending upon the geographic location, taxes for various services may be levied. Taxes can greatly add to the expenses of doing a fashion show.

PROTECTING PEOPLE AND THINGS

The security of merchandise and equipment is a big concern when producing a fashion show and should not be overlooked during show preparation. The security of the audience and show personnel must also be investigated to ensure safety of the participants and to protect the show against legal damages. Protection of people and materials should be reviewed as the show is finalized. To protect all individuals involved in transportation of merchandise, equipment, locations, or any other materials, agreements should be put in writing and signed by both show personnel and the leasing agent for the venue and the merchandise.

Merchandise Security

Merchandise on loan from retailers for the rehearsals and the show is the responsibility of the show staff. It must be protected from damage while it is being transported and worn, and from theft or vandalism.

Consumer shows on location away from a retail store have special concerns regarding theft. The nature of fashion shows permits many individuals to have access to the stage and dressing areas where merchandise is located during the show preparation and performance. Consequently, merchandise should be protected from potential theft. Show personnel should always be aware of all necessary staff and question any unfamiliar bystanders. Hiring professional models and technicians may cause less concern than using amateurs.

The entire merchandise committee should be assigned the responsibility for organizing, labeling, transferring, and securing the merchandise from the retail store to the show location. This committee should also know what personnel may have direct contact with the merchandise. Shows using amateur models or amateur dressers may ask these individuals to sign waivers making them responsible for missing or damaged merchandise. This contract encourages and strengthens a sense

PERSONAL RESPONSIBILITY CONTRACT

As a participant in (<u>fill in the name and date[s] of the show</u>) presented by (<u>fill in name of group</u>) at (<u>fill in the name of the venue</u>). The show will display merchandise from local merchants and student designers to benefit (<u>fill in the name of the group/organization</u>). I agree to the following rules:

- I accept responsibility for caring for each garment and accessory item that I will be in contact with in a professional manner, during fittings, the dress rehearsal, and the show.
- It is my responsibility to report any damaged or missing items to the merchandise coordinator immediately. I will be held accountable for any damaged or missing merchandise for which I was responsible. I will be asked to pay for damages if I was irresponsible or negligent.
- I agree to act in a professional and reputable manner while participating in this show.
- I agree to attend all of the practices, fittings, and rehearsals to which I am assigned during the 6 weeks prior to the show. If I have more than 2 absences, I will not be allowed to participate in the show.

SIGNATURE_____ DATE_____
PRINT NAME_____
PHONE NUMBER_____
EMAIL_____

Illustration by Carly Grafstein

Figure 3.12
A personal responsibility contract may be developed to assure the dependability and accountability of all of the fashion show models.

of responsibility. Figure 3.12 is an example of a personal responsibility contract for amateur models.

Beyond merchandise security against theft or damage, couture or prestige merchandise must be protected against **design piracy**. Stealing designs and creating **knockoffs**, or copies of designer originals at lower prices, are so commonplace in the fashion industry that European designers hire security agents during collection openings. The agents do not allow any individuals to see the collection until it is presented on the runway. Timing is crucial in the presentation of these design ideas. They are so secret that a show can be ruined if the design ideas are leaked before the proper time. Some designers, including Tom Ford, have kept their designs secret for as long as possible. They hold private fashion shows for a limited number of magazine editors and celebrity clients so that their designs are not immediately displayed on the Internet and duplicated before they even reach the retail stores.

Venue and Equipment Security

Show staff also has the responsibility of securing the location and any borrowed or leased equipment. **Lease agreements**, contracts between leasing agency and users, should be written before the show. If necessary, security personnel should be hired to keep watch over the equipment.

Hotels, auditoriums, restaurants, and other locations may provide insurance policies to cover show liabilities. The show coordinator should know where the responsibility for fashion show insurance lies, with the show personnel or with the venue. If insurance is provided, show planners should make sure it covers the period of time when the merchandise is transported from the retail store or showroom to the show location. The policy should also cover the audience and personnel of the show against accidents or injury as a result of attending the fashion show. If the location does not provide insurance, the fashion show committee may wish to take out a policy to protect merchandise, equipment, personnel, and guests of the show. It is better to have coverage than leave the show organization open to lawsuits, which may be very costly.

Audience Security

The audience must also feel safe at the location and be protected from equipment used during the show. Electrical cords, used for sound equipment or lighting, that cross audience walkways should be taped securely to the floor. It is necessary for show personnel to make sure fire codes have been met at the location. Fire extinguishers and other safety equipment should be available. Entrances and exits should be marked for the audience in case of emergency. Aisles should be spaced properly to allow for easy access.

Staff Security

In addition to being concerned about audience safety, fashion show planners need to assure the safekeeping of all the models, announcers, technicians, makeup and hair personnel, dressers, show coordinators and staff, and backstage guests. Care must be taken with garment steamers, electrical cords, merchandise fixtures, hair appliances, trash, and any equipment that might be dangerous.

Security should never be overlooked in show preparation. The show director is responsible for accidents or injuries of the audience and staff; professionally, the director must assure the safety of the garments and accessories; personally, the director must show confidence to the staff and crew that safety will be assured.

FINALIZING THE FASHION SHOW PLAN

The **fashion show plan** (Fig. 3.13) is a document that describes all of the preliminary decisions made to produce the fashion show. It serves as a guide to setting up a more detailed action plan. The fashion show plan includes the following information:

- Name (theme) of the show
- Themes of each scene (if used)
- Names and titles of the fashion show leadership team
- Type of show
- Type of merchandise
- Schedule, including date and time of rehearsals as well as of the actual show
- Venue
- Planning calendars (Fig. 3.14)
- Target audience for fashion show attendance
- Planning budget

It is a mistake to overlook the importance of planning and budgeting; therefore, effort needs to be put into the preliminary stages of the fashion show to make the process go smoothly. Often, excitement and enthusiasm overshadow the details necessary to produce a successful fashion show. One such detail that cannot be ignored is the budget. Controlling costs will add to the profit if the show is intended to make a profit. Accurately

FASHION SHOW PLAN

Name (theme) of the show_____

Date_____

Time of Show_____

Themes of each scene (if used)

_____

_____

Names, titles, and contact information of the fashion show leadership team

Director_____

Student or Organization Director_____

Budget Coordinator_____

Merchandise Coordinator_____

Model Coordinator_____

Promotion Coordinator_____

Stage Manager_____

Type of show_____

Type of merchandise_____

_____

_____

_____

Names and contact information of retailers and/or designers

_____

_____

_____

_____

Schedule, including dates and time of rehearsals and the actual show

_____

_____

_____

_____

Venue

Venue name_____

Venue address_____

Venue Contact_____Phone_____Email_____

Planning calendars and timeline (attach)

Target audience for fashion show attendance

_____

_____

_____

Planning budget (attach)

Figure 3.13
A fashion show plan will guide all of the people involved in producing a successful fashion show.

Illustration by Carly Grafstein

OCTOBER

Sunday	Monday	Tuesday	Wednesday	Thursday	Friday	Saturday
					1 Model Casting Contact student designers	**2** Model Casting
3	**4** Contact retailers Planned budget due	**5** Contact retailers Scene titles due Visit & confirm venue	**6** Contact retailers Model Practice 8pm	**7** Contact retailers Invitations, posters & ticket rough drafts ready to proof	**8** Contact retailers	**9**
10	**11** Confirm Retailers & Designers	**12** Invitations, tickets & posters go to printer	**13** Model Practice 8pm	**14** Ideal Charts Due	**15**	**16** Make-up model practice
17	**18**	**19** Invitations, tickets & posters delivered from printed	**20** Model Practice 8pm	**21** Invitations sent	**22**	**23** Make-up model practice
24 **31**	**25**	**26** Music selections due	**27** Model Practice 8pm Tickets go on sale	**28** News releases drafted Photos for taken	**29** Student designs due	**30** Make-up model practice

NOVEMBER

Sunday	Monday	Tuesday	Wednesday	Thursday	Friday	Saturday
	1	**2** Posters printed Scripts completed	**3** Model Practice 8 pm	**4**	**5** News releases distributed	**6** Make-up model practice
7	**8** Hair & makeup looks demonstrated	**9**	**10** Model Practice 8 pm	**11**	**12** Facebook page, blog & other social media goes live	**13** Make-up model practice Model fittings
14 Model fittings	**15** Model fittings	**16** Model fittings Pick up Silent Auction items	**17** Model Practice 8 pm Pick up clothes	**18** Pick up clothes Organize clothes by model	**19** SHOW DAY! Set the stage Rehearsal 9 am Doors open 5:30pm	**20** SHOW DAY! Doors open 11:30 am Return clothing after show
21	**22** Write thank-you notes Committee budgets due	**23**	**24** Thanksgiving Break	**25** Thanksgiving Break	**26** Thanksgiving Break	**27**
28	**29** Committee Diaries Due	**30** Final Income Statement due				

Figure 3.14
Planning calendars help everyone working on the show to know what activities are taking place and when the deadlines will occur.

Illustration by Carly Grafstein

projecting ticket sales will enable fashion show planners to set realistic expectations for spending money on such things as venue and model expenses, hospitality, and staging expenses. In evaluating the success of a show, fashion directors and retail executives will always want to know if the show was within the budgetary estimates set prior to the show. If the show comes within budget, the executives are more likely to look favorably on this type of promotion and be responsive to future fashion show productions. The more planning that goes into the show the more confidence the show director and fashion show staff will have when it comes time to present the fashions. Planning will not prevent all problems associated with fashion show production, but it will help to eliminate many concerns and make the entire experience enjoyable.

So, You Want to Be a Fashion Stylist? . . .

Reah Norman

Courtesy of Reah Norman

A career as a fashion stylist is filled with photo shoots, celebrities, exotic locations, beautiful models, gorgeous clothing and accessories, industry events, and rubbing elbows with the "who's who" of the industry. I get e-mails daily from aspiring stylists asking me for advice. Here is the lowdown on what it really takes to become a stylist.

What Is a Fashion Stylist?

Fashion stylists are trendsetters, image consultants, fashion forecasters, personal shoppers, fashion show coordinators, fashion writers, magazine editors, and bloggers. Stylist categories include the following:

- **Celebrity**—dressing public figures for the red carpet and special events
- **Wardrobe**—dressing actors for movies, television shows, commercials, and music videos
- **Print and editorial**—dressing models for advertising campaigns, magazines, and other publications
- **Fashion shows**—dressing models for fashion runway presentations
- **Image consulting and personal shopping**—dressing private clients who want assistance with wardrobe selection, shopping, closet organization, and packing for travel
- **Model portfolio development**—advising and styling aspiring models on their portfolios and working with the agent to create looks that will appeal to the model's potential clients
- **Fashion writing**—contributing to magazines, blogs, and other publications as a fashion expert
- **Product styling**—products photographed without a model in a studio or on location
- **Prop styling**—creating an environment for a shoot or event, including anything from a small table setting to a complete room

Stylists often wear several different hats, and our focus shifts as we work with different clients. I offer all of these services in my business, but other stylists choose to focus on just one category.

What Skills and Traits Are Needed to Be a Successful Stylist?

Stylists should be artistic, creative, fashionable, confident, personable, well spoken, outgoing, and, most of all, highly organized with a strong attention to detail. These are just a few of the skills that shape a successful stylist.

Be Organized

Being organized with a strong attention to detail is the most important part of being a successful stylist. This shapes your day-to-day business—on a job as well as during pre- and post-production. Time management is essential. As a freelance stylist, I set my own time, scheduling clients and business meetings, doing fittings, and meeting deadlines. I organize my fashion shoots, which involves labeling and putting the clothing in order on the clothing rack; laying out shoes and accessories; and keeping receipts, tags, and shopping bags ready for returns. Then I pin a garment onto a model, tape the bottom of shoes, and keep accessories separate in bags.

Know Fashion, Art, and Design

Stylists are artists. Having a strong artistic perspective and being proficient in basic art and photography skills are just as important as having a strong fashion sense. Of course, I put my artistic touches into the looks I coordinate.

Stylists need to have an overall knowledge of fashion and all that it encompasses, including design, merchandising, marketing, textiles, and retail. Having knowledge of clothing construction and how garments fit on the body is also helpful. I also use my knowledge of fabrications, textiles, fashion terminology, marketing, and selling when speaking with clients and designers. Being educated on the history of fashion is also essential. Every era of fashion is unique, and these eras continue to influence today's fashion collections. You must know where to draw inspiration from, especially when the concept is period specific.

Understand Customer Service and Communication

As a stylist, I use my customer service proficiency every day. I am so thankful for my days working as a receptionist and in a retail store where I learned these skills. I am constantly working with new, creative personalities and must be able to adapt to those personalities, interact graciously, communicate ideas and concepts eloquently, and establish trust that will allow the professional relationship to grow. Because stylists are asked to speak as experts at fashion presentations and workshops, being comfortable in front of an audience and public speaking is also important.

What Is Involved in the Business of Being a Stylist?

As a freelance stylist, I am running my own small business. There is much more that goes into it than simply styling a client. Having a formal college education has definitely been an asset to my business in many ways. I am much more confident in my abilities, not just as a stylist, but also as a small business owner. There are specific skills, including marketing, accounting, communication, merchandising, photography, art, and public speaking, that I learned in college and use every day.

The business of styling has a huge financial responsibility. Stylists must have established credit—and lots of it—in good standing! Stylists use their credit cards to make purchases for the job, and are reimbursed after the job is done—anywhere from 30 to 90 days after the job is completed. In many cases, stylists are given a budget by the client or producer. Then, the stylist will shop using her own credit cards to put looks together for the shoot. Items that are not used for the project are returned after the shoot. Daily accounting and managing finances are essential so that you are not charged late fees or interest.

How Can You Get Started as a Stylist?

My journey to a career as a fashion stylist started as a young girl, playing "photo shoot" in my bedroom "photo studio." It was fully equipped with a white sheet tacked to the wall, a Fisher Price camera, and my dolls and stuffed animals as models. I have always loved creating magic with pictures. Throughout high school, junior college, and at the university, I took photography courses. I received my B.S. in merchandising with a minor in photography from Northern Arizona University. After graduation I moved to Los Angeles and completed a visual communications program at the Fashion Institute of Design and Merchandising (FIDM). I was certain that I wanted to pursue styling as my career path, and upon graduation I landed my first job as a stylist.

Many stylists get their start by working as an intern or assistant for a working stylist or at a fashion house, magazine, or PR agency. Assisting established stylists is the best way to get firsthand experience—working and learning the "ins and outs" of a stylist's daily tasks. Many interns and assistants do not get paid at first. If you have a great work ethic and prove yourself, the stylist will eventually hire you to work on paid assignments and will recommend you to other stylists as well. Your work is your reputation and word-of-mouth recommendations carry a lot of weight. This business is all about building your reputation, networking, and getting recommendations from satisfied clients.

Does this sound like you? If so, go for it! Being a stylist is creative and rewarding. If all of this makes sense to you, styling is definitely a dream job!

Reah Norman graduated from Northern Arizona University and served as the Merchandise Coordinator for the fashion show *Wear to Go*. She lives in Los Angeles and regularly commutes to New York City for assignments. She is a well-respected fashion and product stylist, a plus size fashion expert, and the Executive Fashion Director for *PLUS Model Magazine*.

Budgeting Is Vital for a Successful Fashion Show

Cynthia Tripathi

Courtesy of Cynthia Tripathi

Budget—it's not exactly the most exciting or creative part of developing a fashion show. For me, however, it was the perfect job. As a junior in college studying merchandising, I took the role of budget coordinator for our biennial fashion show. Not many other students were jumping at the chance to take on this role, so why did I want to take the lead on the budget as opposed to the fun job of coordinating the merchandise, for example?

Directing the budget is a way for someone to be involved in every aspect of a fashion show. It is also vital to the success of the show. Every committee has its own responsibilities. *Get Your Fashion Fix on Route 66* was composed of the merchandise, model, stage, publicity, and, of course, the budget committees. What does each of these committees have in common? They all have necessary expenses in order to carry out their duties. That's where I stepped in.

A fashion show requires planning. The budget is perhaps the most important part of the planning process. One simply cannot spend freely on whatever he or she wishes. Every show, whether small or large, will need to stay within a budget. Estimating costs is significant, especially if the show plans on generating a profit. *Get Your Fashion Fix on Route 66* was produced to raise money for the Merchandising Leaders of the 21st Century Scholarship fund at Northern Arizona University. Staying within a reasonable budget meant the opportunity to raise more money for the scholarship, which was beneficial to many of the merchandising students.

How does one even begin planning a budget? Because our show was biennial, I began by looking at previous budgets. This gave me an idea of all the expenses that would go into the production of the event. I asked each committee to draft a budget for all of their projected expenses. I took these documents and examined them carefully. I added a miscellaneous section to each budget to account for anything that may come up in the course of production. After adjusting some numbers, I compiled a master planning budget.

Although a budget needs to remain flexible, it is also critical to uphold control of all expenditures. I asked all the committee coordinators to approve any spending with me and the faculty director prior to making their purchases. Upon my approval, they gave me every single receipt. This helped me not only to control the outflow of funds and stay within the budget, but also to keep track of all expenses and reimbursements accordingly.

Now one may think that the budget is the only responsibility of a budget director. Although it is the primary duty, I was also in charge of tickets, sponsorships, donations, and various other tasks. Organization is key in successfully developing and maintaining a budget. I had to keep track of all tickets, receipts, money, donations, letters, and so forth. It is essential to be organized and keep a record of everything.

Money

All fashion shows need funds to produce and execute the event successfully. A good source of income is fund-raising. *Get Your Fashion Fix on Route 66* relied primarily on ticket sales, silent auction sales, as well as sponsorships from friends, family, and the community. As with any facet of preproduction, this too requires planning in advance. My budget team was responsible for contacting local businesses to ask for sponsorships and donations. I drafted letters explaining the details of our show and how the proceeds would go to a scholarship fund to benefit hardworking merchandising students. Individually, members of my team each went to various businesses around the community with the letter in hand.

Businesses will only be willing to donate and support an event that carries a professional image. When physically contacting businesses, I ensured that my team dressed professionally, kept a positive attitude, possessed confidence about our show, and always had a smile. Professionalism is absolutely crucial in any event planning.

Directing a team for the first time gave me hands-on experience in how to be an effective leader. The two main points of advice I would give anyone who is in charge of a team is to have open lines of communication and delegate tasks among members. Communication is imperative among team members and all staff involved in production. It is necessary to be available at all times to solve problems and deal with any issues that may arise.

As the budget coordinator, I had to make certain that all of my team's obligations ran smoothly. Leading a team doesn't mean taking charge of all tasks. I learned that it is necessary to delegate tasks appropriately because it is nearly impossible to prepare everything on your own. Directing involves overseeing the work of your subordinates and providing the necessary guidance and support to ensure tasks get completed in an efficient manner. I constantly asked my team for their opinions and ideas for improvement throughout the course of our work. This is where communication was vital and completion of work provided immense contribution to the fashion show itself.

After months of planning and hard work, the day of the show finally arrived. The work, however, wasn't complete. As a team, my committee was mainly in charge of ticket sales on show days. We checked guests into the show and kept their tickets in order to track attendance. We also set up a table for additional donations, purchased food for everyone involved behind the scenes of the production, and ran several errands to guarantee the show ran smoothly.

Watching *Get Your Fashion Fix on Route 66* finally come together was an indescribable feeling. Almost an entire year of planning and work went into the production, and in the end it was worth it. It was a huge accomplishment knowing that I, and countless others, contributed to producing an entire fashion show.

After the show was over, I completed a final budget. This showed actual expenditures, revenue, and total profit from the event. We remained well under budget and were able to make a generous deposit to the Merchandising Leaders of the 21st Century Scholarship fund. I also sent out thank-you letters to all the friends, family, and businesses that supported our production.

Directing the budget committee was a valuable experience. It certainly wasn't an easy job by any means. Dedication and persistence were necessary on my part throughout the planning process. It was rewarding to see that our show was produced well under the planned budget, and we were able to play a significant role in providing for the scholarship fund. I eventually came to be one of the recipients of the scholarship and took pride in the fact that I made an impact in helping scholarship recipients, such as myself, to pursue academic success.

Cynthia Tripathi, from Tucson, Arizona, graduated with a B.S. in Merchandising from Northern Arizona University where she was the Budget Coordinator for *Get Your Fashion Fix on Route 66*. She completed two different minors in business and in photography. In addition to her involvement in fashion, she is a certified personal trainer.

THE PLAN—A RECAP

- The first step in creating a fashion show plan is to develop leadership, which differs between professional designer industry events and consumer-oriented retail, educational, or charitable events.
- Responsibility documentation helps keep all people involved in the production aware of what needs to be accomplished and when the deadlines are.
- The target audience for fashion week shows includes traditional and digital media journalists, influential customers, friends of the designer, and celebrities.
- For consumer shows, audiences include fashion-forward trendsetters, working women searching for new career-oriented looks, or individuals on holiday wanting souvenir apparel; audiences are targeted based upon demographic and psychographic characteristics.
- Scheduling and timing the show are set by industry standards and educational institution expectations. The day, date, and time of the show must be established early in the planning process.
- Fashion shows will have a theme with a creative title, which defines the nature of the fashion show and assists the fashion show staff in promotional activities. If the show promotes several themes, each scene will also have a theme connecting it to the overall show theme.
- The planning budget is an estimate of the revenues—income from ticket sales, silent auctions, donations, sponsorship, or vendor support—and expenses—model fees, staging costs, venue rental, food and refreshments, hair and makeup artists, and any other costs necessary to produce the fashion show.
- The security of merchandise, equipment, audience members, and show personnel must also be investigated to ensure safety of the participants and protect the show producers against legal damages.
- The fashion show plan defines the theme, leadership team, type of show, schedule, place, target audience, and planned budget.

KEY FASHION SHOW TERMS

budget	knockoff
budget coordinator	lease agreement
celebrity stylist	merchandise coordinator
created audience	model coordinator
demographics	nonprofit organization
design piracy	planning
diary	program editor
editorial stylist	promotion coordinator
Fashion Calendar	psychographics
fashion director	responsibility sheet
fashion show director	show producer
fashion show plan	stage manager
gratuities	theme
guaranteed audience	usher
host	venue

QUESTIONS FOR DISCUSSION

1. Were you on a prom, a wedding, or an anniversary planning committee? What steps did you take to make it a success? What would you do differently next time?
2. How does the leadership differ between an industry show and a consumer-oriented show produced by a school or charitable organization?
3. How does the audience differ between that of a designer industry show and an audience attending a school or charitable organization show? How do you attract the target audience to your show?
4. Discuss the advantages and disadvantages of holding a fashion show at a hotel, restaurant, or campus venue.
5. Who creates a fashion show theme?
6. What types of expenses should be included in a fashion show budget for a show you plan on presenting? How far in advance should you start planning the budget?
7. What should be included in a fashion show plan?

FASHION SHOW ACTIVITIES

1. Break into teams of four or five students or fashion show volunteers. Each group should suggest a theme for a fashion show. The team will present their ideas to the group, explaining why they think it would be a good theme for your group's fashion show.
2. What kinds of permissions will you need to put on a fashion show at your school? Put together a list of all the people with their contact information whom you will need for approval of your fashion show.

THE CAPSTONE PROJECT

It is time to start planning your fashion show. Put together a fashion show plan, which includes the following:

CD-ROM

- leadership job descriptions
- process for selecting merchandise, model, budget, stage, promotion, and budget coordinators
- show type, show theme, and scene themes
- show date, time, and location
- target audience characteristics and size
- planning calendars for each team
- anticipated revenues from ticket sales, sponsorships, donations, or advertising
- anticipated expenses for each team

Templates for the fashion show plan and budget are available on the CD-ROM included with this book. Please refer to the CD-ROM for tools that may assist you with this section of the fashion show planning process.

References

Agins, T. (2006, February 9). Who's the coolest kid at fashion week? Some say the stylist. *Pittsburgh Post-Gazette.* Retrieved from http://www.post-gazette.com

Blankfeld, K., & Bertoni, S. (2011, May 5). The world's top earning models. *Forbes.* Retrieved from http://www.forbes.com

Fernandez, S. M. (2011, November 29). Inside Victoria Secret's sexy $12 million fashion show. *Hollywood Reporter.* Retrieved from http://www.hollywoodreporter.com

Mariano, K. D. (2011, November 9). Victoria's Secret revealed: Details of VS fashion show leaked. *International Business Times.* Retrieved from http://www.au.ibtimes.com

Mears, A. (2011, September 14). Poor models. Seriously. *The New York Times.* Retrieved from http://www.nytimes.com

Menkes, S. (2012, June 11). Ferragamo takes stage at the Louvre. *The New York Times.* Retrieved from http://www.nytimes.com

Swanson, K. K., & Everett, J. C. (2007). *Promotion in the merchandising environment* (2nd ed.). New York, NY: Fairchild Books.

Trebay, G. (2011, February 16). At Marc Jacobs, the show before the show. *The New York Times.* Retrieved from http://www.nytimes.com

Vilaseca, E. (2010). *Runway uncovered: The making of a fashion show.* Barcelona, Spain: Promopress.

Widdows, L., & McGuiness, J. (1997). *Catwalking: Working with models.* London, UK: Batsford.

Wilson, E., McCants, L., Fung, S., & Kletter, M. (2000, August 24). Selling the shows: Would a new owner spoil a good thing? *Women's Wear Daily,* pp. 6–7.

CHAPTER FOUR
The Message

AFTER READING THIS CHAPTER, YOU SHOULD BE ABLE TO DISCUSS:

- The role of promotion and branding in fashion show production

- Definitions of *advertising, public relations, direct marketing, interactive* and *social media*, as well as such other promotion strategies including *personal selling, special events,* and *visual merchandising*

- How to prepare media kits, news releases, photographs, and other support materials to attract media coverage for your event

- What the purpose of sponsorship is in promoting a fashion show and how to prepare a sponsorship pitch

- How to create a "brand" for a fashion show through a visual image that can be used for advertising, poster, invitation, and ticket design

- How to determine which promotion activities are best to use for communicating information about your fashion show to your target audience

Courtesy of WWD/Steve Eichner

Fashion involves change. The fashion business fully embraces new communication technologies, including the Internet and social media, as some of the best ways to get noticed almost instantaneously. "Fashion aims to be at the cutting edge, but in the days of round-the-clock tweets, Facebook updates, editorial content, multiplatform strategies, and image-driven Instagram and Tumblr posts, it's hard for designers to keep up with the constant change in the social media world," according to Rachel Strugatz (2011, p. 35).

DKNY PR Girl is a prominent figure on Twitter and Facebook, with nearly 380,000 followers (Chang, 2012). When DKNY PR

Figure 4.1
Aliza Licht uses social media and posts regular Tweets as DKNY PR Girl.

Courtesy of WWD/Steve Eichner

Girl decided to reveal her true identity as Aliza Licht (Fig. 4.1), the senior vice president for global communications at Donna Karan International, she did so on YouTube. Originally, her job at DKNY consisted of classic PR, including distributing news releases, arranging fashion show seating, and handling celebrity dressing. Then she added social media to her portfolio. Ms. Licht's contributions to the online fashion initiative made her the big winner at the Style Coalition Fashion 2.0 Awards (Style Coalition, 2012), which honor the most innovative fashion brands for outstanding achievements and communication strategies across a variety of digital media channels. She was given awards for Best Twitter and Best Blog by a Fashion Brand.

While today's message may be similar to those in the past, evolving promotional techniques are combined with traditional communication methods by fashion brands to reach the always evolving fashion consumer. This chapter focuses on both traditional and innovative communication strategies used by fashion designers, retailers, charitable organizations, and educational institutions when producing fashion shows.

Media coverage is a contributing factor to the increase in popularity of the various fashion shows and fashion events. We introduced haute couture shows and ready-to-wear industry oriented shows in Chapter 2. These shows are extravagant promotion tools used to get the media and potential customers excited about the fashion messages of the new season. Consumer show producers also depend on promotion efforts to assure an audience for their productions. Without pre-show promotion creating excitement about the show, the audience enjoying the children on the runway in Figure 4.2 would not be there.

Figure 4.2
This audience learned about the fashion show through various communication methods, such as a mailed invitation, an article in the local newspaper, or via a Facebook invitation.

Courtesy of Christopher C. Everett

PROMOTION

Promotion is a comprehensive term used to describe all of the communication activities initiated by the seller to inform, persuade, and remind the consumer about products, services, and/or ideas offered for sale. In addition to fashion shows, common promotion activities in the fashion field involve advertising, direct marketing, interactive and social media, personal selling, public relations, special events, and visual merchandising. In practice, there is some confusion in how these terms are used. For example, some people use the term *publicity* when they are actually describing *advertising*. The definitions presented in this chapter should help differentiate what is meant by each of these terms when used to promote fashion and fashion shows.

Within the fashion industry, branding has become an influential part of the promotion strategy. According to the American Marketing Association (2012), a **brand** is a name, term, design, symbol, or any other feature that identifies one seller's good or service as distinct from those of other sellers. A brand may identify one item, a family of items, or all items of that seller. A brand can be visually identified by a *logo*—a graphic symbol or a word mark using the company's name; a *font*—a range of letters and numbers with a particular typeface; a *color scheme*—GAP uses white on blue; a *symbol*—Coach uses a silhouette of a horse-drawn carriage; and a *sound*—a unique tune or set of notes that can symbolize a brand. The brand may be developed to represent implicit values, ideas, and even personality.

If the name or features of its designs are registered with the appropriate government office the brand is called a trademark. This protects the trademark owner from any unauthorized use of the brand name or logo. Dana Thomas (2007, p. 25) traced the first luxury brand to Georges Vuitton, who placed the words, "Marque Louis Vuitton

Deposée" (*marque desposée* means "registered trademark") within some squares on the Damier checkerboard print in 1888. Burberry had the foresight to register its iconic camel, black, and red check in 1924, when it was first used as the lining in the Burberry trench coat (Posner, 2011). The British firm has exclusive rights to use this plaid fabric, and it is protected from being counterfeited, pirated, or used without authorization.

Mark Tungate, author of *Fashion Brands: Branding Style from Armani to Zara,* wrote, "You don't buy clothes, you buy an identity" (2008, p. 1). Branding creates an image, a lifestyle, and a desire that is much greater than the clothing, accessories, or perfume that is made available to consumers. Thus, branding the image and message for such luxury companies as Chanel, Hermès, or Prada has become increasingly important. Branding has also trickled down to moderate and lower priced fashion goods. For example, Swedish retailer H&M—with Karl Lagerfeld, Lanvin, and Versace—and American retailer Target—with Missoni, Jason Wu, and Liberty of London—have used branding to create desire with its designer collaborations.

Natalie Sanger Gendle (personal communication, January 24, 2011), a lecturer in textiles and clothing, reports that Iowa State University branded its show as *The Fashion Show.* The benefits of branding a fashion show such as this one includes name recognition, an image of quality, and the impression of experience and reliability. Future students, sponsors, and audience members are much more likely to remember the show by name. They will also associate the show with greater value and with more anticipation than an unbranded show. Developing a brand image (Fig. 4.3) for a show through interdisciplinary collaboration is discussed in Notes from the Runway: Branding a Fashion Show. Also see Color Plate 6.

All fashion shows need promotion to create interest in attending the show and in raising awareness about the brand. Who is responsible for the promotion of a fashion show? Ultimately the success of promotion lies with the show director, but specific responsibility is often delegated to a promotion coordinator, who is one of the fashion show coordinators introduced in Chapter 3. In the fashion industry, the role of promotion is frequently relegated to a public relations specialist. Understanding communication in all forms—oral, written, and visual—is key to the success of an industry public relations specialist or an educational or charitable organization's promotion coordinator. This person will oversee the creation and distribution of advertisements, television commercials, radio spots, media kits, news releases, photographs, direct marketing pieces, and interactive and social media as well as all other forms of promotion.

ADVERTISING

Advertising is any nonpersonal message, paid for and placed in the mass media, and controlled by the sponsoring organization (Swanson & Everett, 2007). Advertising can also be classified by its purpose, including product (action) advertising, institutional (nonproduct or image building) advertising, commercial (for profit) advertising, or noncommercial (nonprofit) advertising. Promotion of specific goods or services is the objective of **product advertising.** Consumers are urged to take quick action toward purchasing a product. A fashion show audience member might respond by instantly purchasing a garment or accessory presented at a fashion show. **Institutional advertising** is focused upon building the reputation and fashion leadership of the company or sponsoring organization. It is designed to enhance civic responsibility and community involvement to develop a

(a)

(b)

(c)

(d)

Figure 4.3(a–d)
These figures illustrate the stages in developing the brand identity for *Get Your Fashion Fix on Route 66*. This was a collaboration between merchandising students and visual communication students under the guidance of Patricia Murphey, faculty director of the VisualDESIGNLab.

long-term relationship between the customers and the firm. Either product or institutional advertising can be considered **commercial advertising**, which is advertising with the purpose of making a profit for the firm. If the firm is in the nonprofit sector, use of **noncommercial advertising** is directed toward gaining support for its charitable work.

Fashion show advertising is information, paid for and controlled by the sponsoring organization, that notifies the public about an upcoming production. As long as standards are acceptable for print publications, broadcast media, or online media, advertisements or commercials are published or run as submitted by the sponsoring organization.

To use advertising for a fashion show, show producers will buy space in print media, buy time in broadcast media, or produce materials for the Internet. Advertising can be purchased in newspapers and magazines; broadcast on network television, cable television, and radio; or purchased on online publications, for example, as a banner ad.

Marc Jacobs was successful in using banner advertising on the online version of the *New York Times* to publicize his fashion week shows.

The cost of advertising is based upon specific rates of a publication or network. Rates for advertising units are published for all media on **rate cards**. The costs are based upon specific rates of time, frequency of the advertisement or commercial, and special requirements of the publisher or network. Rate cards are available to the public by calling or writing to the media outlet or by checking the company's website; many media outlets post their rate cards on the Internet.

Newspapers

One of the most common forms of advertising for a retail or consumer-oriented fashion show is through local or regional newspapers. Newspapers reach a local audience efficiently and are more cost effective than magazine or television advertising. Advertising in newspapers is commonly sold by **standard advertising unit (SAU)**. An SAU is $2^1/_{16}$ by 1 inch. Ad prices are based on 1 SAU. The basic rate of a newspaper advertisement allows the advertiser to run an ad at a **run-of-paper (ROP)** rate. This means the newspaper can choose to run the adver-

tisement on any page in any position within the paper. If the advertising budget is large enough, it may be beneficial to pay a slightly higher rate, called a **preferred position**, and specify the page or position where the advertisement will be placed within the paper.

The *Tampa Bay Times* is Florida's largest newspaper, providing comprehensive daily coverage of Florida's west coast. The newspaper has a daily circulation of 240,024 copies and 403,229 copies on Sunday ("Media Kit," *Tampa Bay Times*, 2012). This newspaper is typical of many national and regional newspapers, with readership peaking on Sunday.

The *Tampa Bay Times* provides an extensive media kit (Fig. 4.4) online. The newspaper offers a wide range of advertising rates for regional retailers—permanent, qualified retail outlets located within the state of Florida selling direct to consumers—as well as national rates—for ads that are placed by non-regional manufacturers, wholesalers, jobbers, or distributors, and national transportation/travel companies. Classified rates are also offered for short advertisements, which are grouped into categories or *classes*, and typically placed by private individuals with single items they wish to sell or buy. The *Tampa Bay Times* offers advertisers full-run or zoned editions. **Full-run**

Figure 4.4
The *Tampa Bay Times* offers an extensive media kit on its website.

Courtesy of Tampa Bay Times

means advertising will run in all editions of the newspaper. **Zoned editions** means advertising can be selectively placed in only one or a few geographically selected editions.

Similar to many other regional newspapers, the *Tampa Bay Times* offers a weekly online entertainment guide, *Things to Do*, at tampabay.com/things-to-do. This guide suggests activities and events occurring during the week that would be interesting to local residents and tourists, from new recipes, food festivals, and restaurant reviews to theatrical performances, museum exhibits, and concerts. Events of the week are submitted on the website and some events are featured for free on the weekly calendar of events. A fashion show producer may also pay for an advertisement on this website. This format would be an ideal medium for fashion show advertising and publicity. If the target audience includes college-age students, school newspapers are a good choice for advertising.

Preparing Newspaper Advertisements

The first consideration is the size of the advertisement, which is based on the cost of the space and whether color will be used. Newspaper advertisements may be created by fashion show personnel or by the newspaper's advertising department.

A newspaper advertisement is composed of copy, art, and white space. The text within the advertisement is designated as **copy**. Illustrations or photography are **art**, and space between the copy and art is designated as **white space**.

Copy may include one or several of the following components: headline, subheadline, body, slogan, and logo. **Headlines** attract the attention of the reader and create interest in the advertisement and may contain the words *fashion show* or the theme of the show. **Subheadlines** are used to further explain the headline. They may inform the reader

of the intended audience or promote the sponsoring organization or retailer. **Body** includes the important details needed in the advertisement, such as the day, date, time, location, ticket price, and where to buy tickets for the fashion show. The body should further stimulate the reader to want to attend the event. The **slogan** is usually a catchy phrase that is appealing when spoken or viewed in print. The theme of the fashion show may be used as a slogan, which should easily be remembered by the reader. If the fashion show is produced in cooperation with a retailer or sponsoring organization, a **logo**, which is a copyright-protected symbol or phrase, should be incorporated in the advertisement. Repeating a logo in an advertisement creates immediate identification to the reader and increases interest in the event.

Illustrations, photographs, graphic designs, or clip art are considered artwork in the advertisement. An **illustration** is artwork for a printed advertisement that is created using pen, pencil, brush, or crayon. **Photography** is the reproduction of images created by a camera. Artwork must effectively create a visual message promoting the fashion show and attracting the reader's attention. **Graphic design** involves the art or profession of using design elements, including typography and images, to convey information or create an effect. Graphic designers frequently use desktop publishing software, such as Adobe Illustrator, Photoshop, or InDesign. **Clip art** images, or prefabricated illustrations, are popular when creating advertising artwork.

Copy, art, and white space must be arranged within the boundaries of the advertisement layout. If the fashion show producers are using the newspaper's advertising department to create the advertisement, rough sketches of a layout are presented to the newspaper's representative. The art department of the newspaper will produce the rough draft, which is called a **paste-up**. This is given to the advertiser for review before final production is run. When both the advertising sponsor and the newspaper have approved the advertisement, the newspaper will put the advertisement into production. Upon final printing, the newspaper will deliver a **tear sheet** to the sponsor. The tear sheet is the advertisement, torn directly from the newspaper or magazine, to show proof of publication to the advertiser. With the increase in online advertising, tear sheets frequently appear as a PDF file, called a **virtual tear sheet**. The tear sheet or virtual tear sheet should be saved and included with other items submitted for evaluation after the show. Fashion models also include tear sheets from advertisements as well as editorial work in their portfolios, which are discussed in Chapter 6. Figure 4.5 shows a final fashion show advertisement for Mercedes-Benz Fashion Week.

Figure 4.5
Mercedes-Benz Fashion Week is advertised in *Women's Wear Daily*.

Magazines

WWD Collections (Fig. 4.6), *Vogue, InStyle, W,* and *Elle* are just a few of the national and international magazines that cover haute couture and ready-to-wear fashion shows. Photographers from publications such as *WWD Collections,* a trade publication, and *Vogue,* a consumer publication, have premiere positions at the end of the runway. Magazines, as compared to newspapers, have excellent reproduction qualities that make fashion photography pop off the page. The excellent reproduction quality also makes this medium more expensive to produce than newspapers.

Magazine advertising is generally used to reach a national or international audience. Very little advertising for fashion shows appears in national magazines, except for magazine tie-in shows as discussed in Chapter 2 or large regional mall shows that are co-sponsored by a magazine.

While fashion trends, looks, and themes present well in magazines, the lead time necessary to get specific events published inhibits the widespread use of this medium for fashion show promotion. Magazines are usually published monthly, so advertising or news releases must be delivered six weeks to two months or more before the publication date. This is the **closing date**, the date when all ad copy must be received by the magazine for inclusion in the next issue. For example, *Vogue* has an early closing date for the September issue, which typically has more advertising pages than other issues. The closing date is June 29, and the magazine goes on sale in mid-August. This means there is nearly a three-month lead time to publicize a September event. Many fashion shows are not planned this early in advance, causing national magazine advertising to be excluded from the promotion plan.

Figure 4.6
WWDCollections is a special edition of *Women's Wear Daily* that covers fashion weeks held in New York, London, Milan, and Paris. It is published twice each year.

Courtesy of WWD

Local or regional magazines, such as *Los Angeles, Chicago, Denver, Atlanta, Toronto Life,* or *Northern Arizona's Mountain Living,* are better publications to promote a local or regional event. Not only are advertising rates lower, closing dates are also shorter. It is more likely that the target audience will be reached.

Magazines sell space by the page or portion of a page, and similar to newspaper advertising, rates are published on rate cards. *Vogue* magazine, with a circulation of over 1.2 million, sells advertising space in the following page portions: 1 page, ⅔ page, ½ page, ⅓ page, or ⅙ page. A one-page advertisement in four-color print costs $165,232 ("Standard Rate," 2012). As with newspaper advertising, magazine advertising generally allows discounts if a certain number of pages are guaranteed over a 12-month period. *Vogue* gives a 3 percent discount for 3 pages up to a 10 percent discount for 12 pages over a 12-month period.

A fashion show produced for a local audience should consider placing its advertising in a local magazine. For example, Canada's *Toronto Life* publishes its *Stylebook* as a special interest publication annually in the fall ("Media Kit," *Toronto Times,* 2012). The closing date for ads is July 13, with ads due on July 27 for a magazine that goes on sale August 23. A full-page ad, which is 8 by 10.75 inches, costs $5,365, whereas an eighth of a page ad, measuring 3.375 by 2.291 inches, costs $1,285. A fashion show planned for September could economically advertise in this special interest issue or another issue of the monthly issue of the magazine. An eighth of a page, one-time ad in the "going out" section of the main book costs $3,000. Figure 4.7 shows *Toronto Life*'s *Stylebook.*

Network and Cable Television

Television is the most influential type of advertising available, and the most expensive. Only the largest fashion show budgets are able to afford television advertising. The costs of television advertising are based on

the length of the advertisement—15, 20, 30, or 60 seconds—and the specified time the advertisement will run. Prime time, from 7:00 p.m. to 11:00 p.m., will have the highest rates and the most viewers. The rates to advertise on television should be carefully evaluated before deciding on this type of advertising for fashion shows.

To advertise on television, the sponsor must buy time as either network advertising, spot advertising, or local advertising, with local advertising being the most economical. **Network advertising** is time bought on one of the major networks during a specified show. Costs are the greatest for network commercials because they are produced nationally. According to an *Advertising Age* survey, Sunday is the most expensive night to advertise, with 30-second spots costing from $79,742 to $512,367 to broadcast ("American Idol," 2011). An average 30-second network spot on Sunday night is around $150,000.

Time bought on independently owned stations is considered **spot advertising**. Advertising is purchased by quantity and generally run in a specific timeframe rather than during a specific show. Commercials on these stations are produced both nationally and locally, and can service a specific geographic area. Spot advertising is much less expensive than network advertising but still may range in the thousands of dollars.

Local advertising is time purchased on local television stations by businesses or organizations. Advertising costs at these stations more readily fit into fashion show budgets because the shows are produced in and for the immediate area. If merchandise used in the fashion show is borrowed from a local retailer, it may be wise to ask if the retailer is willing to share in the cost of the commercial because both parties will benefit from the

Figure 4.7
Toronto Life publishes its *Stylebook* each year in the fall.

Courtesy of Toronto Life Stylebook

advertising. Some advertisers will participate in creating the commercial while other advertisers leave it to the station. A 30-second commercial should have approximately 70 words, and photography should be in the form of video. Charitable organizations and educational groups are encouraged to advertise on television but they should be highly organized with just one or two people, such as the promotion coordinator in consultation with the budget coordinator, making decisions. If the decisions need to be discussed with all the members, too much time is wasted and production engineers may lose their patience.

The fashion show as entertainment has been a theme throughout this text. Cable television has encouraged this trend with such shows as *Project Runway* (Fig. 4.8) and *America's Next Top Model*. These programs have a high-profile presence and show the cable television industry's commitment to bringing high fashion to a mass audience.

Radio

Radio is considered to be a cost-effective medium compared to other broadcast media. Radio advertising is sold in 10-, 20-, 30-, and 60-second spots. Portions of shows may also be purchased and sponsored by the advertiser. Prime time is considered drive time in the morning and the evenings, from 6:00 a.m. to 9:00 a.m. and from 4:00 p.m. to 7:00 p.m. When advertising fashion shows, it may be best to use only local or regional radio. Different fashion show audiences will listen to different radio stations, so it is important to match the show to the station. Check with local stations to determine rates.

Because of the many varieties of radio stations, on-the-air radio commercials must target specific audiences more than print media. Commercials must be brief but they must get the message across. A 60-second commercial should be limited to 125 words. Shorter commercials should be planned accordingly. Radio commercials can be prepared in two forms: they can be read live on the air or taped in advance and played on the air. If the fashion show budget does not include a prepared radio commercial, news releases should be delivered to all radio stations in a community 2 to 4 weeks before the event. Like other media, public service announcements (PSAs) will be broadcast if the event is perceived by

© Everett Collection Inc/Alamy

Figure 4.8
Tim Gunn, Heidi Klum, Michael Kors, and Nina Garcia celebrate on the popular television show *Project Runway*. This show would be an appropriate broadcast medium for advertising a big fashion show or special event.

the news director as noteworthy. Figure 4.9 is an example of a radio-advertising script.

A promotion coordinator who is considering television or radio advertising should seriously evaluate the use of a professional advertising agency or student media center to produce the commercial. Professionals have studio space, equipment, and design talent not available to the layperson. Commercials, to be effective, must be of the highest quality to retain viewers or listeners.

Advertising should be used as the fashion show budget allows. Advertising is paid for with the guarantee that it will run, but is often too expensive to be used extensively by charitable and educational organizations. In those cases, the organization may choose to use public relations to attract an audience.

PUBLIC RELATIONS

Public relations (PR) is the management function that establishes and maintains mutually beneficial relationships between an organization and the public on whom its success or failure depends, according to Glen M. Broom (2009). Therefore, public relations is an important communication resource that can help influence public opinions and create programs to improve relationships between the firm and its public. In fashion, public relations is crucial to the ongoing success of the fashion firm. We learned earlier in this chapter that advertising depends upon paid funding to be placed in the media, but public relations and publicity, a tool of public relations, do not require payment for placement.

Communication that is initiated by public relations personnel is considered **editorial content** because the media outlet, not the advertiser, determines the final message and whether the piece will even be published. Readers or viewers of traditional print media, such as the *New York Times*, consider its stories as editorial content, representing the opinion of the journalist, to be more objective than **advertising content**. For example,

Agency	E&S Advertising		Writer	Kaci Shields
Client	University Fashion Show		Producer	Amanda Briggs
Project	Radio Spot		Station	KNAU Radio
Title	"Get your fashion fix"			

"GET YOUR KICKS ON ROUTE 66" INSTRUMENTAL VERSION IN BACKGROUND

ROUTE 66 WAS BORN IN 1929 AS THE MAIN STREET OF AMERICA, CONNECTING PEOPLE TO PLACES … FROM THE EAST TO THE WEST. TRAVELERS HAVE INCLUDED LEATHER-CLAD BIKERS AND MIGRATORY SNOW-BIRDS TO TRAVELING SNOW-BIRDS AND YOUNG LOVERS. SEE WHAT TODAY'S TRAVELERS ARE WEARING FROM MAIN STREAM TO LESS SEEN ON THE CAMPUS OF NORTHERN ARIZONA UNIVERSITY ON FRIDAY, NOVEMBER 19TH AT 7 PM OR SATURDAY, NOVEMBER 20TH AT 1PM. TICKETS FOR *"GET YOUR FASHION FIX ON ROUTE 66"* ARE AVAILABLE AT THE DOOR OF NAU'S PROCHNOW AUDITORIUM.

Figure 4.9
This is an example of a radio-advertising script created for the fashion show *Get Your Fashion Fix on Route 66*.

Illustration by Carly Grafstein

an article written by *New York Times* journalist and fashion critic Cathy Horyn about Italian designer Roberto Cavalli's fashion show is considered to be a more objective critique of his work than a paid advertisement for Cavalli's brand (Fig. 4.10).

Fashion businesses achieve success in promotion efforts by balancing editorial content and advertising content. Businesses show support for the media outlet by purchasing advertising; in return, the media shows support for the fashion business by running public relations pieces.

Publicity is information with news value, uncontrolled by the source because the source does not pay the media for placement, and is provided by public relations specialists to be used in the mass media (Swanson & Everett, 2007). Thus, publicity is a public relations tool that involves communication initiated by the firm seeking to tell others about a product, service, idea, or event. Publishing or broadcasting content is at the pleasure of the editor of a print publication or the director of a broadcast show. Editors and news directors read many news releases every day and determine which, if any, will run in print or be broadcast on air. Therefore, the information must be presented to the media in a newsworthy manner so that the editor or news director will see the news value of the event and pass it on to their readers or viewers.

A **publicist** is the individual hired to publicize a client or client's product in the

> "For the amount you invest in a show, you can generate between ten and a hundred times the cost in free advertising, in terms of photos in magazines and newspapers, television coverage and so forth. One designer told me that if he does a good show he doesn't have to buy advertising space for a year."
>
> —Thierry Dreyfus,
> freelance lighting designer

media. According to Crosby Noricks (2012), there are three options for working as a publicist in the fashion industry: work on several accounts for a fashion PR agency, such as People's Revolution, owned by Kelly Cutrone; work in house for a single brand or retailer, such as Aliza Licht for DKNY; or work as a freelance fashion PR practitioner, also known as an independent contractor. In Notes from the Runway: Public Relations for a Luxury Fashion Retailer, Miss PR Diva, a public relations manager who works for an upscale retailer, shares details about her in-house public relations job.

Figure 4.10
The fashion designer company Roberto Cavalli controlled and paid for the placement of this advertising message. It is considered *advertising content*, not *editorial content*.

As an in-house publicist, the employee is an integrated member of the team with access to all of the news, updates, and activities. This environment is helpful when brainstorming with other professionals to come up with new ideas and identify PR opportunities. On the downside, working on a single brand can become monotonous. Working for a fashion PR agency gives the staff member experience with multiple brands with various specializations. Working on several different accounts requires time as well as client management skills. One day might be filled with research, while the next is spent scouting a new fashion show venue or stuffing envelopes with invitations to an event.

Freelance fashion publicists work on their own, contracting with a few agencies on a project-by-project basis or specializing in one area of public relations. Freelancing can be difficult for some because the publicist is responsible for finding work, getting health insurance, and paying quarterly rather than annual taxes. On the positive side, the freelancer gets to work with clients she wants to work with and executes the public relations strategy she creates, while setting her own hours.

Publicity is released to the media through news releases, photographs, and media kits.

Common outlets for sending publicity include local print publications (e.g., newspapers and magazines), TV stations, and radio stations. For national or international coverage, publicity may be sent to national print publications, national broadcast networks, and wire services. Newspaper options include daily or Sunday editions; living, style, or fashion sections within the daily or Sunday editions; and community weekly editions. At the national level, trade publications such as *Women's Wear Daily* cover fashion shows. Magazine coverage may include regional publications or national and international publications. Broadcast outlets include local or regional network affiliates, cable channels, and local radio stations. In addition, the Internet and social media have become major outlets to share fashion show information.

One of the first tools a promotion coordinator should generate is a **media list**, a list of all media outlets (local, regional, national, or international) that might be used to publicize the fashion show. All contact information should be provided on the media list: name of media outlet, contact person(s) and titles, mailing address, phone number, fax number, and e-mail address or website, if appropriate. Figure 4.11 is an example of a media list.

MEDIA LIST

ORGANIZATION	NAME	TITLE	ADDRESS	PHONE	EMAIL
Lumberjack	Betsy Weaver	Lifestyle Editor	Box 5555 Flagstaff, AZ 86011	928-523-5551	brw@gmail.com
Daily Sun	Sara Miller	Lifestyle Editor	532 Main Street Flagstaff, AZ 86001	928-525-5552	sim@hotmail.com
Mountain Living	Ann King	Editor	532 Main Street Flagstaff, AZ 86001	928-525-5553	ask@flaglive.com
ASU Press	Jeff Hutchins	Sun Devil Editor	934 Rural Road Tempe, AZ 81502	480-225-5554	jkh@asu.edu
U of A State Press	Kim Wales	Wildcats Editor	1134 Campbell Rd. Tucson, AZ 89100	520-346-5555	ksw@ua.edu
KNAZ-TV	Joan Burg	Morning Anchor	2201 N. Vicky St. Flagstaff, AZ 86001	928-526-5556	jeb@hotmail.com
KJAK-Radio	John Allen	News Director	Box 5556 Flagstaff, AZ 86011	928-523-5557	jaa@gmail.com
KNAZ-Radio	Theresa Brown	News Director	457 Main Street Flagstaff, AZ 86001	928-523-5558	teb@gmail.com

Figure 4.11
This is a media list, which has been updated with the current contact information of the regional journalists who will receive media kits about the upcoming show.

Illustration by Carly Grafstein

When developing a media list, media outlets should be contacted to verify contact information. This is a good time to get specifics about how the information should be delivered. Send an e-mail message about the story, tailored specifically to the recipient's interest in the story, and ask how he or she would like to receive the materials, either mailed or via e-mail with the press materials as attachments.

If the organization producing a fashion show is a nonprofit, the promotion coordinator should consider using PSAs as a part of the promotion plan. **Public service announcements** are print or broadcast spots that run free of charge to charitable organizations (Swanson & Everett, 2007). Advertising and the other promotional tools discussed in the following sections have expenses attached to them. The only expense associated with a PSA is the staff time required to write and deliver the PSA to the media. The promotion coordinator should set as a priority the distribution of PSAs to all outlets on the media list.

"The press release is a reflection of the product to be sold. It must be carefully designed and reviewed to ensure there are no typos or errors."
—Sarah Cristobal, fashion editor, Stylelist.com

Media Kits

If the proposed fashion show is a large event in which many media outlets are to be invited, the use of a media kit may be a better promotion solution, compared to news releases and photographs alone. A **media kit** (often called a *press kit*) is a collection of public relations materials delivered or mailed to the media, often in a colorful folder with pockets. The folder, sometimes called a *shell*, is usually illustrated graphically to present the theme of the event and reinforce the importance of the event to the editor or director.

Media kit modernizes the term *press kit* because a press kit implies the materials included are only for newspapers or other traditional print media. *Media kit* is a more inclusive term that suggests the prepared materials are appropriate for both traditional and new media, although many practitioners continue to use the phrase *press kit*.

The media kit should be tailored for an intended media outlet. A media kit prepared for a broadcast media outlet should include a video or voice interview, whereas a media kit that is prepared for a newspaper or magazine should include a news release and photographs.

Media kits developed for fashion shows may include a combination of any of the following elements: news releases and photographs, as well as ancillary materials such as a cover letter, fact sheets, a program of events, a list of participants, biographical information, a straight news story, and a feature story. Figure 4.12 is the cover of a media kit prepared for *Runway to Wonderland*, which reinforces the brand image of the show.

News Releases

A **news release** (also called a *press release* or *media release*) is an article on a newsworthy event sent to editors or news directors for publication or broadcast in the media. The term *press release* is still commonly used, although some practitioners are moving toward using the term *news release*.

"The primary reason for the press release is to get the public relations

Figure 4.12
This is the cover of the media kit that was developed for the fashion show *Runway to Wonderland*.

message to the media and obtain coverage for the story," according to Gerald Sherman and Sar Perlman (2010, p. 174). The information includes all the details about the event and is written to gain the attention of an editor or news director. How well the news release is written has a bearing on whether the message will be covered. If the editor or news director finds the message or event interesting and well written they will run the narrative in their media, frequently just as the release is written.

To gain the editor's or news director's interest, the news release should not be too long—usually one to three pages. Longer news releases lose the reader's attention. News releases should be mailed first class or e-mailed. News releases are not specific to fashion show publicity. Variations of style may occur, but they follow a general format and are used by any organization or individual wishing to publicize an event or brand.

Guidelines for News Releases

Each company, organization, or school typically develops its own guidelines for news releases. These guidelines provide a consistent and professional image for messages delivered from the group. Normally, the print release is prepared on 8½ by 11 inch paper or on the company's letterhead, which includes the logo. It is best to submit the release on white or light-colored paper using only one side. A clear, black typeface with an average font size of 10 to 12 points makes the release easy to read. The words *News Release* near the top of the page indicate that the document is an official news release. This allows the media to use any of the information from the release for its story and assures that all quotes have been approved for use by the attributed source (Sherman & Perlman, 2010). If letterhead is not used, the news release should include the company name, address, phone number, and e-mail address.

The headline is the first sentence of the news release, which sets the tone with a strong and appealing synopsis of the purpose of the release. The headline is frequently emphasized in a larger font size than the rest of the content. It should be centered and typed in sentence case, which means capitalizing the first word and any proper nouns. The headline should be the title of the release and include the news value of the story, using an action verb. It is not necessarily the title the publication will use for the story.

A dateline and release date should be included to inform the editor when the release should run in the media. The **dateline** refers to the opening of a news report that indicates where and when the story was written. For a print story, the dateline is traditionally placed in the first line of the text, followed by two dashes, as shown in Figure 4.13. The date the news release is written is considered to be the **release date**. Editors prefer an actual date more than the statement "For immediate release." The contact person's phone number and e-mail address should be near the top of the first page. This individual may be the publicist who wrote the news release or the promotion coordinator of a school show. Figure 4.13 illustrates a news release

NORTHERN ARIZONA UNIVERSITY

COLLEGE OF SOCIAL AND BEHAVIORAL SCIENCES
SCHOOL OF COMMUNICATION
P. O. Box 5619 Flagstaff, AZ 86011-5619
928-523-2232

NEWS RELEASE

CONTACT:
Alexandra McLendon
Promotion Coordinator
(702) 332-5124
agm32@nau.edu

Follow Fashion Down the Rabbit Hole

FLAGSTAFF, AZ, October 31, 2008—"How do you know I'm mad?" asked Alice. "You must be," said the Cat, "or you wouldn't have come here." Fall down the rabbit hole and experience a twisted trip through runway fashion.

Runway to Wonderland is making its debut Thursday, November 20, 2008, and Friday, November 21, 2008, at the duBois Ballroom on the Northern Arizona University south campus. Tickets cost $10 in advance, $15 at the door. Advance sale tickets are available at the NAU ticket office.

Runway to Wonderland is a student-produced fashion show that was presented as a concept nearly one year ago. This theme and the promotional strategies for the show were developed during the spring semester by the MER 332 Merchandise Promotion class. During the fall semester MER 434 Fashion Show Production class produces the show. Students are divided into five committees: merchandise, model, promotion, stage and budget.

This fashion show features six scenes: *Stuck in a Dream*—sleepwear, *Chasing the White Rabbit*—active and outdoor wear, *Afternoon with the Caterpillar*—casual wear, *Meeting the Queen of Hearts*—career wear, *Mad Tea Party*—date attire, and *A Twisted Affair*—student designs. Retailers include: Target, Old Navy, PJ Chilcottage, Decker's, Aspen Sports, Mountain Sports, Babbitt's, Gap, Raci Thredz, Basement Marketplace, Dillard's, Black Hound Gallerie, Carol Anderson by invitation, and Premier Designs Jewelry.

# # #

Figure 4.13
The promotion coordinator for *Runway to Wonderland* lets the media know about its fashion show through this news release.

written about *Runway to Wonderland*. This document was placed inside the media kit shell.

The **lead** is the most important part of the news release. It is the first paragraph that summarizes the importance of the story, which should be created to grab the attention of the editor. The lead paragraph has to be strong and informative, giving news value to the reader. Information including who, what, where, when, and why should be addressed.

After the lead, the copy follows. The copy (or *main text*) is the actual material or content for the news story. This section provides additional information and facts, which may be one or several paragraphs always written in diminishing order of importance. If there is limited space available to an editor, he or she may chose to omit some of the copy at the end of the news release. It is imperative to list the most important information first.

News releases should be written objectively, not subjectively, from a third-person point of view. Do not use *I, we,* or *you* when writing the release. The writer should not show biased interest in the event by using opinionated words when describing the event. Fill the news release with facts, not opinions. It is important to follow the correct format so the news release will not be discarded before the content is read.

The distribution of news releases should be looked at as a strategy, not a mass distribution. Each medium should be considered separately and contacted in the most appropriate manner for that medium, either by mail or e-mail.

The news release and photographs should be sent to the media at least 2 weeks before the event is staged to give the publication plenty of time for the editor to review the materials. Save-the-date news releases are often delivered to the media a full month before the event is held.

Photographs

Photographs are prepared specifically for use in media to accompany news releases or to be included in a media kit. Photos are selected to emphasize a specific fashion, look, or person. Each photograph should communicate a message about the fashion or the trend and enhance the written communication of the news release. Avoid photographs that have busy backgrounds or those that do not convey a specific message about the intended subject.

The fashion company or charitable or educational group should own the rights to the photos, or have written permission to use the photos from the photo's owner. **Photo credit**, identifying the photographer or owner of the photo, should be included with the photo. A **cutline**, which is a photo caption, is placed directly below or next to a photo, and describes what happened in the photo. The cutline should also identify the people in the photograph. People should be identified from left to right with full name, title, and firm affiliation. Although photo captions are offered, a publication may write its own caption for the photograph.

The fashion industry communicates in a visual manner, making photographs and video footage extremely important. In addition to providing some photographs in a media kit, the fashion show promotion team should set up a **photo opportunity** to accompany a news release whenever possible. A photo opportunity is any photo or video that serves as a visual enhancement to the news story. According to Sherman and Perlman (2010), there are six main types of photo opportunities, including the headshot, group shot, grip-and-grin, the product shot, the action shot, and the video opportunity.

Headshot

The **headshot** (sometimes called a *mug shot*) is a small photo of a person's face, typically a portrait, cropped from the chest or bottom of the neck to the top of the head. If someone is quoted in a news release, a headshot puts a face to a name.

Group Shot

Group shot involves a photograph of several people lined up. These individuals, who are part of the news story, are placed against a wall to be shot—by a camera (hence why they are often called *execution-at-dawn* photos). These photo ops are used at fashion shows or red carpet events, where a number of people pose for a group photograph.

Figure 4.14 is a photo of all of the class members, models, and faculty members involved in producing *Get Your Fashion Fix on Route 66* at Northern Arizona University.

Grip-and-Grin

People receiving awards, passing out scholarships or fund-raising checks, or cutting ribbons are often posed in **grip-and-grin** photographs. These types of photos have a group of people holding an award or oversized check, or shaking hands. At a fashion show, this type of photo may be used to recognize the winner of a design competition or the recipient of a scholarship. It might be more interesting to have a photo of the recipient being surprised with the award or scholarship than a dull photograph of two people shaking hands or holding an oversized check.

Product Shot

The **product shot** emphasizes the fashion item by itself or with other fashion items.

Courtesy of Christopher C. Everett.

Figure 4.14
Here is a group shot of all of the participants involved in *Get Your Fashion Fix on Route 66*. It took a large number of people to make a show like this happen.

A studio or environmental shot of a model wearing the clothing and accessories that will be on the runway at the fashion show is useful for a media kit. This type of photo does not always include people. A product shot may also be taken in a studio setting as a tabletop shot if the item or items are photographed on a table or counter. Tabletop product shots may be used in coordination with a fashion show to emphasize designs or brand extension accessories that will be shown on the runway.

Action Shot

The **action shot** is a photograph of the product in action. After each fashion week, several action shots of models on the runway are featured in *Women's Wear Daily* and *the New York Times*. Photos from charity events, including walk-a-thons or designer fashion sales for-the-cause, fall into this category. Figure 4.15 demonstrates action on the runway for the Louis Vuitton show in Paris. Designer Marc Jacobs had models getting off a train to awaiting porters who carried each model's Louis Vuitton bags.

The Video Opportunity

The fashion industry offers many occasions, such as fashion shows or fund-raising events, as video opportunities. A **video opportunity** (also called a *b-roll*) involves a news story that is captured on digital video. It is an audiovisual story ideal for television stations or video websites to create a television segment or YouTube video.

Ancillary Materials for the Media Kit

A variety of supporting documentation may be included in the media kit. These elements include a cover letter, fact sheets, a program of events, a list of participants, biographical information, a straight news story, and a feature story. The **cover letter** introduces the media kit and informs editors or producers why the event deserves attention in the media. Figure 4.16 is an example of a cover letter.

The media kit may include two types of fact sheets. A **basic fact sheet** offers details about the fashion show and explains its significance in a factual manner. Essential facts are presented in a list. This fact sheet should include the contact phone number and address in case it gets separated from the rest of the kit, as well as the date and time of the show, the participants, and retailers or organizations backing the show. Figure 4.17 is an example of a basic fact sheet. An additional **backgrounder** (*historical fact sheet*) may also be included. This fact sheet tells when the show was first held, where, who attended and their significance, milestones in the event's history, and other historical facts about the show. When discussing historical facts, always make clear the significance of each fact. For universities or organizations that host annual fashion shows, the backgrounder may be particularly valuable.

A **program of events** (also called a *schedule of activities*) is a detailed description of the time schedule for the show. Broadcast media frequently rely on this information and may also want to have a script if one is available. A complete **list of participants** highlighting their contributions to the event and their relationship to the organization may be part of the media kit. Supplemental to the participation list is **biographical information** of the principals, including headshots if available.

Figure 4.15
Marc Jacobs's inspiration for the Louis Vuitton fashion show always starts with the bags, which were prominently featured by porters carrying real trunks and cases for the elite train-traveling models.

Courtesy of WWD/Giovanni Giannoni

NORTHERN ARIZONA UNIVERSITY

COLLEGE OF SOCIAL AND BEHAVIORAL SCIENCES
SCHOOL OF COMMUNICATION
P. O. Box 5619 Flagstaff, AZ 86011-5619
928-523-2232

October 31, 2008

Betsy Weaver
Lumberjack, Lifestyle Editor
Box 5555
Flagstaff, AZ 86011

Dear Miss Weaver:

Every other year, the Northern Arizona Merchandising Association produces a fashion show, and this year we are proud to present *Runway to Wonderland,* a fairytale fashion show extravaganza. With the hard work of the merchandising students, *Runway to Wonderland* will be a whimsical must-see event.

The show raises money for the Merchandising Leaders of the 21st Century Scholarship, as well as gives the participating students a fantastic learning experience. The show will be held on November 20 and 21, 2008, in the NAU duBois Ballroom on south campus.

We look forward to your support for this event. In this media packet, we have included two news releases, a backgrounder, a fact sheet and a flyer. We are very excited about *Runway to Wonderland* and with your help and enthusiasm we can make this a fanciful event on our campus. I look forward to speaking with you in the near future.

Thank you for your support,

Alexandra McLendon

Alexandra McLendon
Promotion Coordinator
(702) 332-5124
agm32@nau.edu

Figure 4.16
A cover letter such as this one introduces a media kit.

NORTHERN ARIZONA UNIVERSITY

COLLEGE OF SOCIAL AND BEHAVIORAL SCIENCES
SCHOOL OF COMMUNICATION
P. O. Box 5619 Flagstaff, AZ 86011-5619
928-523-2232

CONTACT:
Alexandra McLendon, Promotion Coordinator
(702) 332-5124 or agm32@nau.edu

BIENNIAL FASHION SHOW
FACT SHEET

- Show logistics: Thursday, November 20, and Friday, November 21, 2008, 7:00 p.m., duBois Ballroom on the south campus of Northern Arizona University.

- Theme: *Runway to Wonderland.*

- Theme influence: Lewis Carroll's fairytale, *Alice's Adventures in Wonderland* and Disney's animated movie, *Alice in Wonderland,* provided the inspiration for checkerboard floors, stripped walls and mixed proportions to create a vibrant childhood fantasy and romantic nostalgia of innocent times.

- Clothing scenes include sleepwear, active wear, casual wear, career wear, "after five" date attire and student designs.

- All show proceeds go to the Merchandising Leaders of the 21st Century Scholarship, generated through student projects in the merchandising program for over 20 years.

- Two previous fashion shows have won NAU's Service Learning Award.

- The show is student-produced by the MER 434 Fashion Show Production class with ideas and promotion tactics generated by the spring MER 332 Merchandise Promotion class.

- Northern Arizona Merchandising Association (NAMA), a university sanctioned, student organization affiliated with the merchandising program, and student volunteers help as models and provide assistance in many other tasks.

Figure 4.17
A basic fact sheet is frequently included in a media kit.

Two news stories can be included—a straight news story and a feature story. A straight **news story** gives basic information about the fashion show in a news announcement approach. For print media, this story should be approximately a page and a half, double-spaced on a 60-space line. For broadcast media, the article should be one or two short paragraphs, triple-spaced. If you are presenting the information to a broadcast outlet, include the print story also. A longer general news story that ties the background information may be as long as three double-spaced pages for print media and one full page for broadcast media. A **feature story** is an article that provides insight to the event. It may focus on one particularly interesting aspect of the show. Both kinds of stories can be included if appropriate. This story is written only in the format for print media (as long as three double-spaced pages) but may be included in the broadcast media kit.

It is important to match the message with the event. If the show is large with great fashion influence, a media kit should be preplanned to reach national magazines and online channels, among other media. If the show is smaller, organizers should take advantage of local media opportunities, creating a newsworthy event for a local audience.

In this section we have discussed publicity as editorial content in a publication or broadcast medium. Next, we look at direct marketing strategies. Direct marketing as a promotion strategy is very old, beginning with catalog sales in the late 1800s. However, technological advances, including the Internet and database management, have reinvigorated direct marketing as a major promotion tool. Some of the direct marketing strategies discussed next have particular value in promoting a fashion show.

DIRECT MARKETING

In addition to advertising and public relations, some fashion show producers promote directly to potential members of the fashion show audience through direct marketing techniques. The marketing process by which organizations communicate directly with target customers to generate a response or a transaction is called **direct marketing** (Swanson & Everett, 2007). Direct marketing often relies on **direct response media**, which include both traditional as well as rapidly evolving innovative media. Direct marketing materials require a direct reply, for example, an RSVP to a mailed invitation or an interactive response to an e-mail or Facebook event posting. The goal of direct marketing is to go directly to the consumer with the message to generate a response, such as to invite a consumer to attend a fashion show.

Traditional direct marketing involves broadcast media—television and radio as well as direct mail. In a local or regional market, fashion show personnel may use television or radio advertising to make a personal appeal to a bride-to-be, her mother, and her friends to attend the fashion show at the bridal fair. This encourages the bride and her entourage to attend the event and view the many dress options.

Direct mail includes all direct response communications delivered through the mail. Mailed pieces with relevance to fashion shows typically include advertisements with personal solicitations, invitations, and promotional postcards. Fashion show personnel create mailing lists from previous participants, sponsors of prior shows, the families and friends of current participants, fashion show class members or models, alumni, or, in the case of charities, previous donors.

The Online Environment

Since we wrote the last edition of this book, technological advances have led to the most rapid and groundbreaking changes in communication that we have ever seen. Today, interactive media allow for a back-and-forth flow of information in real time. Internet advertising has become a popular way for sponsors to communicate their message to consumers, with consumers providing feedback almost instantaneously through innovative media, such as the Internet, mobile devices, and tablets. The development of the Internet has created a digital revolution. The speed and convenience of accessing information are mind boggling.

Nearly every commercial business or news organization has an online presence. According to Tim O'Reilly and John Battelle (2009), the Web 2.0 Conference in 2004 helped restore confidence to an industry that had lost its way after the dot-com bust of the early 2000s. Web 2.0 introduced a new role for the Web—building Web applications with two-way communication through various collaboration techniques. These two-way communication changes helped make possible innovations such as searchable websites (e.g., Google, YouTube), wikis (e.g., the Wikipedia encyclopedia), and social media (e.g., Facebook, Twitter, and LinkedIn) possible. Technological innovations have also changed the way we access the Internet. Easily transported devices, such as laptops, netbooks, smart phones, and tablets, have made digital connections available almost anywhere we go.

The term *app* has been used as shorthand for *application* in the information technology community for a long time. **App** describes mobile applications used by smart phones and tablets (see Fig. 4.18), especially after the creation of Apple's iTunes App Store in 2008 ("Definition of: App," 2012). It is just as correct to say "iPhone application" as it is "desktop computer application." Because *app* is shorter and computer people love to abbreviate, the term *app* came into popular use as mobile devices and apps became more available.

Made Fashion Week is an interactive app that broadcasts live images of runway shows and fashion week presentations as they develop (Lipke, 2012). For anyone attending an event at Milk Studios, a live slide show is pushed to the app placed on the attendee's iPhone, iPad, or Android device. The attendee can "like" an individual

> "Covering a fashion week online is like participating in a long-distance race, madness!"
> —Laird Borrelli, fashion editor, Style.com

Figure 4.18
App on a cell phone.

look for later reference, type notes on specific looks, tweet about the show with the "#madefw" hashtag automatically applied, and e-mail all of her looks to herself or others. Designer biographies, inspiration statements, and contact information are attached to each show. Information is also made available after the event on Tumblr. MAC Cosmetics is the principle sponsor of *Made Fashion Week*, which makes the live-streaming video available to viewers who were not able to attend the actual show.

Advertising on the Online Environment

The Internet is a widely used platform for advertising. Whether you are on a newspaper, magazine, retailer, or social media website, advertising is there.

The most common type of Internet advertising is the **banner ad**, which is an advertisement embedded into a web page (Belch & Belch, 2012). Banner ads are intended to attract traffic to the advertiser's website by linking to it. The banner advertisement is an image, sometimes enhanced with animation, sound, or video to create greater attention. Banner images are typically wide and short or tall and narrow, similar to a physical banner. Banner ads are usually placed on affiliates, including newspapers or blogs with many followers, with interesting content. Affiliates earn money, usually on a **cost per click** (*CPC*) basis. Every time a unique user clicks on the ad, the affiliate earns money.

Other forms of Internet advertising include sponsorships, pop-ups/pop-unders, interstitials, links, paid searches, online commercials, video on demand, and webisodes (Belch & Belch, 2012). **Internet sponsor-**

ships involve an organization that subsidizes a section of a website or provides content to a website. **Pop-ups**, which appear as a window or animated creature when a website is opened, and **pop-unders**, which appear underneath the website after the user leaves a website, are designed to grab your attention. Not everyone likes this kind of distraction. Computer programmers have developed pop-up blockers to prevent this kind of advertising. Consumer complaints have influenced some websites against accepting this type of advertising. **Interstitials** are ads that appear on screen while a website's content is being loaded. Negative consumer reaction to interstitials is similar to that of pop-ups and can also be prevented by pop-up blockers. **Links** (*hyperlinks*) are underlined references within Web text that take the user to additional information or related material on another website. Although some people do not think that links are a type of advertising, links do serve a similar purpose. **Paid search** (*search engine advertising*) involves an advertiser paying only when a consumer clicks on its ad or on a link from a search engine page. For example, Google AdWords are ads that are linked to keywords that have been created by the advertiser. When Google users search the advertiser's keywords, the ad pops up. The advertiser pays only if the consumer clicks on the ad.

Online commercials are the online equivalent of a traditional television commercial. Some firms create commercials that are exclusively broadcast on their websites, whereas other firms broadcast the commercials that were created for television. An ad created to launch during the Super Bowl or during the Academy Awards program could be rebroadcast or enhanced as an Internet broadcast. **Video on demand** uses video clips of various types of entertainment or sports activities. If the Mercedes-Benz or *Women's Wear Daily* website presents fashion shows from various fashion week shows, it is an example of video on demand. **Webisodes** are short films created by the advertiser and shown on the Internet. Target has used webisodes to promote its brands.

Direct Marketing on the Online Environment

E-mail is essentially the electronic version of traditional mail. Each time you receive a personal e-mail message or blast from an online or bricks-and-mortar retailer, it is direct marketing on the Internet. Have you received an e-mail from Amazon.com or some other website offering suggestions about a new book or piece of clothing that you might like? That is direct marketing, using your past purchases as a predictor of your future purchases. Some consumers have become frustrated by unwanted e-mails. These unsolicited and unwanted e-mails, called **spam**, are the electronic equivalent of junk mail.

Infomercials, which originated as a long, 30- to 60-minute television commercial, have found their way to the Internet. These commercials are presented as if they were regular television shows. The **home-shopping channels**, which also originated on television, now are multiplatform shopping sites. QVC, HSN, and Shop NBC have websites in addition to their television broadcasts. Consumers can watch Isaac Mizrahi, Lori Goldstein, or Rachel Zoe on television or on their computers.

Public Relations on the Online Environment

As we learned earlier in this chapter, public relations activities are very useful to compa-nies promoting fashion and fashion shows. Many firms maintain websites that devote a portion of their content to the firm's public relations activities, including philanthropic activities such as Macy's Passport or Ralph Lauren's Pink Pony, annual reports, product registration, awards received, scholarships offered, news articles, news releases, and more.

Social Media

Social media use web-based and mobile technologies to turn communication into interactive dialogue. According to Andreas Kaplan and Michael Haenlein (2010), there are six different types of social media:

- collaborative projects, such as Wikipedia
- blogs and microblogs, such as Twitter
- content communities, such as YouTube
- social networking sites, such as Facebook
- virtual game worlds, such as SocioTown
- virtual social worlds, such as Second Life

Although fashion aims to be always forward thinking, these days of round-the-clock Tweets, Facebook updates, multiplatform strategies, and image-obsessed Instagrams make it hard for the fashion industry to keep up with the constant change in the social media world. Figure 4.19 is a humorous way to look at the various types of social media that can be used to promote a fashion show.

Some fashion businesses, including Burberry and DKNY, are using social media better than others. Burberry was recognized by Digital IQ Index, the New York University think tank Luxury Lab (L2), as the top fashion brand ranked by online competence. This honor was due to Burberry's actions as one of the first fashion brands to stream its runway show live and in 3-D (Fig. 4.20), launch a successful global website, create a

SOCIAL MEDIA EXPLAINED

TWITTER	I'M WATCHING A FASHION SHOW
FACEBOOK	I LIKE THIS FASHION SHOW
FOURSQUARE	THIS IS WHERE I WATCH FASHION SHOWS
INSTAGRAM	HERE'S MY PHOTO FROM THE FRONT ROW
YOUTUBE	HERE ARE THE MODELS ON THE RUNWAY
LINKED IN	MY SKILLS INCLUDE FASHION FORECASTING
PINTEREST	HERE ARE MY FAVORITE LOOKS
LAST FM	NOW LISTENING TO THE SOUND TRACK
G+	I'M A GOOGLE FAN WATCHING FASHION SHOWS

Figure 4.19
Social media coverage of fashion is explained in a humorous way.

Illustration by Carly Grafstein

Figure 4.20
This Paris audience was treated to a 3-D live stream of the London Burberry Prorsum fashion show.

Courtesy of WWD/Thomas Iannaccone

mobile-commerce site, and offer its customers the opportunity to purchase selected goods directly from the runway show. The Burberry brand, which is over 155 years old, has more Facebook friends, YouTube uploaded videos, and Twitter and Instagram followers than most younger fashion brands.

According to Shenan Reed, co-founder and chief media officer of Morpheus Media, "'transmedia storytelling'—or using the various social media platforms to tell a story in a way that it is fitting for each medium—is vital to designers' and retailers'

digital strategy" (Strugatz, 2011, p. 35). Retailer Bergdorf-Goodman provides a good example of multiplatform versatility. Bergdorf-Goodman's transmedia storytelling activities include the following:

- Instagram—The "Shoes About Town" project encouraged users to use Instagram to share photos of shoes taken against cityscapes and other backdrops.
- 5th/58th blog—images of the shoes from "Shoes About Town" were placed

on an interactive city map along with photos from fashion week, store windows, and other store features.

- Polyvore— The "Dress Bergdorf-Goodman's Linda Fargo for Fashion Week" challenge was created on this community fashion site known for sets and collages. Users competed to design sets using clothing items curated by Linda Fargo, Senior Vice President, Fashion Office and Store Presentation, with the hopes of winning a $2,500 shopping spree and a ticket to Michael Kors's fall fashion show
- Facebook—Bergdorf's with Fendi staged a handbag design contest. Users entered to win a chance to model in the store's "Faces of 5F" fall ad campaign. The winner appeared in *Lucky* magazine and starred in a shoppable video, which allows consumers watching the video to purchase the merchandise shown.
- Twitter, bergdorfgoodman.com, YouTube, Foursquare, Tumblr, and Hunch—All are other types of digital media used by Bergdorf-Goodman.

Fashion enthusiasts look to all kinds of media to learn about fashion trends during the fashion week marathon. Fans of bloggers eagerly await the comments from these social media entrepreneurs. *Women's Wear Daily* writer Rachel Strugatz (2011) identified Bryanboy, Kelly Framel of *The Glamourai*, Susie Lau of *Style Bubble*, Leandra Medine of *The Man Repeller*, and Rumi Neely of *Fashiontoast* as top bloggers who "have become as relevant as the shows they blog

about" (p. 36). With about 4 million page views per month, Kelly Framel ranks as one of the most popular bloggers. Having a degree in fashion design, combined with work experience at Naeem Khan, helps make her *The Glamourai* blog about personal style and interior design convincing.

> "The digital show format is a tool that will change the landscape of fashion week and allow us to see fashion shows through a different lens."
> —Prabal Gurung, fashion designer

By the time this book is on your shelf, new types of social media may very well be the craze. The only thing that we can say for sure about fashion shows and social media is that both will continue to change. Our students keep asking, "What will the next big thing be?" We wish we knew. Maybe one of you will invent it!

OTHER FORMS OF PROMOTION

Although most fashion shows use some form of advertising, public relations, direct marketing, or social media, the forms of fashion promotion known as personal selling, visual merchandising, and special events are not always associated with fashion show production. Next, we will consider the contributions of these forms to fashion show promotion.

Personal selling is the direct interaction between the customer and the seller for the purpose of making a sale (Swanson & Everett, 2007). Although some practitioners do not consider personal selling a form of promotion, it is one of the most successful forms. It enables the salesperson to promote the characteristics of the product and overcome any objections raised by the customer. Some customers see this personal attention as validating their selection of a product. In fashion show production, personal selling is a very effective way to sell tickets to potential audience members. A student, designer, or model involved in a class fashion show is often the most enthusiastic promoter of the event.

Visual merchandising is the physical presentation of products in a nonpersonal approach (Swanson & Everett, 2007). This form of fashion promotion may include window, interior, or remote displays. In the case of fashion shows, producers or designers often use mannequin modeling or stationery mannequins to display garments. This technique was used at the Los Angeles Fashion Week shows (Fig. 4.21).

A **special event** is a one-time occurrence with planned activities, focused on a specific purpose—to bring attention to a brand, manufacturer, retailer, or organization, or to influence the sale of merchandise (Swanson & Everett, 2007). The range of these activities is vast, from large-scale storewide celebrations to singular product promotions in one department. Store image is differentiated through execution of special events. It is an important device to draw customers into the store during off-peak selling seasons. Fashion shows may be a part of a special event.

Promotion is a necessary element of all fashion shows. Although personal contact is one of the best methods to communicate a message, it is not always possible. A successful promotion plan will incorporate both editorial content (public relations) and advertising content to assure communication between the sponsoring organization, the media, and readers or viewers of the media. Not all shows will include all the promotion tools that have been discussed in this chapter. It is up to the show director and the promotion coordinator to plan a promotion campaign that will best fit the needs of the targeted audience and the sponsoring organization.

SPONSORSHIP

Sponsorship involves schools, companies, or other supporters that lend their name to an event through monetary and/or some type of contribution, as a way to underwrite

Figure 4.21
Los Angeles Fashion Week included this instillation of garments worn by models imitating mannequins.

Courtesy of WWD/Amy Graves

production costs of the event. Sponsorship is gaining in importance in the fashion world and should be considered when planning a fashion show. An example of a sponsorship pitch is shown in Figure 4.22.

Although such brands as Mercedes-Benz, Vodafone, Canon, MasterCard, and others are the primary sponsors of fashion events, other sponsors also support these large events as well. For example, makeup brand

COLLEGE OF SOCIAL AND BEHAVIORAL SCIENCES
SCHOOL OF COMMUNICATION
P. O. Box 5619 Flagstaff, AZ 86011-5619
928-523-2232

March 28, 2008

Donna Crews
5600 Loop Road
Kent, Ohio 44240

Dear Ms. Crews:

What does Alice from Wonderland have to do with the Northern Arizona University merchandising program? She and her whimsical friends are the theme for *Runway to Wonderland* the merchandising program's biennial fashion show to be held on November 20 and 21, 2008. Will you consider being a sponsor for this show?

The show, which is completely student produced, is part of the merchandising curriculum and a fundraiser for the Merchandising Leaders of the 21st Century Scholarship fund at NAU. Sponsorships will be directly deposited into the scholarship fund.

Your business will receive various benefits for being a sponsor, including positive exposure and recognition in the program and signage at the event. Levels of sponsorship are included with this letter. The greatest benefit you receive is tremendous goodwill in knowing you are an essential part of a program which prepares future leaders of the merchandising industry.

We are confident that this show will turn heads, educate students, entertain the crowd, and raise money for our scholarship fund. Please reply by April 30 so that we can include you in the execution of this dynamic show. The merchandising program appreciates your support.

Sincerely,

Kris Swanson

Kris Swanson, Ph.D.
Merchandising Faculty Member

Katie Schmalzel

Katie Schmalzel
Merchandising Student

(a)

Courtesy of Christopher C. Everett

Figure 4.22
This sponsorship package was created to help raise funds for a scholarship. Part **(a)** is the sponsorship letter, **(b)** indicates the sponsorship levels, and **(c)** is the contribution form. (*Figure continues on following page.*)

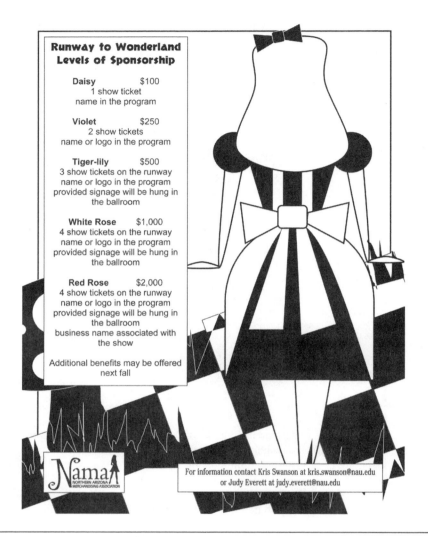

**Runway to Wonderland
Levels of Sponsorship**

Daisy $100
1 show ticket
name in the program

Violet $250
2 show tickets
name or logo in the program

Tiger-lily $500
3 show tickets on the runway
name or logo in the program
provided signage will be hung in
the ballroom

White Rose $1,000
4 show tickets on the runway
name or logo in the program
provided signage will be hung in
the ballroom

Red Rose $2,000
4 show tickets on the runway
name or logo in the program
provided signage will be hung in
the ballroom
business name associated with
the show

Additional benefits may be offered
next fall

For information contact Kris Swanson at kris.swanson@nau.edu
or Judy Everett at judy.everett@nau.edu

(b)

Runway to Wonderland

Thank you for using this contribution form to support Runway to Wonderland. Your sponsorship will be directly deposited into the Merchandising Leaders of the 21st Century Scholarship Fund. We thank you for your support!

Please use the enclosed envelope to return this contribution form.

_____ Yes, I will become a sponsor! Please indicate your sponsorship level.

$100 _____ $250 _____ $500 _____ $1,000_____ $2,000_____

_____ No, I can't contribute at this time but thank you for asking.

Organization: _____

Contact Person: _____ E-mail address: _____

Address: _____ Phone: (_____)_____

City: _____ State: _____ Zip: _____ Fax: (_____)_____

Please make checks payable to the NAU Foundation.

For information contact Kris Swanson at kris.swanson@nau.edu
or Judy Everett at judy.everett@nau.edu

Figure 4.22 (cont'd)

(c)

Maybelline sponsored 12 shows during New York Fashion Week and had 120 makeup artists working backstage (Born & Brookman, 2012). Besides New York, Maybelline also sponsors fashion weeks in Amsterdam, Berlin, Kiev, Lodz, Moscow, Tel Aviv, Tokyo, Toronto, and Ukraine. Damien Bertrand, Maybelline's global brand president, said, "For me, what's very important is not only Lincoln Center, it's bringing the trend to the world . . . taking them from the catwalk, bringing them to the sidewalk" (Born & Brookman, 2012, p. 33). Bertrand also suggested that Maybelline's goal in fashion show sponsorship is to democratize beauty trends and have its products become synonymous with style.

When a company sponsors an event, it generally contributes through monetary and/or in-kind contributions. Corporations use sponsorship as a public relations strategy to enhance image. Other reasons that corporations sponsor events are to improve customer relations, increase employee morale, and fulfill civic responsibilities.

Businesses can sponsor an event in several ways. They can lend their name to the event, such as the Mercedes-Benz Fashion Week. This enhances the image of both the event and the sponsoring organization. Along with name recognition, the company also contributes financially to ensure the event will be successful.

Contributing door prizes and giveaways and providing refreshments are two other ways companies can sponsor a fashion show. Gifts, offered as silent auction items, can be used to raise money. Other gifts can be used as door prizes, awarded by a drawing or raffle, to thank audience members for buying a ticket. Giveaways are items given to every member of the audience. A swag bag, perfume sample, or discount coupons left on each chair are examples of a giveaway, and the sponsoring fragrance company or retailer is acknowledged as a sponsor.

Door prizes and giveaways are used to build interest in the show and thank the audience for attending. Depending on the type of show, few or many of these presents may be used. Gifts may be large items such as weekend getaways, DVD players, or diamond jewelry, or small items such as cosmetics, tote bags, water bottles, T-shirts, accessories, or other mass-produced premiums. At fashion shows, it is also common to see gift certificates for manicures or haircuts as part of sponsorship.

Sponsors may directly buy the gifts, or contribute money and allow the fashion show committee or staff to buy appropriate gifts. Often, gifts with the corporation's logo are part of the giveaways, reinforcing brand recognition with the company. Providing refreshments is also a way for corporations to sponsor events. Again, the company may provide actual product or provide money to buy the food and beverages. Local soft drink bottling companies often sponsor refreshments by contributing beverages for the event.

CREATIVE DEVELOPMENT OF PROMOTIONAL MATERIALS

Fashion show announcements, invitations, or promotional posters left on the counter at a retail store or posted on a bulletin board are used to create a brand image for the show. They are useful in attracting attention to the show and recognizing sponsors and donors. The elements and principles of design are used in the creative development of promotional materials.

Posters, Flyers, and Invitations

Often, the first place to start in developing a promotion package is with a poster design. Posters (8½ by 14 inches or 11 by 17 inches) are easy and effective ways to promote a fashion show. Posters can be read easily and quickly from a distance and the elements can be modified for use on tickets, the program, and other printed materials. Posters can also be placed at store entrances, near elevators, or used as in-store signage. The poster design can also be used for e-mail invitations or announcements.

The keys to an effective poster are eye-catching visuals and easy-to-read information. Visuals should be large and have appeal when viewed from a distance. Generally, one visual element is enough when text is being included on the poster. Fonts should be large and easy to read from a distance, and according to accepted design rules, no more than three fonts should be used on one poster (including any fonts within visual elements). It is better to stay with one or two fonts and change the point size to create variety.

The poster should include a prominent design element or a logo for the show as well as the following information:

- Show title reflecting the theme of the show
- Day, date, and time
- Location
- Ticket information and costs
- RSVP if necessary
- Sponsoring organization
- Logos and brand images for the show and sponsors
- Any other useful information

The best piece of advice for creating a poster is to *simplify*. Information should be stated as simply and specifically as possible. Proofreading by multiple committee or staff members is a must. As the poster is proofed, unnecessary words should be eliminated. Ideally, the poster is printed on card stock. Figure 4.23 is a poster for *An Evening of Innovation*, a fashion show produced at Philadelphia University.

Flyers—often a smaller version of the poster on 20 pound bond paper—are excellent for reaching general audiences such as a student body or mall shoppers. Standard sizes for flyers are 8½ by 11 inches, or half sheets, 5½ by 4¼ inches. Flyers can be folded in half or thirds and mailed. Flyers can also be distributed in person or used as a newspaper insert.

Invitations include the same textual information as the poster, but are printed on high-quality paper with a more elegant look. Invitations are more expensive to produce and should be sent to a more specific, targeted mailing list, including the sponsoring retailer's customer list. When developing an invitation, work with a printer who is familiar with standard invitation sizes. The minimum size for first class mail is 5 by 3½ inches. Certain sizes are considered irregular by the U.S. Postal Service and will require additional postage.

When considering print media, printing and postage costs should be evaluated. The addressee should receive mailed flyers or invitations at least 2 weeks in advance of the event. This gives the potential audience member enough time to make plans for the event. A save-the-date notice could be e-mailed to potential audience members a month or more in advance, if the show is likely to attract out-of-town participants.

Mailing lists are an important tool when using direct mail. Membership lists and customer lists should be used whenever possible to generate an audience. When developing a mailing list it is extremely important not to duplicate mailings. An item mailed twice to one address aggravates the recipient and is costly to

Figure 4.23
The fashion show An *Evening of Innovation* at Philadelphia University was promoted with this poster.

the organization. Many computer programs are available that can generate a database list and eliminate duplicates. A committee member should take on this responsibility as part of the show planning and organization.

Tickets and Programs

When planning the poster and other printed materials, it is easy to design tickets and programs at the same time. Tickets serve many purposes. For the show committee, they are a good way to control the number of attendees. For the attendee they serve as a reminder for the event. Mailing lists for future events can be generated from tickets if the voucher has a space for the attendee to write his or her name and address, or other contact information. Tickets can also be prepared with a perforated section so that part of the ticket can be returned and part held by the audience member to use for door prizes.

It is always an issue whether to sell or give away tickets. Some schools cannot sell tickets to campus events; others need to sell tickets to cover the cost of producing the show or to provide scholarships. There are advantages to both free and sponsored shows. Shows free to the public are common in retail stores. The cost of producing the show is usually recovered in retail sales after the show. Response rates increase if the show is specialized, such as a bridal show, and if tickets must be picked up at a certain location, such as at the information booth of the retail mall.

Charging for tickets lends a degree of exclusivity to the show, causing it to have greater importance to the ticket holder. When tickets are sold, the number of tickets distributed will be lower but the percentage rate for those who attend will be greater. Plan for a 15 percent no-show and print that many extra tickets. Tickets can be printed at local print shops or purchased in rolls at stationery or office supply stores. If the show is being produced at an auditorium or a theater, the cost of printing the tickets may be part of the rental fee. Or the facility may require use of a ticketing agent, such as Ticketmaster. Check with the venue management to be sure about ticket regulations.

Tickets should be carefully proofread to make sure day, date, time, and location are correctly printed. When these errors are not caught in time, the fashion show staff must either correct the tickets by hand or spend additional money to reprint them. If reserved seating is used, then tickets must be marked with the seat number. Tickets should be designed to complement the rest of the printed material, contributing to a well-coordinated package.

Printed programs serve as an outline or guide of the merchandise being presented. Programs may or may not be used, depending on the type of show. Mall shows with audience members filtering in and out may not need programs, perhaps a simple flyer identifying the retail participants would help guests find items they would like to purchase. Programs for special event shows may help the audience keep track of the garments they intend to try on after the show. Figure 4.24 is an example of a student getting a fashion show program ready to hand out to guests.

Models' names may or may not be used in the program, depending upon the type of show. Price is seldom listed. Programs may also acknowledge the sponsors, producers, designers, models, manufacturers, retailers, or any additional staff who volunteered their time to produce the show. This not only thanks those people who helped, it provides some publicity for businesses such as printers, photographers, hair stylists, cosmeticians, or technicians that have provided assistance. It can also serve to reinforce the charity and group sponsoring the show.

Figure 4.24
This student is getting programs ready to distribute to the audience during the fashion show's rehearsal.

Courtesy of Christopher C. Everett

As with all printed materials, the design of the programs should emphasize the established theme, not detract from the show. It is better to have no program than a program that was slapped together at the last minute. Advertising space may be sold in programs. Rates are usually determined by the sponsoring organization. This is a way to increase profits of the show or cover advertising expenses.

PROMOTIONAL STRATEGIES THAT WILL WORK FOR YOUR SHOW

The promotion coordinator must be careful in his or her choice of communication channels. Although Mercedes-Benz Fashion Week is a large enough fashion show event to receive coverage on *Good Morning America*, most local events should focus on local media. To get the message across, the channel must be one that the target audiences will receive and believe. Mass media such as newspapers, radio, and television are the best media for fashion show coverage. Magazines are also excellent channels for fashion show coverage, but they require a longer lead time for publication than is available to many fashion show planners.

People are also channels for communicating messages. Person-to-person meetings or person-to-group interactions are very good channels to promote fashion shows, particularly within a local community or on a university campus. In addition to face-to-face communication, e-mail can be effective in delivering personal communication. Finally, another communication channel is direct marketing such as flyers, personal invitations, or other promotional pieces to get the fashion message across to the public.

The Internet provides a very cost-effective way to promote a fashion show. The fashion show promotion team can create a web page for the show. If your school or charitable organization has an e-mail newsletter, you can place an announcement there or you can create a Facebook page and event listing. If your school permits off-campus ticketing, you can announce your event and sell ticket through Evite.

Branding a Fashion Show
Patricia Murphey

Courtesy of Patricia Murphey

In fall 2010, the merchandising professors from the School of Communication at Northern Arizona University (NAU) approached me with the idea of having my design students collaborate on a project with their merchandising students. The project scope was to have my design students help develop a strong brand identity to promote the merchandising students' fashion show.

I have always believed in exposing students to challenges with real-world expectations, and in this case, it was to work together with students from another discipline. My students had to understand the merchandising students' needs and, together, develop a well-thought-out brand identity.

The designers of this project were two of my VisualDESIGNLab (VDL) students. The VisualDESIGNLab is a design studio in the visual communication program at NAU, where students have the opportunity of working with real clients and real projects. They learn how to take on projects from conception to execution, dealing with contracts, budgets, project briefs, group collaboration, project delivery, guidelines, and printing. I work with students and clients to develop visual solutions that represent the client's vision in a professional and accessible manner.

The design team decided to approach this project as any other; the merchandising class would be our client. We would do our best to transform their vision into a strong visual identity.

For 3 months, the design team worked on understanding the needs of the project and on developing a brand identity that would materialize the show's theme. Faculty involvement was minimal, interjecting only when needed and only to guide the process and give feedback. The faculty agreed from the start that the goal was for us to create an environment that inspired creative collaboration, not one that dictated results.

The first step in the process was for our client, the merchandising students, to decide among themselves the theme of the show and create a promotion committee to work with the design team. Once the theme was established, they brought the idea to my class and together brainstormed ideas on how to best visually portray the concept of the show. The theme of the show was *Get Your Fashion Fix on Route 66* and they wanted the show to reflect the experience of traveling through the Southwest and Route 66 in the old days. The client wanted the design team to be inspired by the vintage artifacts and memorabilia found on Route 66 when designing the brand identity.

With this theme in mind, the designers went into research mode, creating mood boards that translated these ideas into visual representations. The VDL designers gathered magazine clippings, landscape photos, jewelry, fashion drawings, and all sorts of objects and images that would visually embody what they understood of the theme. The result of this research was a series of sketches of possible "Fashion Fix" marks (logos), typographic choices, and a unique color palette. The design students drew their ideas as they do in other design classes, in an attempt to describe many different ways of designing for this theme. The students understood that their ideas would help communicate and promote the tone of the fashion show and that the mark would be the visual expression of the theme, creating unity, consistency, and a memorable identity throughout all the promotional pieces.

There were some power struggles between the two groups because they were both passionate and had strong opinions. I had to tell my design students to "wow" their client; the client had to be convinced that the idea was a regurgitation of their creative brief. During the next creative meeting, the design students were ready to impress and refined their ideas into colored compositions and mock-ups of the printed pieces. It worked!

Each element of the identity was used to enhance the representation of the Route 66 theme. The typography evoked an Old West poster feel; the blue color chosen represented the turquoise stones and skies of the area, and the red reflected both the mountains and a vintage color palette. The design of the mark was both a challenging and fun process. The students, both designers and clients, wanted the mark to reflect both fashion and the amateur aura of a student fashion show. The designers started developing the Route 66 girl (mascot), dressed in a fashionable jean jacket, boots, a cute beanie, and a long scarf that turned into a road. The feedback from the merchandising students was great.

As the team started the refinement phase, they discussed proper fashion-drawing proportions, fashion trends, and line quality and my students went on to refine their ideas, incorporating the valuable feedback they received. Photos showing the stages of creations of the mark from rough sketches through refinement appear in Figure 4.3.

Once the logo was finalized, the design team created posters, tickets, postcards, and T-shirts to promote the show; the clients were so happy with the identity we developed that they decided to dress one of the runway models as the Route 66 girl. This unified the theme really well.

Collaboration was the key for the success of this project and it allowed for a result that encompassed ideas from both groups and generated a sense of accomplishment and participation. The lesson was clear: both groups had strong talents. By working together, they were able to take advantage of their diverse expertise and prove that producing and promoting a fashion show definitely requires a team effort. This one, even with its few bumps, serves as a success story of cross-disciplinary education that mimicks the context of a professional environment. These working partners developed a relationship of professionalism and trust, and from that relationship, the project developed into a coherent product.

Patricia Murphey has been working as a designer, art director, and creative director for the past 20 years in Chicago, San Francisco, Rio de Janeiro (Brazil), and Flagstaff, Arizona. She has been an assistant professor at Northern Arizona University since 2006, teaching graphic design, typography, branding, and portfolio classes. She is also the principal at Patricia Murphey Design and continues to be an award-winning design professional.

Public Relations for a Luxury Fashion Retailer

Miss PR Diva

Courtesy of WWD/Giovanni Giannoni

My role for a luxury retailer is to promote the brand by planning and executing merchandise-driven events such as fashion shows. I coordinate with local press to cover events, which in turn gains visibility for the company, resulting in increased sales.

As a retailer, we host many types of events including designer fashion shows, local charity luncheons, trend fashion presentations, and private VIP receptions. Each season, I determine what events will affect the business and develop a plan of action to execute them. Depending on the event, I have to determine who the audience will be and the best way to invite and promote the event.

When hosting a private fashion show, we usually invite a charity or special audience. For this type of event, I pull a list of names from our existing database to mail a printed invitation. Occasionally I will produce one via Evite, but use that more as a reminder than an invitation. In some cases a ticket price is determined, usually to raise money for a charity or to cover the cost of the event. It is important to have press events such as these to help build your company's brand image and reputation in the community.

Once the fashion show or event is planned, I prepare a media kit to send to the local media. The kit should be compelling enough to gain the media's interest, but not have too much information or they will be overwhelmed. In the world of public relations, you have no control over how the media will present your information or if they decide to use it at all. The more creative your pitch is, the more likely they will cover your event. I always include the press release with details of the event, photos of the designer or trends that will be featured, and an invitation to the event. Building a relationship with the media is key! The more interaction you have with them, the more credibility you will gain.

Traditional media such as magazines, newspapers, and television need ample lead time for stories to be published. Timeliness is important! I make sure to give magazine editors plenty of time to run news releases in their upcoming issues. Post-event coverage is just as important as pre-event coverage! At every event we designate a table or special area just for press and photographers. Most publications or newspapers will print event photos in their social pages following the event.

The use of social media has become a very important way to connect with the target audience for events. Everyone is connected to a smartphone device, which allows you to give instant information. Social media channels that may have worked one season can completely change the next! It is an exciting world, but you have to be educated and tech savvy to keep up.

Here are a few different forms of social media that that I use to affect my brand image and promote events:

- **Facebook** is the most popular form of social media I use to promote events. I am able to update followers instantly with photos and event invitations. I can also create photo albums to showcase pictures from the show or event.
- **Twitter** is a microblogging service that enables you to send and read text-based posts of up to 140 characters, known as "tweets." I create "hashtags" that will identify the event and cause this word to appear in the search engine results. I like to use Twitter to tell my followers what is happening backstage before the show, post Twitpics of the models being styled, and keep them updated on everything in 140 characters or less!
- **Blogs** are online journals that are updated regularly. I work very closely with local bloggers on new product launches and special events. Bloggers have a great network of followers and other fellow bloggers. They are always hungry for new material to write about. If something comes up at the last minute and the magazines have gone to print, bloggers are a perfect solution to get the word out. I find this a great resource for reaching new audiences to attend my events. If you think about it, any time you post an opinion online you are in effect a blogger.

At the end of the day, it is very rewarding to see customers excited to come to our shows and events. The best feeling to have as a retailer is knowing the customer enjoyed the experience and wants to come back. You can plan and execute a flawless show, but it won't benefit you if there is no audience. Exposure is everything!

My fashion career began a decade ago with an internship in retail management at a luxury retailer. After successfully completing my internship, I advanced within the retail company to a position in public relations. I have a B.S. degree in fashion merchandising and a minor in advertising from Northern Arizona University. I was the president of Northern Arizona Merchandising Association, the student organization that sponsors the biennial fashion show and a model in *Rock the Runway*.

THE MESSAGE—A RECAP

- All of the communication activities initiated by the seller to inform, persuade, and remind the consumer about products, services, and/or ideas offered for sale are known as promotion.
- Fashion companies rely heavily on branding by creating a name, term, design, symbol, sound, or any other feature that identifies a seller's goods or services as distinct.
- Fashion promotion involves a variety of activities including advertising, direct marketing, fashion shows, interactive and social media, personal selling, public relations, special events, and visual merchandising.
- Advertising is any nonpersonal message, paid for and placed in the mass media, and controlled by the sponsoring organization. Advertising can also be classified by its purpose, including product (action) advertising, institutional (nonproduct or image building) advertising, commercial (for profit) advertising, or noncommercial (nonprofit) advertising.
- Public relations is the management function that establishes and maintains mutually beneficial relationships between an organization and the public on whom its success or failure depends. Publicity, a tool of public relations, is information with news value, information that is uncontrolled by the source because the source does not pay the media for placement, and is provided by public relations specialists to be used in the mass media.
- A media kit is a collection of public relations materials, such as news releases, photographs, basic fact sheets, historical fact sheets, names of participants, biographical information, news story, or feature story delivered, mailed or e-mailed to the media.
- The marketing process by which organizations communicate directly with target customers to generate a response or a transaction is called direct marketing, which relies on traditional and innovative direct response media.
- The Internet and advances in technology allow for a back-and-forth flow of information in real time, rapidly changing the types of direct marketing opportunities that are available. Social media, such as Facebook and Twitter, use web-based and mobile technologies to turn communication into interactive dialogue.
- Personal selling, visual merchandising, and special events are other types of promotion that can be used by fashion show producers.
- Sponsorship involves schools, companies, or other supporters that lend their name to an event through monetary and/or some type of contribution as a way to underwrite production costs of the event.
- The elements and principles of design are used to create fashion show announcements, invitations, or promotional posters that help brand the show.
- The message is most useful when it is targeted to the prospective audience and when the appropriate media is used to promote the show.

Key Fashion Show Terms

action shot	media list
advertising	network advertising
advertising content	news release
app	news story
art	noncommercial advertising
backgrounder	online commercial
banner ad	paid search
basic fact sheet	paste-up
biographical information	personal selling
body	photo credit
brand	photographs
clip art	photography
closing date	photo opportunity
commercial advertising	pop-unders
copy	pop-ups
cost per click	preferred position
cover letter	product advertising
cutline	product shot
dateline	program of events
direct mail	publicist
direct marketing	publicity
direct response media	public relations (PR)
editorial content	public service announcement
feature story	rate card
full-run	release date
graphic design	run-of-paper
grip-and-grin	slogan
group shot	social media
headline	spam
headshot	special event
home-shopping channels	sponsorship
illustration	spot advertising
infomercials	standard advertising unit
institutional advertising	subheadline
Internet sponsorships	tear sheet
interstitials	video on demand
lead	video opportunity
links	virtual tear sheet
list of participants	visual merchandising
local advertising	webisodes
logo	white space
media kit	zoned edition

QUESTIONS FOR DISCUSSION

1. What is the difference between promotion and branding?
2. What types of advertising would you recommend to the organizers of a fashion show for a charitable organization, such as breast cancer awareness? How would your recommendation change if you were working for H&M? Macy's?
3. What is the difference between advertising content and editorial content? Which is better for a fashion brand, such as Tommy Hilfiger, to use?
4. If your show has a very limited budget to spend for promotion, what kind of promotional activities would you plan?
5. What are some of the limitations of using only social media as a promotion tool?
6. How are personal selling, visual merchandising, and special events used to promote a fashion show?
7. How can you find a sponsor for your show?
8. If you are presenting a regional fashion week, such as Chicago Fashion Week or Atlanta Fashion Week, what types of promotion activities would help you draw the biggest audience?

FASHION SHOW ACTIVITY

Divide into teams of four to five members. Each team is responsible for setting up a photo shoot for an upcoming fashion show. Determine what types of photos—headshots, group shots, grip-and-grin, product shots, or action shots—would be best for the theme of the show. Find friends or use team members as models, stylists, and photographers. Locate a site for the photo shoots to take place. Each team should have a minimum of five different photographs, using at least three different types of photographs.

THE CAPSTONE PROJECT

CD-ROM

1. Create a brand image or show logo to use for an advertisement, poster, tickets, program cover, or any other promotional items, such as T-shirts, water bottles, key rings, or tote bags.
2. Produce an advertisement that can be placed in your school or local newspaper for your show.
3. Prepare a media kit for your show. Include a cover letter, news release, five to ten photographs with captions, a fact sheet, a program of events, a list of participants, biographical information, historical information, a straight news story, and a feature story.
4. Use your brand image as a media kit cover and place your team's promotional materials in your portfolio.

Please refer to the CD-ROM for tools that may assist you with this section of the fashion show planning process.

REFERENCES

American Idol, N.F.L. duke it out for priciest TV spot. (2011, October 23). Advertising Age. Retrieved from http://adage.com

American Marketing Association. (2012). Brand. Retrieved from http://www.marketingpower.com/_layouts/Dictionary.aspx?dLetter=B

Belch, G. E., & Belch, M. A. (2012). *Advertising and promotion: An integrated marketing communications perspective* (9th ed.). New York, NY: McGraw-Hill/Irwin.

Born, P., & Brookman, F. (2012, March 9). Maybelline's masterminds. *Women's Wear Daily BeautyInc.* Retrieved from http://www.wwd.com

Broom, G. M. (2009). *Cutlip and Center's effective public relations* (10th ed.). Upper Saddle River, NJ: Prentice-Hall.

Chang, B.-S. (2012, February 15). P.R. girl revealed as P.R. executive. *The New York Times.* Retrieved from http://www.nytimes.com

Definition of: App. (2012). *PC Magazine encyclopedia.* Retrieved from http://www.pcmag.com/encyclopedia

Kaplan, A. M., & Haenlein, M. (2010). Users of the world, unite! The challenges and opportunities of social media. *Business Horizons.* 53, 59–68.

Lipke, D. (2012, February 6). Made Fashion Week launches interactive app. *Women's Wear Daily.* Retrieved from http://www.wwd.com

Media kit. (2012). *Tampa Bay Times.* Retrieved from http://www.tampabay.com

Media kit. (2012). *Toronto Life.* Retrieved from http://www.torontolife.com/

Noricks, C. (2012). *Ready to launch: The PR couture guide to breaking into fashion PR* [Kindle edition]. Retrieved from http://www.Amazon.com

O'Reilly, T., & Battelle, J. (2009). Web squared: Web 2.0 five years on. Retrieved from http://www.web2summit.com/web2009/public/schedule/detail/10194

Posner, H. (2011). *Marketing fashion.* London, UK: Laurence King.

Sherman, G. J., & Perlman, S. S. (2010). *Fashion public relations.* New York, NY: Fairchild Books.

Sifferlin, A. (2012). *The digital runway: How social media is changing fashion.* Retrieved from http://www.time.com/time/nation/article/0,8599,2106921,00.html#ixzz2CQ9B7Jls.

Standard rate and data system. (2012). *Vogue.* Retrieved from http://www.srds.com

Strugatz, R. (2011, November 13). Nobody does it better. *WWD Collections, Spring 2012,* pp. 35, 36.

Style Coalition. (2012, February 12). Style Coalition announces winners of the 3rd Annual Fashion 2.0 Awards. Retrieved from http://stylecoalition.com/awards

Swanson, K., & Everett, J. (2007). *Promotion in the merchandising environment* (2nd ed.). New York, NY: Fairchild Books.

Thomas, D. (2007). *Deluxe: How luxury lost its luster.* New York, NY: Penguin.

Tungate, M. (2008). *Fashion brands: Branding style from Armani to Zara* (2nd ed.). Philadelphia, PA: Kogan Page.

Vilaseca, E. (2010). *Runway uncovered: The making of a fashion show.* Barcelona, Spain: Promopress.

CHAPTER FIVE
The Workroom and Runway

AFTER READING THIS CHAPTER, YOU SHOULD BE ABLE TO DISCUSS:

- The process used to select merchandise for a fashion show

- How to categorize merchandise and develop an ideal chart

- How to plan merchandise to show rhythm and flow within a show scene

- The translation of merchandise categories into show scenes tied to the show theme

- Professionalism and retailer relationship building

- Elements of the merchandise pull

- The differences between tentative lineup and final lineup

- The process of merchandise fittings

Courtesy of WWD/Kuba Dabrowski

Tracy write a cover letter

The *raison d'être* for producing fashionshows is to present merchandise. The starting point of the cycle comes from the designer's inspiration, which is a never-ending process of presenting collections and going back to the drawing board to start the next season's merchandise collection. Inspiration comes from many sources. To introduce New York Fashion Week, *Women's Wear Daily* featured designers' inspirations as cover stories. Designers for Marchesa, Georgina Chapman, and Keren Craig found inspiration from an 1878 painting called *A Soul Brought to Heaven* (Fig. 5.1a) and used it as the show's theme for a fall line ("God Help Us," 2012). Judy Garland (Fig. 5.1b) was the muse for Chris Benz, who designed a line celebrating the casual richness of American sportswear ("'Tis the Season," 2012). Michael Kors was inspired by a cozy, snow-covered cabin in the woods, and Betsey Johnson found inspiration from the 1960s iconic model Twiggy.

Colors and shapes, words and mathematics, ice-skating and sci-fi warrior heroines, even listening to J. S. Bach were just a few of the diverse inspirations cited by designers for their merchandise collections presented on fashion week runways during that season. It just goes to show that inspiration can come from anywhere or anything!

> Zac Posen, fashion designer, when asked what his inspiration for the season was, answered, "The continued exploration of the construction, heritage and evolution of glamour."

This chapter takes us from the designer studios, where merchandise is created, to the runway, where the latest trends are presented to the media, retail buyers, and influential customers.

MERCHANDISE SELECTION PROCESS

Merchandise selection is the designation of apparel, shoes, and accessories for presentation in a fashion show to the target customer (Fig. 5.2). Several factors must be considered when selecting merchandise. Because many fashion shows are produced to sell clothing, selected merchandise

Figure 5.1
Women's Wear Daily featured designer inspiration as the cover story for several editions during fashion week. **(a)** The painting *A Soul Brought to Heaven* provided inspiration for Marchesa designers Georgina Chapman and Keren Craig. **(b)** In another edition, Judy Garland served as a muse for Chris Benz.

(a) *Gianni Dagli Orti/The Art Archive at Art Resource, NY*

(b) *PR Newswire*

(a)

(b)

Courtesy of Christopher C. Everett

Figure 5.2
The coordination of merchandise and model arrangement must be developed and confirmed in advance of the show.
(a) Organization of merchandise is crucial to the smooth running of a show.
(b) Each model's garments are pulled together.

must make a clear fashion statement to the audience to stimulate after-show sales. The merchandise should be suitable to the demographic profile and lifestyle of the audience, and priced appropriately to what they will spend on fashion. Too many times fashion shows display clothing suitable for the models or show planners, rather than the audience. The merchandise must have strong stage presence for everyone in the audience.

Industry shows present garments that show the breadth and depth of the current season's collection, repeating best-selling trends several times throughout the show. Consumer shows display merchandise from one or more retailers, often highlighting seasonal trends. The fashion show may be sponsored by a store, highlighting its merchandise, or a local charity using merchandise from several retailers. Some fashion shows may feature merchandise created by local artists or highlight designers within the community. Adjunct Professor Cynde Koritzinsky was the faculty adviser for a student-produced fashion show at the University of Bridgeport. Her story about merchandise selection is profiled in Notes from the Runway: The Clothing!

Merchandise Categories

The merchandise divisions presented in the show are called **merchandise categories**. Decisions as to what merchandise categories should be presented are made during the planning sessions. Merchandise is selected to fit the fashion show theme according to a plan called an **ideal chart** (Fig. 5.3), which lists categories of merchandise that will be represented in the show. Thumbing through *InStyle* or *Vogue*, or viewing websites such as www.Style.com, or www.wwd.com may help your team identify trends to be included on the ideal chart. Within each category important trends, looks, and accessories are listed so that they will not be missed when selecting merchandise. As a planning tool, ideal charts are completed before merchandise is physically pulled from the stores.

The number of garments per category to be pulled will also be listed on the ideal chart. As Professor Koritzinsky noted, these numbers may be double the amount of merchandise that will actually be used in the show. A merchandise planning chart (Fig. 5.4) helps estimate the number of garments needed for the show. When planning the merchandise for a show, plan for a minimum of one garment per minute depending on

decide on categories

go line up retailers to borrow from

Runway to Wonderland Ideal Chart

Scene 1- Stuck in a Dream (Sleepwear)
- Approximately 15 outfits
- Retailers: Target, Old Navy, PJ Chilcottage
- Flannel pajamas
- Sleep shirts
- Robes
- Slippers
- Nightgowns
- Sleep masks
- Silk pajamas
- Fuzzy socks

Scene 2- Chasing the White Rabbit (Active/Outdoor Wear)
- Approximately 15 outfits
- Retailers: Decker's, Aspen Sports, Mountain Sports, Babbitt's
- Snowboard/Ski pants
- Heavy coats
- T-shirts
- Hiking boots
- Ugg boots
- Active shoes
- Beanies
- Gloves
- Heavy scarves
- Yoga pants
- Puffy vests

Scene 3-Afternoon With the Caterpillar (Casual Wear)
- Approximately 16 outfits
- Retailers: Gap. Raci Threads, Basement Marketplace, Shoes and Such
- Denim jeans
- T-shirts
- Casual dresses
- Leggings
- Sneakers
- Boots
- Fedoras
- Headbands
- Lightweight scarves
- Suspenders
- Cardigan sweaters

Scene 4- Mad Tea Party (After 5/Date Attire)
- Approximately 15 outfits
- Retailers: Dillard's, Blackhound Gallerie, Basement Marketplace
- Premier Designs Jewelry
- Short cocktail dresses
- Bow ties
- Top hats
- Dressy skirts
- Collared shirts
- Tights
- Dressy jackets
- Heels

Scene 5- Meeting the Queen of Hearts (Business Attire)
- Approximately 12 outfits
- Retailers: Dillard's, Carol Anderson by Invitation
- Blazers
- High waist trousers
- Button down shirts
- Pencil skirts
- Pumps
- Dressy vests
- Trench coats
- Pantyhose
- Ties

Scene 6- A Twisted Fantasy (Student Designers)
- Approximately 25 designs from local student designers

Figure 5.3
An ideal chart is a projection of the merchandise to be presented in each fashion show scene. This ideal chart was created for *Runway to Wonderland.*

Illustration by Carly Grafstein

	NUMBER OF OUTFITS	NUMBER OF MODELS	TIME (minutes)
Small Show	25–40	4–6	15–20
Medium Show	40–65	8–10	25–39
Large Show	66 or more	12 or more	45–60

Figure 5.4
A merchandise planning chart helps the merchandise and model committees assess the number of outfits and models needed for the show.

Illustration by Carly Grafstein

the length of the runway. Many shows plan one outfit every 30 seconds to hold the audience's attention. A 45-minute show presents a minimum of 45 garments, with closer to 90 garments for a faster-paced show. Most shows do not exceed 1 hour and 15 minutes for nonfashion portions of the event, including refreshments and announcements, and 45 minutes for fashion presentation. Designers may show up to 100 outfits per show, sometimes more.

After developing the ideal chart for consumer shows, the merchandise team should visit local retailers to review available merchandise to determine what trends identified on the ideal chart will work for the show. Merchandise should not be reserved at this time. It may be important to visit a store several times to check out new arrivals, especially during seasonal transition periods. The merchandise selection committee needs to be familiar with the fashion preferences of the local market so they can know what merchandise to select.

Merchandise within categories should be grouped in a pleasing manner indicating a rhythm or flow among looks. Pieces within a category may be grouped according to color, styling details, design sophistication, popularity of the trend, or some other identifiable theme. Something as simple as a ribbon (Fig. 5.5) or models wearing a top hat, or other matching accessory, can add rhythm to a merchandise category.

Common categories for merchandise groupings include *play/casual clothing, intimate apparel/lingerie, career/business clothing, leisure/active/sport clothing, date/cocktail/evening clothing,* and *bridal/special occasion clothing*. Variations of these categories based on the show theme are common in many presentations. When plenty of merchandise is available, a show may divide *active* and *leisure* into two categories. For other shows, categories may be combined. Some shows may focus on one category, such as bridal wear or lingerie. A bridal show may categorize the merchandise according to styling details such as A-line dresses, ball gowns, trumpet or mermaid silhouettes, sheath dresses, and Empire waist bridal dresses. Victoria's Secret classifies garments for its annual fashion show by collection: Angels by Victoria's Secret and Victoria's Secret Pink, among others. The finale always includes a beautiful, bedazzled, winged angel.

The merchandise flow is critical to an exciting presentation. Effective merchandise flow allows the audience to visualize how garments may be worn together. Coordinated pieces should be shown in succession. Models might switch jackets on the runway to show the audience the versatility of the collection. The audience may also visualize the combination of new pieces with fashions they already own.

Color Plates 8 through 11 show thumbnail photographs from a spring

 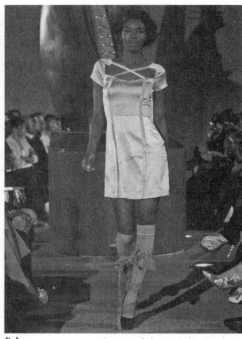

Figure 5.5 (a–b)
Phoenix fashion designer Caroline Monick used ribbons to accent her models and demonstrate rhythm within a scene at Phoenix Fashion Week.

(a)

(b)

Courtesy of Phoenix Fashion Week, LLC

couture collection designed and produced by Karl Lagerfeld for Chanel. The show is featured in its entirety as we discuss merchandise flow and rhythm for a show. The Chanel show took place inside of a mock airplane and descriptors such as "The sky's the limit" and "Karl's Rhapsody in Bleu!" were used by journalists to describe the remarkable show ("Chanel Spring Couture," 2012). The Chanel show can be broadly interpreted in four sequences, indicated by hem length. Sequence one represents day wear with a casualness represented by knee-length garments, followed by the second sequence showing day wear, but in floor-length silhouette. The third sequence represents cocktail dresses but returns to knee length, whereas the final sequence shows elegant eveningwear at floor length.

The first sequence of a show must be exciting and capture the audience's attention. The Chanel show captured the audience's attention with an explosion of blue, pale blue, bright sky blue, royal blue, ombré blue, and iridescent blue, all sophisticatedly accented with neutrals. Lagerfeld described the countless shades of blue as a monochromatic rainbow ("Chanel Spring Couture," 2012). The first sequence showed day dresses, two-piece suit dresses, and dress/coat ensembles, casual in nature for a couture show, and similar color-blocked dresses and repetition of interestingly wide necklines to emphasize looks of the moment. Two dresses accented with navy lamé created the high point of the sequence as the merchandise transitioned into black for the next grouping.

When producing a fashion show, planners should decide how merchandise category transitions are to be executed. In shows such as the Chanel couture show, the model parade is not interrupted; rather, a transition is indicated through merchandise flow. Other show types may pause the action with scene changes similar to a dramatic play or use music to indicate a transition. Dancing or theatrical readings may be used to create a transition to the next themed merchandise category.

In the Chanel show, the second sequence featured dresses, ensembles, and coats for day wear, similar to the first sequence, but floor length. The procession was rhythmic, continuing with black from the first sequence, and repeating in five successive looks a very stylized three-quarter-length voluminous sleeve to emphasize the unique silhouette. Then a series of jacketed dresses and jacket and skirt ensembles paraded the runway, keeping the silhouettes similar but at the same time transitioning into sheer, chiffon-like skirts, and then moving to shades of blue and blue prints, repeating the wide neckline introduced in the first scene. The sequence reached its finale with a dramatic giraffe-inspired print dress.

Merchandise flow must make sense. The third sequence in the Chanel show took on a decidedly more elegant look but returned to the knee-length silhouette. The scene began by focusing on embellishments, first with all-over roses, then a beaded bodice, and progressively repeating ruffles and beading at the hemline. The silhouettes repeated with various accents and reintroduced the pop of blue tones seen in previous scenes before finishing the scene with black.

> "Our themes are decided by a majority consensus based on all the ideas developed by the students in the class. Everyone gets a chance to present an idea to class. Then the class votes by anonymous clicker to decide the theme. Everyone's ideas matter and everyone's vote counts. We get the best themes through this inclusive process."
>
> —Natalie Sanger Gendle, Iowa State University

The last sequence must be equally thrilling, leaving the audience on a high note. The final sequence of the Chanel show presented floor-length, sophisticated dresses that began with similar black sheer skirts, then moved toward sequined sheaths in blue tones and black, and finally presented elegant gowns in sheer, pale-toned blues. The show finished with a wedding dress, traditionally the finale of a fashion show, and designer Karl Lagerfeld walking the runway.

Merchandise Theme Coordination

The next step in merchandising planning is to translate the broad merchandise categories into the scene themes developed earlier during the planning stage.

The ideal chart (Fig. 5.3) includes the scene themes for a show. The overall show theme was *Runway to Wonderland*, inspired by the Lewis Carroll book, *Alice's Adventures in Wonderland*.

The scene themes evolved from the overall show theme and allowed distinction between merchandise categories. Sleepwear began the show and was given the theme "Stuck in a Dream." The next scene featured active/outdoor wear and was titled "Chasing the White Rabbit." Skiwear, hiking apparel, and yoga pants were among the featured items. Casual wear, including leggings, jeans, and casual dresses, was featured in the next scene, "Afternoon with the

Caterpillar." When looking at the merchandise listed within the two scenes—activewear and casual wear—it might seem similar. Merchandise coordinators need to pay special attention to differentiate comparable scenes through the use of different retailers, fabric weight, color stories, or styling details.

After 5/date wear was featured in the scene "Mad Tea Party," followed by business attire featured in a scene titled "Meeting the Queen of Hearts." The showstopping final scene featured student designers and brought the show together in a scene titled "A Twisted Fantasy." This title worked well because it was inclusive and allowed many different designer items to be featured together.

Consumer show merchandise should reflect two groups. The first group should be clothing that the audience can wear and afford. The second group should be showstopper items—experimental items—that the audience will enjoy viewing and possibly experimenting with after the show. Affordable, wearable clothing should make up 75 percent of the collection with showstopping garments accounting for 25 percent of the collection. Creating this balance will reassure the audience that the producers understand them while showing them ways to have fun expanding their wardrobe. The industry calls this 75/25 percent balance "merchandising to your audience."

Fashion designers from the community or local design schools are often a source for showstopping merchandise. Using local designers is a way to create excitement for a show and give these designers exposure. Figure 5.6 is an example of a flier calling for fashion designers to submit their entries for a local fashion show. It is important to remember that designers need a much longer lead time to design garments for inclusion in a show. Local designers may have a collection they can pull from. Student designers may need a semester or more to complete garments to present in a show. If you are going to use designer garments, getting the call out to designers must be one of the earliest tasks to be completed.

When using retailers, the fashion show director or merchandise coordinator for shows produced by a charitable organization or school should make sure the retailers selected have enough merchandise of the right types and quantities to match the merchandise categories planned. It is poor planning to select a merchandise category and then later realize that the retailer carries only limited selections within that category. When retailers agree to lend merchandise for a charitable or school show, merchandise categories should be tailored to match the store offerings.

Merchandise should be new to the audience and represent the latest trends to create as much excitement as possible. Merchandise that the audience has already seen in the store will not encourage sales of the goods. Trends may be influenced by past seasons, but it is important to select details that reflect the current season.

Using merchandise from more than one retailer has both advantages and disadvantages. The advantages include having more items to choose from and having more categories from which to draw for ideas. Small stores, which may carry limited merchandise, also have the opportunity to participate because they do not have to worry about providing large quantities of clothing. Using more than one retailer may be considered a disadvantage if favoritism is shown to one store or if uniqueness among retailers' merchandise is not evident. All retailers should be aware of other participating merchants, and the same policies should be enforced for all retailers.

Northern **A**rizona **U**niversity's Fashion Show Production
and
Northern **A**rizona **M**erchandising **A**ssociation are . . .

Calling all
fashion designers!

Get Your Fashion Fix on Route 66

What: Northern Arizona University needs your designs for our Student Design Segment in our runway scene November 19 and 20

When: All garments must be submitted by October 29

Where: Please be in touch with your instructors and NAU will send students to your school to pick up submissions

Why: Get Your Fashion Fix on Route 66 will be a professional runway show in Flagstaff. Designs accepted will be shown in two shows. This will give up and coming designers a chance to show what they've got!

If you have any questions, please contact NAU student and Student Director, Emilee Dunn via email at ekd23@nau.edu.

NAMA and the NAU fashion show production class thank you in advance for the amazing designs that you will submit. We look forward to working with you!

Courtesy of Northern Arizona University

Figure 5.6
A flier, "Calling All Fashion Designers," puts out the word for designers to submit their designs for a fashion show.

A charity or school team should not try to use a retailer just because it volunteers clothing. Show coordinators may be initially excited to use this merchandise, only to realize later that it does not fit the audience. If a junior store, specializing in small sizes aimed at the tween and young adult market, asks to be part of the show, but the audience attending the fashion show is composed of misses clothing customers, then the fashion show will be of little benefit to the merchant or the audience. Merchandise from all the retailers used should match the theme of the show and the needs of the audience, as discussed in Chapter 3.

RELATIONSHIPS WITH MERCHANTS

A good working relationship with retailers is crucial for a successful show. A professional image must be projected at all times. You are representing your show, your organization, your school, and, most important, yourself. Your actions directly reflect on the show, school, or organization. Merchants are reluctant to participate in current shows if they have had poor experiences in the past with show staff that was unprofessional. Speaking directly to students, you might participate in a show only once, but the reputation of your school, department, and faculty lives on in the community for many years. Your actions, positive and negative, will affect the opportunity for future students to be able to borrow merchandise for their fashion show.

In most cases, merchandise used in the show is "on loan" from stores. Merchandise loan procedures vary from store to store and it is best to ask merchants how they prefer to inventory borrowed merchandise. Show personnel are responsible for lost or damaged merchandise and will be held accountable. A prepared merchandise team will provide a **merchandise loan record**, which is a standardized form used to record details of the borrowed merchandise. Figure 5.7 is a sample merchandise loan record. The loan record should include a description of the garment, the manufacturer, color, size, price, date of loan, store authorization, merchandise department, when it will be returned, and who will be responsible for returning the merchandise. One copy should be kept by the store lending the merchandise and another by the person responsible for returning the merchandise. Inform the merchant of security measures that will be taken to ensure the safety of the garments while they are out of the store.

MERCHANDISE PULL

A **merchandise pull** is the physical removal of merchandise from the sales floor to an area reserved for storage of fashion show merchandise. Twice as many garments should be pulled, as will be used, to avoid problems at fittings. By pulling extra merchandise, last-minute frantic searches for replacements can be prevented. Merchants may limit the number of items and the amount of time items may be pulled to avoid having too much merchandise off the sales floor. Merchants may also indicate that, although the merchandise has been pulled, they may sell it if necessary.

Ideally, pulling the merchandise should begin 2 to 4 weeks before the show to give ample time for fittings and deciding the final lineup of the show merchandise. Unfortunately, that is not always possible. Basic seasonal items may be pulled first, whereas new looks may not be available until closer to show time. Merchandise for apparel mart shows is often pulled 24 to 48 hours in advance of the show.

MERCHANDISE LINEUP

When merchandise grouping is completed, it is necessary to create a tentative show lineup. A **tentative lineup** includes the order of the models and the proposed merchandise from the theme groupings, prepared before fittings. The tentative lineup is created using the **model order**—the rotation in which the models will appear throughout the show. The merchandise is in unconfirmed order. If the lineup has to be changed, the coordinator must try to change the order of the merchandise without upsetting the theme or model rotation previously established. Changing the order of the models should be a last resort because this adds confusion during the presentation. Changes in the lineup

MERCHANDISE LOAN RECORD

Date_____   Department_____

Store_____

Show_____   Date of Show_____

Issued to_____

Qty	Style #	Size	Color	Description	Price

Received in Stock by_____   Date_____

From_____

Illustration by Carly Grafstein

Figure 5.7
The merchandise loan record provides documentation about where the merchandise is borrowed from and when it is returned.

are made during the fitting and rehearsal sessions. These changes result in a **final lineup**—a complete listing of merchandise and models in order of their appearance—that is prepared and distributed to everyone after the dress rehearsal. Sample tentative lineup and final lineup charts are shown in Figures 5.8a and b.

The final lineup is used for many different purposes throughout the show. Dressing areas are organized according to this lineup, placing each model in a specific area to avoid confusion (Fig. 5.9). Dressing area organization is discussed in Chapter 7. The dressers, fitters, backstage manager, and cue personnel follow the final lineup for order. Choreographers, music technicians, and lighting technicians can record any cues on their copies of the lineup.

MERCHANDISE FITTINGS

Fittings are planned and executed when the tentative lineup is completed. **Fittings** involve matching the models to the merchandise

TENTATIVE LINEUP
Runway to Wonderland

Order of Appearance
Scene 1: Stuck in a Dream
(Sleepwear–25 outfits)

1	Alexia
1	Michelle
1	Joan
1	Tammy
1	Pam
2	Erica
3	Carl
3	Brett
4	Sara
4	Jenny
4	Melissa
5	Kenny
6	Natasha
6	Jasmine
7	Marcy
7	Jessica
8	Dawn
8	Dusty
8	Cathie
9	Whitney
9	Bart
10	Breezy
11	Paige
11	Terry
12	Angel

Scene 2: Chasing the White Rabbit
(Active/Outdoor Wear–20 outfits)

13	Kari
13	Dan
13	Jennifer
14	Lisa
14	Susanna
15	Andrea
16	Mike
16	Tom
16	John
17	Joan
17	Jose
18	Pam
18	Chris
19	Sally
19	Jenny
19	Tim
20	Kerry
20	Sylvia
20	Kaley
21	Sam

(a)

FINAL LINEUP
Runway to Wonderland

Model Order	Outfit	Accessories
Scene 1: Stuck in a Dream (Sleepwear–21 outfits)		
1 Alexia	flannel pants, thermal top-red	each model carries
1 Michelle	flannel pants, thermal top-orange	a stuffed animal
1 Joan	flannel pants, thermal top-yellow	
1 Tammy	flannel pants, thermal top-green	
1 Pam	flannel pants, thermal top-blue	
2 Erica	holiday print pajamas	red moccasins
3 Carl	deer print flannel pants, navy hoodie	fuzzy slippers
3 Brett	bear print flannel pants, brown hoodie	fuzzy slippers
4 Marcy	red snowflake leggings, white tank	red booties
4 Jessica	white snowflake leggings, green tank	green booties
5 Sara	gray sweat pants, purple baseball shirt	mules
5 Jenny	navy sweat pants, gray baseball shirt	mules
5 Melissa	navy sweat pants, purple baseball shirt	mules
6 Kenny	brown plaid pants, green long sleeve t-shirt	brown moccasins
7 Natasha	navy sweatpants, gray sweatshirt	fleece slippers
7 Jasmine	navy sweatpants, light blue sweatshirt	fleece slippers
8 Dawn	green stripe PJs	moccasins
8 Dusty	purple stripe PJs	moccasins
8 Cathi	blue strip PJs	moccasins
9 Whitney	white bathrobe	slippers
9 Bart	blue bathrobe	slippers
Scene 2: Chasing the White Rabbit (Active/Outdoor Wear–15 outfits)		
10 Kari	black jeans, red down jacket	cowboy hat
10 Dan	black jeans, white down jacket	cowboy hat
10 Jennifer	black jeans, purple down jacket	cowboy hat
11 Lisa	teal yoga pants, print tank top	yoga mat
11 Susanna	navy yoga pants, print tank top	yoga mat
12 Andrea	pink ski pants with matching parka	snowboard
12 Sandy	white ski pants with matching parka	snowboard
12 Tara	navy ski pants with yellow parka	snowboard
13 Mike	black ski pants, red parka	Panda knit cap
13 Tom	black ski pants, yellow parka	Cat knit cap
14 Jake	running pants and hoodie dark green	running shoes
14 Pam	running pants and hoodie burgundy	running shoes
14 Joe	running pants and hoodie navy	running shoes
15 Tim	sweats (campus logo) blue	green Vans
15 Jenny	sweats (campus logo) yellow	red Vans

(b)

Figure 5.8
(a) The tentative lineup is created before fittings. Compare this lineup to the final lineup **(b)** which is established after model fittings and before the rehearsal.

Illustration by Carly Grafstein

Figure 5.9
The final lineup is used in many ways, including organizing the model's dressing area.

Courtesy of Christopher C. Everett

(Fig. 5.10). Fitting sessions are scheduled to avoid wasting models', coordinators', and merchants' time. If professional models are being used, they are paid for their time at fittings, and this cost must be budgeted. Shows involving only a few models may schedule individual fittings. Shows involving 15 to 20 models should schedule 3 or 4 models at a time to avoid mass confusion within the store. Apparel mart or trade shows may use standard size fitting models. When professional models are used, the fitting may be the first time the model wears the garments. Anyone who has regularly watched episodes of *Project Runway* has seen designers anguish at model fittings when the real model was not the same size as the dress form.

Some retailers will reserve a specific area in which show coordinators and models can work so that they will not disturb

Figure 5.10
Making sure the model and the merchandise are complementary takes place during the fittings. The lineup sheet can be finalized after the models try on garments.

Courtesy of WWD/Steve Eichner

customers. Other retailers with limited space may ask show staff to work around regular store hours, customers, and dressing rooms. With retailers it is critical to act professionally and not distract the store's clients.

Fitting Sheets

A fitting sheet should be prepared for each outfit as the tentative lineup is determined. The **fitting sheet** (Fig. 5.11) is an information sheet coordinated to the merchandise and model. It should include sizing information, the order number in the lineup, and a detailed description of the garment. The description must have enough detail to easily locate the garment within the store. During the fittings, coordinators and models should list accessories to be worn with the ensemble during the show. If an accessory must be worn in a certain way, this detail is included. The coordinator may choose to put the model's name on the fitting sheet prior to the fittings if the model order will not be altered. Fitting sheets and the tentative lineup are used to prepare the final lineup. One set of fitting sheets should be organized in a notebook to serve as a running checklist as accessories are gathered and alterations are completed.

Fitting Supplies

Before beginning the fittings, the merchandise committee should gather needed materials. A fitting supply checklist should be

---

FITTING SHEET

Store or Designer_____

Fitting Time_____

Scene_____

Position Number_____

Model Name_____

Garment Size:

Dress_____ Shirts/Sweaters_____

Bottoms_____ Shoes_____

Garment Description_____

_____

Accessories_____

_____

_____

Models need to bring_____

_____

Staff need to bring_____

_____

Figure 5.11
The fitting sheet is used to record the garments and accessories that a model will wear. It is completed during the fittings.

Illustration by Carly Grafstein

used to avoid forgetting important items. Once the checklist has been designed, it may be used repeatedly for many shows. Fitting supplies should include the following items: fitting sheets, garment tags, pens, pencils, and staplers for record keeping. Straight pins, safety pins, tailor's chalk, scissors, and measuring tapes should be available to assist with alterations, if alterations are permitted. Miscellaneous materials to help protect the merchandise, including cellophane tape, masking tape for protecting shoes, garment and accessory bags, hangers, dress shields, and scarves to protect garments from model's makeup, should also be part of fitting supplies. Accessories, shoes, and innerwear garments should also be gathered (Fig. 5.12).

Pre-Fitting Organization

Model sizes must be known, and the merchandise tentatively selected, ordered, and matched to the model before he or she arrives for the fittings. Store staff that understand the look should also be included when fitting merchandise to models. In ideal situations, a model arrives at a prearranged time to find specific looks ready and waiting to be tried on. The fitting is handled quickly and efficiently with little interruption to the retail environment.

In the worst-case scenario, all models arrive at the same time to find that merchandise has not been selected or pulled and their sizes were not provided by the show producers. Extraneous friends are in the way, distracting models and show staff. Merchants are disappointed at the lack of professionalism and leadership within

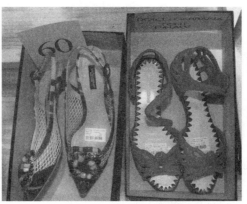

Figure 5.12
Accessories should be tagged and positioned near the merchandise with which they will be worn to allow models and dressers smooth changes.

Courtesy of WWD/Delphine Achard

the group. Precious time is wasted, tempers flare, and the attitudes of all involved become very negative at a crucial time in the show preparation.

To avoid this scenario, plan fittings 10 days to 2 weeks before the show and be fully prepared. The coordinator for school or charity groups should display professional organization to the retailer and the models. Use the tentative lineup and know the specific merchandise that each model will wear before he or she arrives for the fitting. Do not allow models' personal preferences to interfere with the merchandise order. Garments should be exchanged among models only if size or fit problems occur. If a garment cannot be fit to a specific model, it may be necessary to discard the garment from the lineup and use a substitute rather than find a model who may fit the garment but upset the flow of merchandise. It may be advisable to have each model fit into several extra garments at the fitting so substitutions may be made within the lineup without calling the model for a second fitting.

The Clothing!
Cynde Koritzinsky

Courtesy of Cynde Koritzinsky

What makes a fashion show exciting and dramatic? Is it the music, the commentator, the entertainment, or the clothes? In our fashion merchandising department's shows at the University of Bridgeport, we combine each of these for success. The theme of the show is selected first, next the music and entertainment are chosen, the commentator's script is written, and then it's all about the runway, as the models wear the clothes we have selected.

As we get ready for each new show, our students bring in their ideas about the newest fashion trends for the upcoming season. After watching videos of runway shows (our favorites are Betsey Johnson and Victoria's Secret), the class decides how many items should be included in each clothing category, preparing an ideal sheet. Then our modeling committee steps in and finds a group of models with lots of personality from the university campus. Once they have a completed list with sizing information and photos, the modeling and clothing committees head to the stores to shop!

The University of Bridgeport's Fashion Department curriculum is based on marketing and merchandising, not on apparel design. For this reason, our students "borrow" fashionable clothing from local retailers for the show. The five large stores we work with are T.J. Maxx, Marshall's, J.C. Penney's, Loehmann's, and Bob's Stores. In addition, each year we have students in class who work at other local retailers that are always gracious enough to lend us clothes for the show.

The store visits are set at 8 a.m., before the retailers open for business. The students are given racks and they shop the stores to choose what they think would work for the show, keeping in mind the models' sizes, and making sure that they are bringing back enough clothes for each model and for each clothing category. Before checking out, the racks are evaluated one more time to make sure that only the best merchandise is coming back to the school. Sometimes it is hard for the students to understand that what is best for a fashion show is not always what they would choose to purchase for themselves. Garments in a fashion show are all about visual appeal—the audience cannot reach out and touch the apparel; they must be able to see distinguishing characteristics from a distance. The items chosen must be season and target-market appropriate, fashionable, and exciting! Even though black is a huge selling color in stores, it is not a very exciting color on a runway. And, although all of our students wear jeans, we rarely borrow denim from a store for our show.

no denim, avoid black

Once the final decisions are made and the clothes are counted out in the stores, we bring them back to the university where they are counted in again. We are very security conscious—after all, these clothes do not belong to us; they are only on loan. Students in the class write a short description of each style, including vendor name, style number, price, and size. Each store is cross-referenced with a sticker, such as a red star, and this sticker is also placed on all of their garments. We do this to make it easier to figure out which garments belong to which stores after the show. Our show usually has about 175 complete outfits in it, which could be almost 350 separate pieces. We try to bring back twice the number of items to choose from as we want to use in the show. This means that we would need to have close to 700 pieces of apparel. For this reason, we try to be very organized and keep excellent descriptions, so that we can separate clothes by store after the show, without problems.

Once we have all of the merchandise at the university and it has been counted in, we then separate the racks by clothing category (lingerie, swim, casual, work, dinner, club, evening). This makes it easier to place merchandise within the show, because our scenes are created by clothing category. In the final step, the students choose the styles that they feel *must* go into the show, and move them to the front of each of the racks.

Placing merchandise in the fashion show can be a very intense undertaking. Our students try to complete it in a day. A laptop and an Excel spreadsheet are necessities as the students type the master list of the show as placement occurs. We choose the very best outfits with which to start and end each scene. In the beginning, the models are matched to the outfits by size and appearance. As we finish the first scene, we note which models have been placed in it. We make sure that we start the second scene with models that have not yet been used. We try to keep a similar order, because we know that we must have at least 16 runway passes before models can come out again, or they will not have enough time to change into their next outfits. As the apparel is chosen, we have students write up a card for each complete outfit, giving it a scene and an item number. On this card, you can tell when the model will walk, and if he or she is walking alone. It also describes the merchandise to be worn, and any accessories that are included.

We continue, scene by scene, until we are done placing the show. At this point, there is a check done to make sure that the models are all wearing an even amount of outfits. We try not to have one model wear six outfits, whereas another wears only two. We then go through and pull all of the outfits by model. Once the outfits are separated, the students write up the "idiot cards," the complete listings of what each model will wear in what scene for the entire show. We tie these cards over the model's clothing, so that when the models come in for their fittings, we can go outfit by outfit according to their idiot cards.

The fittings are the next step in the process. This can take as long as a day. Every model is given an appointment. Each must try on all of his or her apparel. If something does not fit or looks inappropriate, we make a change. Without the fitting, the model cannot appear in the show. Making a change is a little complicated, because in most cases, the models are not walking alone on the runway. They are either walking with a partner or as part of a threesome, and their clothes must match—if not in color, then in feeling. When we make a change, the individual model's card must be changed, the idiot card must be changed, and the master sheet must be changed.

Once the fittings are all complete, our backstage chairs (student coordinators) take the listing of all models in the scenes and write it up on poster boards. We hang these boards backstage for all models and dressers to see. In addition, copies of the master list are made and handed out to committee chairs.

At this point, we are ready for the dress rehearsal. By going through the full process described above, we rarely encounter any changes going into the dress rehearsal. It is simply a practice for the main event!

Cynde Koritzinsky is an adjunct professor at the University of Bridgeport in Connecticut. She advises students in the production of a fashion show each year.

The Workroom and Runway—A Recap

- Merchandise selection is the designation of apparel, shoes, and accessories for presentation in a fashion show to the target customer.
- Selected merchandise must make a clear fashion statement and be suitable for the demographic profile and lifestyle of the audience.
- The merchandise divisions presented in the show are merchandise categories. Merchandise is selected to fit the fashion show theme according to an ideal chart.
- Merchandise within categories should be grouped in a pleasing manner, indicating a rhythm or flow among looks.
- Merchandise categories should be translated into scene themes. The scene themes evolve from the overall show theme and allow distinction to be made between merchandise categories.
- A good working relationship with retailers is crucial. A professional image must be projected at all times.
- A merchandise pull is the physical removal of merchandise from a retailer's sales floor to an area reserved for storage of fashion show merchandise.
- A tentative lineup includes the order of the models and the proposed merchandise, created using the model order. Changes in the lineup result in a final lineup.
- Fittings involve matching the models to the merchandise.

Key Fashion Show Terms

final lineup	merchandise loan record
fittings	merchandise pull
fitting sheet	merchandise selection
ideal chart	model order
merchandise categories	tentative lineup

Questions for Discussion

1. Why is it important to plan merchandise selection for a fashion show?
2. How does merchandise selection tie in to the overall show planning process?
3. Why is planning with an ideal chart important?
4. What is the difference between a tentative lineup and a final lineup?
5. What are the potential upsides and downsides of working with retailers?
6. Why are merchandise fittings important to the show?

Fashion Show Activity

Divide into teams of four to five members. Each team is responsible for developing a set of professional guidelines for working with retailers. Using these guidelines, each team should develop a fashion show code of conduct. Discuss the different guidelines presented and select the best representation of a code of conduct. Reproduce the code of conduct and have every team member sign a copy to show the importance of professionalism.

THE CAPSTONE PROJECT

CD-ROM

1. Develop merchandise categories and an ideal chart for potential merchandise to be included in the fashion show.
2. Using the overall brand image, show logo, or show theme previously developed, decide on show scene themes, matching the scene theme to a possible merchandise category and the overall show theme.
3. In a coordinated manner, visit local retailers or local design schools to identify potential merchandise for the show.
4. Create a model order and prepare a tentative model lineup.
5. Schedule model fittings.
6. Develop the final lineup.

Please refer to the CD-ROM for tools that may assist you with this section of the fashion show planning process.

REFERENCES

Chanel spring couture 2012. (2012, January 24). *Women's Wear Daily*. Retrieved from http://www.wwd.com/runway/spring-couture-2012/review/chanel

God help us. (2012, February 8). *Women's Wear Daily*, pp. 1, 4–5.

Harris, T. (2012, April 16). State your case. *WWD: The Collections*, p. 12.

'Tis the season. (2012, February 7). *Women's Wear Daily*, pp. 1, 4–5.

CHAPTER SIX
The Catwalk

AFTER READING THIS CHAPTER, YOU SHOULD BE ABLE TO DISCUSS:

- The definition of *fashion model* and the different categories of fashion models

- The types of jobs and places where models find jobs

- The role of a modeling agency in developing and representing a model

- The positive and negative realities of the modeling industry

- The organizations and initiatives to provide a safe and secure working environment for models

- The roles of professional and amateur models in the fashion industry

- How many models and how many changes are needed for a fashion show

- The responsibilities of models during fittings, rehearsals, and the show

- The significance of hair and makeup personnel to the image of the show

- The role of choreography in fashion show production

Jason Wu, Spring 2011. *Courtesy of WWD/Thomas Iannoccone*

Each season, the fashion press watches the international shows to see who will be the "new face" of the season. The print edition of *Style.com* reports the top 10 models who worked the international fashion circuit each season ("The Top 10 Models," 2012). Visitors at the *Style.com* website were asked to vote for their favorite models. The model selected as the top one for the season was Chinese-born Liu Wen (Fig. 6.1), who walked in 50 shows, including Dolce & Gabbana, Balmain, and Stella McCartney, in addition to being a model for Estee Lauder cosmetics. Other top models of the season included Russian-born, German-raised Kati Nescher; Dutch Elza Luijendijk, American Ava Smith, French Aymeline Valade, and American Karlie Kloss. The top models from this season came from all corners of the world. Will any of these girls be the next Karolina Kurkova, Natalia Vodianova, or Coco Rocha?

Figure 6.1
Beijing model Liu Wen first gained attention for her print work in the Chinese editions of *Vogue* and *Harper's Bazaar* before walking the runways of Paris, Milan, and New York.

In this chapter, we discuss the role of the fashion model, including the different model categories, various career opportunities, model resources, training, responsibilities, and the reputation of models and the modeling industry. We also report on the role beauty plays to create a specific look on the runway. Hair and makeup professionals are given the responsibility to create and to present an image that supports the designer's clothing on the catwalk. Finally, we look at the role of choreography as it contributes to the overall impact on the catwalk.

FASHION MODELS

The individuals engaged to wear the apparel and accessories for fashion shows, advertisements, or magazine covers or editorials are known as **models** (*mannequins*). They must be able to effectively promote the image of the clothing to the audience in a believable manner and are very important to the image and success of the fashion show. Models may also infer a standard of excellence, something or someone to be emulated. Many people are inspired to wear and accessorize their clothing in a certain manner after watching and imitating fashion models. To other people, models are exploited as too young, too thin, and a symbol of an unhealthy lifestyle.

The lure of money, a glamorous image, and the ability to wear the latest designer fashions has drawn thousands and thousands of young people from around the world to try modeling as a career. Becoming a fashion model is looked upon as an alluring and celebrated career for young women. Although the possibility of becoming a supermodel—making huge salaries similar to Gisele Bündchen (Fig. 6.2), Kate Moss, Alessandra Ambrosio, or Miranda Kerr—is slim, the industry attracts countless young women (and men) who want to be the next well-known model.

Models should be attractive, not necessarily beautiful. The audience should be able to enjoy the model's appearance, but the model's looks should not deter from the merchandise being presented. A flair for fashion, as well as an instinct about how clothing and accessories should be worn, is helpful. Models are often asked to exercise their fashion sense and enthusiasm in showing clothing to its best.

A model should be well groomed with good hair and skin. The model's figure should be well proportioned and as close to sample sizes as possible, because alterations are expensive and time consuming.

All models, amateur or professional, should project a professional attitude. A professional attitude involves being cooperative with the fashion show staff and other models. Although some models have the reputation for being difficult to work with, moodiness and self-indulgence have no place behind the hectic scene of the fashion show.

The backstage pace at a fashion show is chaotic, as shown in Figure 6.3. When the model rushes to change clothes, she jumps out of one outfit and quickly puts on another with her dresser's assistance. Despite the tension of getting into and out of outfits, the model must be able to promptly gain composure before walking out on the runway. The model must also be able to keep her poise when mistakes or unexpected events happen. An accessory might be forgotten, a zipper might break, or a shoe strap could slip off—the model must be able to gracefully cover up such incidents.

Demanding schedules prevail during market weeks, when a model may do as many as four or five strenuous shows in 1 day. The model must maintain a fresh, enthusiastic, and energetic attitude throughout each

Figure 6.2
Brazilian supermodel Gisele Bündchen is one of the richest models in the world.

Courtesy of WWD/Robert Mitra

Courtesy of WWD/Kuba Dabrowski

Figure 6.3
This model hurries to get ready to walk the runway.

show. With experience, professional models develop an intuition and sense of what to do in any circumstance.

Models do not have to like the particular garments they are wearing. They should respect the clothes and be able to communicate the appreciation of the look or theme of the garments to the audience.

MODEL CLASSIFICATIONS

According to Ashley Mears (2011), female models, called *girls*, are classified as working in either commercial or editorial fields. The commercial side of the fashion industry is concerned with short-term economic profits. **Commercial models** work in the mass-market or for-profit side of the fashion business. The typical jobs for a commercial model involve posing for catalogues, showing clothing in vendors' showrooms for retail clients during market weeks, doing fittings for manufacturers, or posing for television commercials and print advertisements for a wide range of goods, from clothing companies or electronics manufacturers to beauty products. Although commercial modeling is not considered as prestigious, earnings for commercial models are consistent and relatively high. Commercial models have a classic, safe, thin, and youthful appearance.

Editorial models work the runways during international fashion week shows held in the major fashion capitals of the world and pose for editorial sections of high fashion magazines. They also pose for advertisements for prestige and luxury brands. Participants in the editorial side of the fashion field are in fashion for fashion's sake. Editorial producers are interested in making art, rejecting the pursuit of money, chasing after prestige instead (Mears, 2011). Paradoxically, participants are willing to lose money in order to gain social esteem. People working in editorial fashion

may—or may not—make huge financial gains. It is part of the risk that these producers are willing to take. Although status is high for editorial models, earnings are sporadic and low. The image for these models is typically edgy, strange, skinny, and teenage. The audience for editorial models tends to be fashion insiders with interest in being fashion forward by predicting fashion trends, influencing the mass market, and defining brand credibility.

There are physical differences between commercial and editorial models, as seen in Figure 6.4. Commercial models are generally older and larger—still thin, but bigger than their editorial counterparts. Commercial models wear size 2 to size 6, whereas editorial girls range from size 00 to size 4. Editorial models are typically between ages 13 to 22, whereas commercial models are typically at least 18 and continue to work well into their 30s and beyond.

Models in the editorial group have very slim figures and are typically between 5 feet 9 inches and 6 feet in height. Ideal female models have a bust measurement of 34 inches, waist measurement of 24 inches, and hips that measure 34 inches. Although some successful editorial models do not have these exact measurements, this is the size a modeling agency and its clients are typically seeking. There are outliers who do become successful. For example, Kate Moss is only 5 foot 6 inches. However, her extraordinary look and connections in the industry have allowed her to be successful despite not fitting into the ideal size. The career span of a fashion model in the 21st century is typically 5 years (Mears, 2011). A modeling career is considered short term, more of a stint than a long-term occupation.

A rare few models have adapted to this lifestyle, and some have even continued modeling for decades. **Mature models**, also known

(a) *Courtesy of WWD/John Aquino* **(b)** *Courtesy of WWD/Giovanni Giannoni*

Figure 6.4
(a) A commercial model may be older and thin, but not as thin as an editorial model.
(b) Editorial models are younger and extremely thin, with a more edgy look.

as *classic models,* continue modeling well into their 30s, 40s, 50s, and beyond. Carmen Dell'Orefice and China Machado defied the odds and continue to model in their 80s. Style icon Dell'Orefice (Fig. 6.5) started her modeling career at age 15 on the cover of *Vogue* magazine. Proudly displaying her signature white hair, she walked the runways for John Galliano in 2000, Hèrmes in 2004, and Alberta Ferretti in 2011 (Krupnick, 2011). China Machado (Fig. 6.6), another octogenarian, graced the cover of *New York Magazine's* fall fashion issue (Yuan, 2011), and she was one of the models interviewed for HBO's documentary, *About Face: The Super-*

> "We [nonwhites] had no images. We had nothing that told us we were nice-looking. Nothing. So I didn't think of myself as good-looking at all. It never occurred to me. . . . But Richard Avedon did."
> —China Machado, fashion model

models, Then and Now (Greenfield-Sanders, 2012). Ms. Machado started her career after leaving the ruins of Shanghai at the end of World War II (Yuan, 2011). She began her modeling career as a house model for Givenchy, and she eventually became the highest paid runway model of her era—earning $1,000 per day in Paris. During a trip to New York she was discovered by photographer Richard Avedon and Ms. Machado became the first non-Caucasian model on the cover of a fashion magazine.

Jada Yuan (2012, ¶ 1) asked the question, "Is there life after modeling?" Even 20-something models look to their future,

Figure 6.5
Carmen Dell'Orefice started her modeling career at the age of 15 and continues modeling in her 80s.

Courtesy of WWD/John Aquino

Figure 6.6
Model China Machado. China, (pronounced "chenna"), spent three years as a house model for Givenchy before becoming the highest-paid freelance model in Europe during the middle of the twentieth century.

Courtesy of Fairchild Archive

wondering what to do when their modeling career ends. Several options were identified, including the following:

- acting—Milla Jovovich, Amber Valetta, Charlize Theron, Cameron Diaz
- working at a fashion magazine—China Machado, Grace Coddington
- playing music—Karen Elson, Irina Lazareanu
- becoming a photographer—Helena Christensen
- starting a beauty line—Miranda Kerr
- starting a yoga line—Christy Turlington
- starting a clothing line—Kate Moss, Erin Wasson
- starting a furniture line—Cindy Crawford
- becoming the first lady of France—Carla Bruni
- becoming part of a reality television show—Tyra Banks, Heidi Klum, and Carolyn Murphy

Perhaps the wealthiest American fashion model is Kathy Ireland, who started her career in the 1980s as a high school student (Brown, 2012), Discovered by Elite Model Management, she was on the covers of such magazines as *Vogue*, *Cosmopolitan*, and *Women's Fitness* before becoming the cover girl for the *Sports Illustrated* swimsuit issue for 13 straight years. Today, her company, Kathy Ireland Worldwide (KIWW), is a $2 billion brand with her name attached to more than 15,000 stock-keeping units, ranging from furniture, lighting, flooring, windows, jewelry, bridal gowns, to lingerie, with roughly 30 licensees, carried in more than 50,000 stores—all with the promise of simplifying women's lives. In addition to her commercial work, Kathy Ireland is involved in many charitable causes.

Although modeling has been dominated by young, tall, and thin women, the increased awareness of special sizes provides career opportunities for petite as well as plus size models. **Petite models** are generally between 5 feet 2 inches and 5 feet 7 inches tall. Many designers offer clothing in petite sizes; therefore, most petite models work for specialty fashion shows featuring petite sizes or as photographic models for the beauty industry.

Plus size models, also known as 10/20 models, typically wear from a size 10 to 20 plus. Larger women with perfect skin, even features, and long legs and who are able to move well in front of a camera or down a runway are finding work in this market (see Color Plate 12). Most plus size models are 5 feet 8 inches to 5 feet 11 inches tall, with bust measurements between 36 inches and 42 inches, waist measurements between 26 inches and 32 inches, hip measurements between 36 inches and 45 inches, and weight between 140 and 170 pounds. Full-figure model Tara Lynn was featured on a cover of French *Elle* magazine and New York-based Wilhelmina model Robyn Lawley (Fig. 6.7) was the first plus size model on the cover of Australian *Vogue* ("MemoPad," 2012). Although this category of model is becoming better known, it is still difficult for full-figure models to find work walking the runways.

Child models are needed to display merchandise for the baby, toddler, children's,

Associated Press

Figure 6.7
Plus size model Robyn Lawley was featured on the cover of Australian *Vogue* and became the first plus size model for Ralph Lauren.

> "Designers are our last frontier in terms of conquering the fashion industry. There is still unfortunately a stigma that thin is in."
> —Robyn Lawley, plus size model

boys, girls, and preteen markets. In addition, they are prominently featured during the back-to-school season. Although younger children are used in photographic modeling, professional child runway models generally start training from the ages of 5 to 10. Younger girls and boys wear sizes 4 to 6X, and they wear larger children's and preteen sizes as they get older.

It is not surprising that child models are picked from the offspring of well-known models. Ten-year-old Kaia Gerber, daughter of supermodel Cindy Crawford and her husband Rande Gerber—also a former model—was the face of a Versace children's advertising campaign (Torrisi & Fisher, 2012). Kaia's photos looked so similar to her mother's early photographs that criticism followed the distribution of the images. This led Cindy Crawford to bring her daughter's modeling career to a halt until Kaia is at least 17 years old. Meanwhile, Natalia Vodianova's 6-year-old daughter, Neva Vodianova Portman, made her modeling debut wearing a red dress by Caramel Baby and Child, a British children's label (Bergin, 2012). When Karl Lagerfeld wanted a child model for his Chanel fashion show, he called Brad Kroenig, one of his male models, to ask if his son would be able to walk in the show (Wilson, 2012a). At the age of 3, Hudson Kroenig (Fig. 6.8) was already a veteran of his second Chanel fashion show.

Children are great audience pleasers during fashion shows, often earning the greatest audience recognition. But caution must be used to avoid unpleasant scenes with children. It can be very difficult to work with children under the age of 5. Young children may appear able to handle modeling during rehearsals, but they can become frightened when they see a large number of strangers staring at them on the runway. Small children may cry or act out when frightened on stage.

If the show planners decide to use children in the show, the following suggestions may help avoid unpleasant situations. Try to identify children who act somewhat mature, even if they do not understand the idea of a fashion show. It may be helpful to show them videos of other fashion shows in order to teach them what it is all about. These children should be told that an unknown person will help them change clothes and give them stage directions. Introducing them to their dresser before the rehearsal will help overcome their and their parents' fears. It will also be helpful to have child models practice

Figure 6.8
Young Hudson Kroenig started his modeling career walking the Chanel runway.

Courtesy of WWD/Giovanni Giannoni

on the runway in front of an audience made up of show staff and family members to help them feel more at ease in front of a crowd. Mothers or other adults supervising the children should understand the responsibilities of models. A member of the fashion show production staff or parent must be able to watch over the children during all rehearsals and the show.

Although females are dominant in the modeling industry, many men find careers as **male models**. Male models also fit into the editorial and commercial categories, just as their female counterparts. According to Mears (2011), editorial *boys* are young, ages 16 to their mid-20s, and tend to be slim, with 28-inch waists and 36-inch chests. Male models (Fig. 6.9) work the runways in Milan, Paris, New York, and London, just as their female counterparts do. Alternatively, commercial boys—and men—have 32-inch waists and 40-inch chests. These commercial men tend to be older, ranging from 18 years of age to 50 or older.

CAREER OPPORTUNITIES FOR MODELS

Now that we have considered the categories of models, we turn our attention to the various places where models find jobs. Career opportunities are the greatest in large cities with strong fashion design and retail industries such as New York, London, Paris, and Milan. Modeling work in other cities, such as Los Angeles, Phoenix, Chicago, or Toronto, may only be part-time, because the demand for models is not as great. Modeling jobs generally fit into three categories: fashion shows, photo shoots, and fit modeling.

Runway Models

Runway models find jobs during the various fashion weeks at major fashion centers

Figure 6.9
Although male models work the international runways, they don't get the respect, attention, approval, and magazine covers that their female counterparts get.

Courtesy of WWD/George Chinsee

and trade shows around the world. Runway models experience the energy and excitement of a live performance, connecting with the audience and photographers to promote the clothes they are wearing. Models who work the big international fashion shows have style, poise, and confidence to present clothes on the runway. They expect to see their photographs and videos of the runway shows in major newspapers, magazines, television broadcasts, and social media around the world.

Models for Photo Shoots

There are three types of photographic opportunities for fashion models: photo shoots for magazine editorial content, print advertisements, and catalogues. Every up-and-coming model hopes to have her picture in the editorial pages of *Vogue*, *W*, *Harper's Bazaar*, or *Elle*. Although these editorial print modeling jobs do not pay the highest fees, they are considered to be stepping-stones to building a portfolio and other more lucrative, brand-oriented modeling jobs. Models use tear sheets from magazine editorials, which involve non-advertising magazine pages, to find jobs or contracts for major advertising campaigns.

Editorial print modeling involves a cooperative interaction between the model, magazine editor or creative director, photographer, and staff, which consists of a photographer's assistant, stylist, hair stylist, and makeup artist, to find a creative image. Many images are shot to find just the right photograph to capture the look and attract the audience's attention. Once a model has gained some recognition through editorial print work, she may be asked to model for fragrance, cosmetic, or fashion houses for their advertisements.

The purpose of advertising is to promote and sell clothing, fragrances, or other merchandise from the sponsor. **Advertising models** are needed to display and enhance these products for publication in newspapers, magazines, point-of-purchase displays, and digital as well as other media. Depending upon the clothing or cosmetic line, fashion shots for advertisements may be done in either editorial or catalogue style. Advertising modeling fees are among the highest in the modeling industry. An exclusive or contract model can receive several million dollars for his or her work, which excludes the model from working for the competition.

Men and women with attractive hands, legs, feet, and/or hair may find jobs as **body parts models**. This type of modeling is a sub-industry within the modeling industry. Hand models are used for hand lotion, nail polish, or jewelry. Hosiery, shoes, and grooming products are shown on models with eye-catching legs. Some celebrities use body part models as doubles for dangerous or revealing scenes in movies. Ashly Covington is a full-time parts model, earning as much as $1,200 a day (Hare, 2009). Danielle Korwin is the president of Parts Models Agency, an agency in New York that specializes in body parts. She reports that only people with exceptional, veinless, poreless, and flawless hands need apply to her agency. The agency was founded in 1986 to provide hand, leg, feet, and body models for editorial, advertising, and catalogue work ("About Us," 2006).

Because models are confident and composed when photographers take their picture, many models make the transition from fashion modeling into **television commercial acting**. After taking classes in acting and script reading, many models learn how to sound natural for commercials. A great deal of money can be earned from television commercials, especially when the advertisements are nationally distributed. Thousands of dollars in residuals, money paid each time the advertisement is broadcast, are paid to the principal performers featured in commercials. If a model has several commercials running at any given time, his or her income can increase.

Catalogue models are photographed wearing clothing and accessories that will be sold through direct response media such as mail-order catalogues, brochures, and billing statement inserts, and on Internet-based catalogues. It is considered the bread-and-butter job for many models. Catalogue bookings may be for a 1-hour shoot or several days in an exotic location. This type of modeling requires realistic models who resemble the target audience. Catalogue photographs are generally straightforward shots that emphasize the selling features of the garments. Nordstrom gained positive recognition for placing people with disabilities in their wheelchairs as photographic models for some of their catalogues (Fig. 6.10).

Figure 6.10
Commercial models find consistent and well-paid work in catalogues such as this J. Crew catalogue.

Fit and Showroom Models

A designer or manufacturer employs a model, with a particular attitude and specific body measurements that meet a manufacturer's ideal standard size, as a **fit model** (*house model*). Sample garments from the manufacturer's line are adjusted on the fit model. Designers also use their fit models for design inspiration. Designers may use their fit model, a friend, or a celebrity as a **muse**, or an inspiration for their ideal customer. Audrey Hepburn served as the inspiration for Givenchy, whereas Yves Saint Laurent used Loulou de la Falaise as his muse for his couture collections for many years.

A **showroom model** works freelance or as a manufacturer's house model during market weeks. Models wear sample garments at a designer's showroom for a private audience of retail buyers who are evaluating garments for their target customers. The retail buyers are interested in seeing how the garments look on a real person. Because the showroom model wears the season's sample garments, he or she must fit into the company's standard sample size. These models may work for a few days or a few weeks each season.

As we have learned, there are many different career opportunities for models. From informal modeling for a local retailer to walking the international catwalks as supermodels, a variety of modeling jobs are available. We now turn our attention to the resources that help train, build portfolios, and find jobs for models.

MODELING AGENCIES

As we learned in Chapter 1, modeling agencies began in the 1920s with pioneer John Robert Powers. Since then, a number of highly regarded agencies, as well as several disreputable ones, have come on the scene.

Modeling agencies are companies that represent a variety of fashion models and act as scheduling agents for them. Today, many modeling agencies also have a talent division, which is involved with representing actors and performers. Many modeling agencies are structured like FORD/Robert Black. Sheree Hartwell, owner of FORD/Robert Black Agency in Phoenix, Arizona, gives us a look into how model agencies work in Notes from the Runway: Inside a Modeling Agency.

After models are invited to sign with the agency, that agency becomes the model's **mother agency**, which is typically the model's home agency. This agency cares for its models as a mother would, getting the model prepared to work with advice about hair and makeup and test photographs, and developing a portfolio. Once the model is ready, the mother agency helps to place the model in other markets for work opportunities, choosing the best agencies to work with in different cities. New models are placed into the New Faces division. Other divisions in the agency typically include Scouts, Women's Agents and Men's Agents, and the Art Department. The women's and men's divisions are managed by their own set of **bookers** (*agents*), who are the individuals hired by the agency to promote, coordinate schedules, and negotiate fees for the models.

Many young women and men contact modeling agencies for possible representation. Another way for an aspiring model to get recognized is to attend an **open call**, which is held by agencies looking for new faces. **Scouts**, representing the agency, are out in public areas (e.g., shopping districts, school events, sports venues) looking for potential models. If the modeling agency representative chooses a model, he or she will be given a trial period on the test board. Each new model will participate in tests, go-sees, castings, and bookings. Model scouts are searching for new faces that fit into specific guidelines, discussed earlier in this chapter.

Another thing that scouts are searching for is a girl or boy with a **look**. Although it is hard to define, Ashley Mears says that "a look is a reference point, a theme, a feeling, an era, or even an 'essence'" (2011, p. 6). It is much more than being attractive or sexy. A look is a whole package of a model's being, including his or her personality, reputation, on-the-job performance, how they photograph, and their appearance. The model's look is not the same thing as beauty, and models fitting into the editorial category are often referred to as "edgy."

When a client—a designer, department store, or photographer—needs to hire a model, the client will let an agency announce the availability and schedule a **go-see**, which is when models are invited to meet the client. A **casting call** is an appointment to meet with a client for an upcoming job. If the client wants to see a variety of possible looks, any available models are invited to a **cattle call**. If the client asks for a specific model, the go-see or casting is called a **request**. At a go-see, casting, or request the client will greet the model one on one or in a group setting.

Models present their book to the potential client. The book is a **portfolio** containing test photographs that show the model in the most flattering way, along with tear sheets from previous jobs. **Tests** are a variety of photographic shots that show the model's versatility and are put in a model's portfolio. **Tear sheets** from editorial work are added to the portfolio as the model gains experience.

The agency will also suggest creating a **composite** (*comp*), which includes the model's name, stats, and agency contact information with various photographs (Fig. 6.11). The model's **stats** include height, weight,

(a)

(b)

Figure 6.11 (a–b) Information about the model, including his or her photographs, and the agency contact information are printed on comp cards, which are equivalent to a model's business card.

Courtesy of Sheree Hartwell, Ford/Robert Black Agency

suit or dress size, measurements—bust, waist, hips for women; waist, shirt, and inseam for men—shoe size, and hair and eye color. Composites are valuable promotional tools that are sent to prospective clients in order to find jobs. Some agencies combine the composites from several new models into a book, which is distributed to potential clients. Electronic promotion using the Internet is the way many agencies promote their models.

After the casting or go-see, a client selects the top models and invites them to return for a **callback** (*fit-to-confirm*), or a second look. If the client is interested, the client may take the model's picture with a digital camera. For runway bookings, the model will try on several of the client's looks and will be asked to walk in the showroom. The model leaves a comp card with the potential client and offers thanks for being invited. This is generally a quick and informal meeting.

> "Nowadays, everybody wants their child to model. Back in the day, nobody wanted anybody to be a model!"
>
> —Bethann Hardison, fashion model

If the client wants to hire the model for the job, he calls the model's booker. The booker places the model on an **option** (*hold*), which is an agreement between the client and booker that reserves the model's availability. This hold is ranked by the client's order of preference, from first choice to third choice. In the modeling industry, the client may place a hold on a model's time for 24 to 48 hours. Options do not have a fee and are offered as a professional courtesy to the clients. It helps the booker to manage their models' chaotic schedules, especially during fashion week. The job for a runway show or a photo shoot is known as a **booking**.

Although most agencies are legitimate, professional, and have the best interest in promoting careers of young and aspiring models, some agencies have the reputation for unethical practices. Agents from disreputable agencies have asked new models for large sums of money for photo sessions, composites, and other promotional tools with no intention of hiring and booking models. More information about the negative side of modeling is discussed next.

THE DOWNSIDE OF MODELING

Although the majority of people working in fashion act professionally, modeling has had a long-term objectionable reputation. Michael Gross introduced the negative side of modeling in his groundbreaking exposé, *Model: The Ugly Business of Beautiful Women* (2011). He clearly profiled the seedy side of the modeling industry. With vast sums of money at stake, disreputable people have entered the industry. Some agency owners and photographers were exposed for allegedly having sex with underage girls. Rumors of drugging and raping young models were brought out into the open. Some lucky models are never exposed to the corruption and immoral actions by some powerful agents and photographers, but many unlucky young girls are lured by the glamorous-yet-dangerous lifestyle each year. Even today, rumors of these unsavory activities continue to persist in the modeling industry.

About Face: The Supermodels, Then and Now is an HBO documentary film that profiled some of the all-time most celebrated models of the 20th century (Greenfield-Sanders, 2012). Some of the women recall how—in the early days—modeling was considered a small step above prostitution and certainly not viable as a career option. Bethann Hardison, one of the African-American models who participated in the *Grand Divertissement à Versailles* in 1973 (see Chapter 1) said that her mother assumed she was a hooker until she saw Bethann in a TV commercial.

Modeling Scams

Each year, thousands of young girls and boys are scouted for legitimate model agencies, whereas others are scammed by bogus model and talent agencies, modeling schools, or modeling contests. Many complaints are filed with appropriate state or federal consumer protection agencies, whereas other complaints are voiced on Internet web pages. If you have been scouted and find yourself in an office filled with lots of other hopeful models and actors, and the offer to join an agency turns into a high-pressure sales pitch for modeling or acting classes, or for "screen tests" or "photo shoots" that can range in price from several hundred to several thousand dollars, you have probably been scammed.

Here are some common modeling agency advertising claims that should make anyone suspicious:

- *The agency asks for a fee to represent you.* Legitimate modeling agencies make money by taking a commission from its models' work. Some justifiable expenses are incurred by the model: for example, an agency will charge for the model's comp cards to be included in an agency look book that is sent to potential clients, as well as travel and living expenses that are prepaid by the agency.
- *You will earn a high salary.* Only experienced, top models can expect to receive large salaries. The highest salaries earned by models come from contracts with international cosmetic and luxury brands.
- *You can work full- or part-time.* The hours of a model are uneven and sporadic. You will not have the flexibility to choose your own hours.
- *Real people should apply to work for our agency.* Some ads encourage people of all shapes, sizes, and ages to apply for commercial modeling work. But agencies are looking for models within a narrowly defined age and body type. Modeling opportunities are limited even in large cities.
- *The agency charges you money to take their classes, before you are eligible for modeling work.* A genuine modeling agency may provide instruction on applying makeup or walking, but they do not charge you for the classes.
- *The agency sends you to an unprofessional photo shoot.* Models need photographs for their portfolios. But they should be conducted in an ethical manner. A model should not be asked to take off clothing for a photo shoot.
- *The agency requires a particular photographer.* If the modeling agency requires you to work with a particular photographer, chances are the photographer is working with the modeling agency, and they are splitting the fee.

After being scouted, the first thing you should do is ask yourself if you feel that you realistically have the potential to become a professional model, or if you think the agency is just looking for someone who can pay for classes or photographs. Are you strong enough to take all of the criticism that will be directed toward you? To protect yourself, contact other models who have recently worked for the agency and clients that have hired models from the agency. Learn what other models and clients have to say about their experiences with the agency. Also, keep copies of all important papers, such as your contract and agency literature. Be sure to get all promises made verbally in writing. You may need these if you have a dispute with the agency.

But if you feel that your agency is a sham, what should you do? If you have paid money to an agency, you should ask for a refund. If that does not work, you can contact your local consumer protection agency, your state attorney general, or the Better Business Bureau. You also may file a complaint with the Federal Trade Commission (FTC). The FTC works for the consumer to prevent fraudulent, deceptive, and unfair business practices in the marketplace and to provide information to help consumers spot, stop, and avoid them.

Modeling Is a Bad Job

Ashley Mears (2011), an assistant professor of sociology at Boston University, suggested that modeling is a "bad" job. Miss Mears was a model from age 16 to 23, observing the industry as a participant. Although modeling is promoted as a high-paying job, model pay is enormously skewed. Some models earn more than $100,000 a year, whereas others are as much as $20,000 in debt. Work in fashion modeling is typically on a **freelance**, or per-project, basis, similar to day laborers who piece together an erratic living. Such jobs do not require educational credentials, nor do they demand significant entry-level skills. The work provides no health or retirement benefits. Although modeling is considered glamorous, models are regularly subjected to harsh and demeaning critiques from agents and clients.

Perceived high status combined with little entry criteria means that the model market attracts more people than it should, resulting in overcrowding and steep competition. As a steady stream of new faces enters into an agency, old ones are filtered out. Models can be "dropped" by their agencies with little or no warning.

Modeling is also an expensive job. Common start-up costs that require reimbursement to the agency include comp cards, airline tickets, rent to live in a models' apartment, bike messenger services to transport books from one client to the next, and the inclusion of the model's comp card in a "Show Package" mailed to clients in charge of fashion week castings. Typically, expenses build up until bookings surpass the expenses, so many models do not get paid for several months. That is, if the client actually pays the agency in a timely manner or at all.

Ole Schell and Sara Ziff (2010) released a documentary film titled *Picture Me: A Model's Diary*. This video diary follows Ms. Ziff from the time she entered the modeling industry as an 18-year-old fresh face through the 5 years of her career until she left modeling to attend college. At first she is an enthusiastic, young innocent girl, traveling to London, Paris, and Milan, earning pay that seems almost unbelievable to her. Her enthusiasm for modeling starts to wane as she witnesses disregard for child labor laws, the lack of financial transparency, the encouragement of unhealthy eating practices, and sexual harassment in the workplace. She learned that many of the models who achieve a coveted spot walking the runways during New York Fashion Week are never paid at all, instead working for free or for "trade," meaning just clothes. Many young models also become crippled by debt to agencies that charge myriad unexplained fees.

Forging a Better World for Models

As early as 2007, the Council of Fashion Designers of America (CFDA) acknowledged the concerns of extremely young and exceedingly thin models walking in the New York Fashion Week runway shows (Odell, 2012). The CFDA, in partnership with the fashion industry, medical experts, nutritionists, and fitness trainers, created a health initiative to address these issues. The health initiative suggested that models provide identification to prove that they are at least 16 years old on the day of the show. It also suggests that the models should be provided a list of warning signs for eating disorders from the Harris Center for Education and Advocacy in Eating Disorders at Massachusetts General Hospital. Each season the CFDA distributes this information prior to the start of fashion week. Although this is not legally binding, CFDA president Diane von Furstenberg sends members of the fashion industry and media a reminder before New York Fashion Week begins.

> "Designers share a responsibility to protect women, and very young girls in particular, within the business, sending the message that beauty is health."
> —Diane von Furstenberg, president, Council of Fashion Designers of America (CFDA), and fashion designer

As a result of her experiences in the industry, Sara Ziff, with the assistance of fellow models and the Fashion Law Institute at Fordham University School of Law, established the Model Alliance in 2012 (Jothianandan, 2012). The goal of this not-for-profit organization is to give models in the United States a voice in their workplace and to organize to improve their basic working conditions in what is now an almost entirely unregulated industry. The organization provides a platform for models and leaders in the fashion industry to work together to radically improve models' working conditions.

One of the first actions taken by the Model Alliance was to develop a "Models' Bill of Rights" so that models have the right to work in a professional environment, have transparent accounting procedures, control their careers, have negotiable commissions, and for models under the age of 18 to have specific rights that address age-appropriate activities as well as educational opportunities ("The Model Alliance," 2012). The draft of the Models' Bill of Rights (Fig. 6.12) was introduced February 6, 2012, with the intent of being a living document that may be revised periodically.

To help and protect models, Model Alliance Support is the organization's fully confidential grievance reporting system, offered in conjunction with the Actors' Equity Association and the American Guild of Musical Artists. Equity, in partnership with the Guild, advises the Model Alliance and enables Alliance members to report and seek assistance with complaints about inappropriate on-the-job conduct. This is a first step in providing a safe working environment by giving models a place where they can report safely, privately, and confidentially, or request assistance with instances of harassment, abuse, assault, rape, or any unwanted or inappropriate conduct.

A few months after the Model Alliance was formally introduced, Condé Nast

Models' Bill of Rights ~~DRAFT~~

EVERY WORKING MODEL HAS A RIGHT TO...

TO PROFESSIONALISM:

- Agents will maintain a professional relationship with models under contract and will endeavor to ensure that clients and photographers do the same.
- All jobs and castings involving full or partial nudity must be subject to informed, prior consent.
- A model may refuse to accept an assignment or to grant an option.
- The Agency will be a safe, smoke- and drug-free environment and it will endeavor to assure that clients and photographers do the same.
- The Agency will work with Model Alliance Support to ensure models have access to a confidential procedure for reporting harassment or abuse.
- The Agency will work with Model Alliance to ensure that a private changing area, to which photographers will not have access, is provided for changing at castings, shoots and shows.

TO TRANSPARENT ACCOUNTING PRACTICES:

- Models shall be provided by the Agency with a clear statement of account which will include the amounts of compensation received for each booking and the expenses which have been deducted.
- Models shall be advised by the Agency about its collection procedures from clients.
- Models shall be paid by the Agency within a reasonable time after payment is received from the client.

TO CONTROL THEIR CAREERS:

- When reasonably possible, models will be informed of, and agree to, the terms of any booking before confirmation.
- Models may refuse non-paying jobs and jobs that pay only in "trade".
- Models may review the Agency's chart of bookings and options upon request.

TO NEGOTIABLE COMMISSIONS:

- Models are entitled to know that all commissions are negotiable and to have this fact clearly stated in the model's contract in bold type.
- Prior to entering into a management agreement with a model, the Agency will provide the model with an explanation and breakdown of typical start-up costs and terms on which any debt will be held.

SPECIFIC RIGHTS OF MODELS UNDER 18 YEARS OF AGE:

- No model under the age of 17 shall be asked to pose nude or semi-nude.
- The minimum age for runway work at New York Fashion Week is 16-years-old.
- Agents may not misrepresent the age of their models.
- The Agency will endeavor to comply with all current CFDA guidelines with regard to booking models for NY Fashion Week.
- The Agency will work with a model's parent or guardian to formulate an education plan for models of high school age.

Figure 6.12
This is a draft of the Models' Bill of Rights established by the Model Alliance.

Courtesy of Sara Ziff

International chairperson Jonathan New-house announced that 19 *Vogue* editors around the world had signed an agreement and would adopt standards to use models over the age of 16 and stop using models who appear to have eating disorders (Wilson, 2012b). The *Vogue* announcement included the following six-point pact:

1. We will not knowingly work with models under the age of 16 or who appear to have an eating disorder. We will work with models who, in our view, are healthy and help to promote a healthy body image.
2. We will ask agents not to knowingly send us underage girls and casting directors to check IDs when casting shoots, shows, and campaigns.
3. We will help to structure mentoring programs where more mature models are able to give advice and guidance to younger girls, and we will help to raise industry-wide awareness through education, as has been integral to the Council of Fashion Designers of America Health Initiative.
4. We will encourage producers to create healthy backstage working conditions, including healthy food options and a respect for privacy. We will encourage casting agents not to keep models unreasonably late.
5. We encourage designers to consider the consequences of unrealistically small sample sizes of their clothing, which limits the range of women who can be photographed in their clothes, and encourages the use of extremely thin models.
6. We will be ambassadors for the message of healthy body image (Wilson, 2010b).

Top models travel first class, are pampered with the latest beauty innovations and products, and treated like royalty, just for being attractive on a runway or in a photograph. Models are admired as well as exploited. But working conditions and model behavior expectations are under scrutiny.

PROFESSIONAL VERSUS AMATEUR MODELS

Professional models are trained in modeling techniques and are hired through modeling agencies. As we have learned, these models work for the top international designers in addition to other professional shows in smaller markets. **Amateur models** are real people, not trained as professional models, and are selected from other resources. Some effective resources for finding amateur models for school, charitable organizations, or independent retailer fashion shows include a retail store's fashion advisory board, the store's customers and personnel, the members of the organization sponsoring the event, or students from performing arts or fashion schools (Fig. 6.13).

Using Professional Models

The decision to use professional versus amateur models frequently depends upon the show budget. Professional models must be paid. Many fashion show directors feel that using professional models creates a smoother, more sophisticated show. Experienced models can handle last-minute changes and the confusion associated with fashion show production. They have developed an authoritative attitude in presenting clothes properly, which translates as confidence as the professional model walks down the runway. Trained models are quick to pick up modeling choreography and routines. Directions

Figure 6.13
Amateurs may be scouted and trained to model for a fashion student-produced show, such as this one.

Courtesy of Christopher C. Everett

and cues are easily learned and remembered. Appointments are responsibly met. Clothing and accessories are taken care of and respected. Any unforeseen problems or emergencies are maneuvered with expert execution. Professional models frequently make excellent suggestions about how to wear or accessorize an outfit based on their years of experience and love for clothing. Pros know how to stress the importance of the clothes rather than themselves.

Using Amateur Models

Shows working with limited budgets may be restricted to using amateur models, offering them a gift, discount, or gift certificate in lieu of payment. This helps to ensure a positive feeling among all the parties involved. It may also encourage purchases at the store.

The success or failure of months of fashion show preparation can depend upon the performance of the models. Many amateur models take their role very seriously. Unfortunately, some of the disaster stories regarding fashion shows come from the ranks of unprepared amateur models. Without some training and direction, amateur models have flown down runways with arms flapping like birds' wings; others have frozen with fear on the runway after seeing the audience. Untrained models have damaged clothes by not taking proper care of them. Amateur models demand more time and attention to train due to their lack of experience. The show may require a larger number of amateurs than professional models because it will take them longer to change garments.

When selecting the amateur model, the model coordinator and committee need to be sure that the model is willing to make a commitment to participate in fittings, rehearsals, and the show itself. Being a model is not the glamorous job that many amateurs think it is. Having a signed personal responsibility contract, similar to the one shown in Figure 3.12, will encourage professional participation. Stating the model's responsibilities and time commitment helps everyone understand the expectations.

If members of a charitable organization are selected to model, then the model coordinator must use diplomacy in selecting and training participants. Because these members are not always standard model sizes and often have very strong opinions about what they want to wear, fashion show coordinators must be ready to handle objections with tact. Inexperienced models may not understand that a fashion show is an important part of doing business for the store or manufacturer providing the clothes. They may resist wearing anything they dislike.

Despite some of the challenges, amateur models have a great drawing power. Audiences love to see their friends and relatives participating in fashion shows. They can certainly add to the audience's enjoyment of the show. Another reason amateur models contribute to a show is the believability factor. When friends and relatives see garments on "real people," they can see themselves wearing the clothes.

Training Amateur Models

Walking, timing, posing, and turning are very important aspects of the model's presentation on the runway. Confidence and ease in executing these attributes are instrumental for the professional appearance of the fashion show. The show's model committee or choreographer will need to train amateur models.

The model must walk with a smooth light pace. Body weight should be forward. The body should be straight, but not stiff. Arms are placed down at the side seams of the garment with palms toward the body. They should be kept loose and easy and not swing out from the body. Hands and arms may be used to point out some design element such as a pocket of the costume. Using hands gracefully is important to modeling. Hands should be relaxed. A slight bend to the wrist is more attractive than a perfectly rigid, straight arm. Placing the hand in a ballet position or bend will be more becoming. Shoulders should be down, back, and relaxed. The stomach should be flat and buttocks tucked under. The steps should be just long enough to keep the body erect. Reach with the front foot and push with the back foot for the appearance of walking on air. Feet should follow an imaginary straight line on the floor.

The starter or stage manager is responsible for the timing of the show. The speed and pace of walking can accelerate or prolong the show. Models can remain on the runway for longer periods of time, giving other models time to change or get ready, by repeating the basic pattern of walking and turns.

Amateur models frequently walk too fast or want to get off the runway quickly. One technique that helps to keep the pace at a good level is to ask the model to stop and pose on the runway. If a photographer is used, the models can be trained to stop at the end of the runway, pose, and wait for a photograph to be taken. This will help to slow down the pace of a fast-moving model.

Expression and personality are often overlooked in the technical aspects of walking, turning, and posing. Although some designers require a different mood or attitude, smiling is a positive expression to show that the model likes what she is wearing in a consumer-oriented show. The model must be able to communicate a variety of emotions depending upon the type of merchandise or show. The model may be called upon to act in any manner from casual to elegant. If the outfit is fun or casual a smile is very appropriate. On the other hand, if the item being presented is sophisticated or serious then a smile may seem out of place. It is important for the model to practice various expressions in a mirror.

For *Get Your Fashion Fix on Route 66*, Karissa Keiter was the coordinator of the model committee. Her story is profiled in

Notes from the Runway: You Can Find Amateur Models Anywhere, Everywhere. . . . The model committee held model tryouts for amateur models during several open calls in the early part of the academic semester. No prior modeling experience was required. Potential models were asked to fill out an application (Fig. 6.14) and practice some walking routines

---

MODEL APPLICATION

Get Your Fashion Fix on Route 66

Name_____

Phone_____

Address_____

Email_____

_____

Measurements: Women: Men:

Height_____   Bust____   Chest_____

Weight_____   Dress__   Hat_____

Waist_____

Pant Size_____

Shirt Size_____

Hair Color_____

Eye Color_____

Modeling Experience:

If you are selected, you will need to be available on Tuesdays at 7:30pm for practices.

You will need to attend a dress rehearsal on Friday, November 19th, and Saturday, November 20th. Institutional excuses will be available for those who need them.

Thank you for your willingness to be part of our event. We hope you have fun, as we will try to make this a great event.

Figure 6.14
Models who tried out for *Get Your Fashion Fix on Route 66* were asked to complete the application shown here.

Illustration by Carly Grafstein

MODEL RELEASE FORM

Runway to Wonderland

I hereby give the Merchandising Program at Northern Arizona University and/or their designate the absolute and irrevocable right and permission, with respect to the photographs that have been taken of me or in which I may be included with others during the rehearsals and production of Runway to Wonderland fashion show:

(1) To copyright the photographs,

(2) To use, re-use, publish and re-publish the photographs individually or in conjunction with other photographs,

(3) To use my name in connection therewith.

I hereby release and discharge the Merchandising Program of NAU and/or their designate from any and all claims and demands arising out of or in connection with the use of photographs, including any and all claims for libel or invasion of privacy.

_____

Name (print)

_____

Name (Signature)

_____

Date

Illustration by Carly Grafstein

Figure 6.15
This is an example of a model release form from *Runway to Wonderland*, which allows show producers to use the models' images for publicity purposes.

that were demonstrated by members of the model committee. The model committee observed the candidates walking to music and selected the top applicants.

Models were given the dates for each practice, the dress rehearsal, and the show upon their selection. Each model was asked to make a commitment to participate in each of these sessions. Practices took place at a regularly scheduled time once each week for about a month before the show. The model committee spent the first couple of practices teaching models how to walk, turn,

and pose on a floor outlined with masking tape to the dimensions of the runway that was to be used for the show. Model release forms (Fig. 6.15) were signed to allow show producers to use the models' images in a video, as well as in other promotional and print media.

NUMBER AND ROTATION OF MODELS

There are no hard and fast rules determining the number of models needed for a show. The show organizers need to know how many models will appear in a show, and how long each model will need to change outfits between runway appearances. Adequate time must be arranged for models to change clothes and accessories.

Setting up a rotation schedule for models will help the show run smoothly. One way to use models effectively is to arrange a specific order for the models for the first scene prior to the fittings. Then keep the models in approximately the same order throughout the show. For example, if 15 models are needed for a show, these 15 models are placed in order. In this way model 1 would always appear before model 2 and after model 15. The audience will not be able to detect that models are always in the same order, but the plan gives models adequate time to change. It also helps models to recognize when they should be ready to walk.

Each model should be made fully aware of the outfits that he or she will be wearing and the order in which the garments

should be worn. The **individual model lineup sheet** helps to clarify each model's order of appearance, outfit, shoes, hosiery, accessories, props, and whether the model is alone or part of a group. Two types of individual model lineup forms are shown in Figure 6.16.

Depending upon the number of outfits, type of show, facilities, and experience of the models, a 30- to 40-minute show may use as few as 10 or as many as 50 models. A fashion week show in New York generally lasts about 15 minutes or less. During that time 60 or more garments can be presented. Typically, models come on the runway one at a time. But lots of models can appear on the runway at the same time, as can be seen in Figure 6.17, taken at the Chanel show in Paris. Karl Lagerfeld recreated the entrance to the House of Chanel, with the half-opened French windows and the boutique on the ground floor (Horyn, 2008). Stretching in front of the couture

Figure 6.16 (a–b) Here are two different examples of an individual model lineup form, listing or showing the clothing to be worn by each model in the order that the items are to be presented on the runway.

Name of Model _____ Andrea Fried _____

Name of show _____ Fashion Fix _____

Order of Appearance/ Scene	Description of Apparel	Shoes	Accessories or Props
3 / Easy Rider Road	Gap jeans with red turtleneck	Cobalt blue hightop Vans	Green daypack
21 / Snow Bird Boulevard	White down jacket with pink ski pants	Pink uggs	Snowboard
45/ Wheelin' Dealin' Drive	Navy pant suit from Dillards	Red high heel pumps	Navy tote with red print scarf
72/ Road Warrior Way	Gold cocktail dress	Strappy gold high heel sandals	Black evening clutch

(a)

Illustration by Carly Grafstein

house replica was a street, complete with curbs. The show opened with the Madness song "Our House," which gave the audience a lasting impression. The number of models will increase as the designer wants more of a visual statement or the distance between the dressing and stage areas increases.

When selecting and booking models, the model committee should have a few alternative models to prevent the inevitable

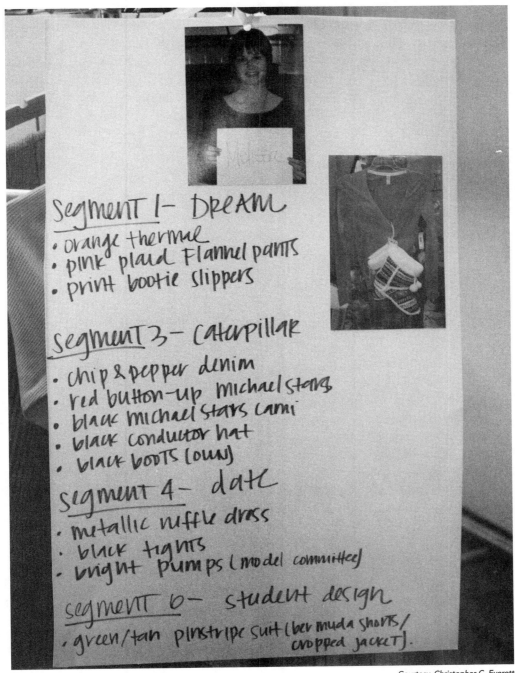

(b)

Figure 6.16 (cont'd)

Courtesy, Christopher C. Everett

Figure 6.17
Various groups of Chanel models walked in front of a full-size façade of the couture house erected inside the Grand Palais in Paris.

Courtesy of WWD/Giovanni Giannoni

disappointment and scramble if it is necessary to replace an absent model. Yes, it happens. Although professional models rarely miss a booking unless there are some extenuating circumstances, using amateur models almost always results in at least one "no show." Contingency plans will help to relieve the pressure of finding a replacement on show day.

After models have been selected, the model committee should prepare a formal model list (Fig. 6.18). A **model list** includes each model's name, telephone number, e-mail address, garment size, and shoe size. Members of the model and merchandise committees will find this information essential.

MODEL RESPONSIBILITIES

Models have a variety of responsibilities during the fittings, rehearsals, and show production. It is most important that, at all times, the models associated with a show cooperate with the show personnel. A positive attitude and professionalism are also appreciated by the fitting, rehearsal, production, and cleanup crews.

Responsibilities during Fittings

Fittings are generally scheduled at predetermined intervals, and the models need to be on time. If a model is late, it can throw off the entire schedule. The merchandise committee or stylist should have a series of garments pulled for each model when she arrives for fittings. The model should be ready to try on clothing. The model should come to the fitting with limited natural makeup, clean and dry hair, and dressed simply without accessories so it will be easy to make several garment changes quickly.

Cooperation between the designer or retailer and show staff as well as the models is very important. The model should never mention whether she likes a garment, unless asked. That is not an important factor when most items are selected to make a fashion trend or color statement.

MODEL LIST

Name of Show_ *Model Behavior* _   Date_ November 20th _

Females

Name	Phone	E-mail	Size Garment	Shoe
Alexia Thomas	532-7127	A.Thomas@gmail.com	10	9½
Joan Points	523 3226	J.Points@gmail.com	6	7
Pam Hiers	774-1718	Pet67@hotmail.com	8	9½
Erica Warren	523-1562	E.Warren@gmail.com	4	8½
Carly Mercier	779-4568	seacat@aol.com	8	9

Males

Name	Phone	E-mail	Size Garment	Shoe
Mike Gibson	526-1287	Mikemouse@aol.com	Large/34	10
Tom Anderson	774-8912	T.Anderson@gmail.com	Medium/30	10
Brett Harwood	525-1025	woody43@hotmail.com	Large/33	11

Illustration by Carly Grafstein

Figure 6.18
After models are selected for the show, a model list with contact information and sizes is created.

Responsibilities during Rehearsals

The rehearsal requires teamwork by all involved. Female models should come prepared with a tote bag containing a few supplies: simple makeup and lingerie, such as a nude bra, a strapless bra, a nude thong, camisole, and slip. She should also bring along a seasonal basic shoe wardrobe including nude and black pumps; casual and dressy flats; and black, silver, or gold strappy sandals. Other items to bring include a scarf to help protect clothing from makeup as it is tried on, pins, a first-aid kit, clear or nude nail polish, simple earrings, clear deodorant, and panty liners. Personal hygiene is very important.

The male models' tote should contain a shaving kit, white briefs, clean white T-shirt, denim jeans, socks (white, brown, and black), belts (brown and black), dress shoes (brown and black), clean sneakers, and deodorant.

All models should also bring along a book or digital device to read, study, or listen to music during their down time.

Caring for clothing is a joint responsibility between the show personnel and the model. The model should never pull a garment overhead without a scarf or head covering to protect clothes from makeup. Merchandise tags should not be removed unless specifically told to do so. Shoes should be removed while stepping into or out of a garment. To protect clothing the model should never sit, eat, drink, or smoke while dressed in garments for the show. Clothing should be returned to hangers and properly stored as soon as possible after trying it on and having it approved. A dresser should be available to help each model with clothing care.

The model should be neat, clean, and pick up personal belongings. The model should not expect the dresser or fitter to be a personal maid. Children and friends should be left at home during fittings and rehearsals. Although children may love to see the process, they will be in the way. Friends may offer helpful suggestions, but they too are in the way.

Responsibilities during the Show

Models should be on time and arrive at least 30 minutes before the start of the show, unless given other instructions. This will be enough time to get ready for the show. Models may need the assistance of hair and makeup personnel on the show day. In any case, models should arrive with their personal supplies in tote bags, as discussed previously. Model responsibilities are listed in Figure 6.19.

Although a dresser is assigned to assist the model, the model should check the clothing and accessories to make sure they are arranged in the order they will be worn during the show. The dresser should prepare the garments by hiding the tags or removing them and putting them in a safe place so they

can be re-attached later when garments are returned to the store. The garments should be ready to step into—zippers are unzipped, buttons unbuttoned, and scarves pre-tied if possible. Shoes and jewelry should be lined up. The model should be aware of the model lineup and where the lineup sheets are posted. This protocol should be followed during all rehearsals using clothing and accessories, as well as during the show.

Models should step into and out of clothes only while standing on a covered area of the dressing room. Once the model is dressed, he or she must follow the rule not to sit down. Smoking, food, and beverages have no place near the merchandise. The merchandise must be kept in immaculate condition and be able to go back into the designer's showroom or retail stock for sale immediately after the show.

Models and dressers should keep conversation to a minimum immediately before and during the show. If it is necessary to speak, use a soft voice. This helps keep the backstage area free from excess confusion.

MODEL RESPONSIBILITIES

Be on time for fittings, rehearsal, and show.

Be cooperative.

Keep merchandise in perfect condition. Clothing and accessories must be ready for sale after show.

Never sit in an outfit.

Do not eat, smoke, or drink around clothing.

Step in and out of clothing in the area wth floor protection.

Use a scarf to protect clothing while pulling clothes over the head.

Keep backstage conversation to a minimum, using a low tone voice or whisper.

Dress and undress quickly.

Line up immediately.

Listen to commentator or cue personnel for instructions.

Do not bring friends or children backstage or in the dressing room before, during, or after the show.

Figure 6.19
A list of model responsibilities provides guidelines for the behavior and behind-the-scenes activities for amateur models.

Illustration by Carly Grafstein

Models need to be cooperative. They should dress quickly and line up promptly. Listening to the backstage starter and watching for any special cues will help to make everything look smooth and polished.

Models should be pleasant, discreet, and poised. If the model has an accident or makes a mistake, he or she needs to continue without drawing attention to the situation. Mistakes such as tripping on the steps or stage, or dropping a prop or accessory, are very common. A professional model will just ignore the circumstances and carry on.

BEAUTY ON THE RUNWAY

Designers cooperate with their fashion show producers to create a story for each of their shows. In addition to using this story for the merchandise, a beauty image is created to further emphasize the vision. From sultry señoritas to rebel chic outlaws, the mood is established for models and merchandise at each fashion show. Next, we look at the show image created by the show staff with the assistance of various beauty professionals.

Show Image

Many people watch the catwalk shows for hair and makeup trends in addition to discovering the changing clothing styles. As we discussed in Chapter 3, the creative director or designer sets the vision for a fashion week show. After the show theme is established, the hair and makeup personnel start working on enhancing the image to be portrayed by the models. For example, designer Francisco Costa for Calvin Klein used the character Lisbeth Salander, from the film *The Girl with the Dragon Tattoo*, as an inspiration for his fall collection (Sardone, 2012). Rooney Mara (Fig. 6.20b), the actress who played the character in the film, sat in the front row of the Calvin Klein fashion show, reinforcing the image of the character's austere beauty. Figure 6.20a

(a) *Courtesy of WWD/George Chinsee*

(b) *Courtesy of WWD/Steve Eichner*

Figure 6.20
(a) Models at the Calvin Klein runway show wear garments inspired by the film *The Girl with the Dragon Tattoo*.
(b) Rooney Mara (seated at right) became the muse for Calvin Klein designer Francisco Costa's fall collection and was invited to sit in the front row for the show.

shows the models wearing the fashions influenced by the film's character. The spirit and aesthetic of the character infused Costa's runway presentation. The stage featured a black floor and walls; all of the girls wore either side-parted ponytails lacquered to a glassy shine or blunt-cut bobs shaved at the nape. The models marched with a thud, wearing thick-heeled shoes or matte crocodile riding boots that echoed over the film's menacing sound track. Costa faintly softened the look by adding vibrant shots of color to the head-to-toe black dress code worn in the film.

A look backstage reveals the beauty trends developed to coordinate with the designer's fashion ideas. Whether the look emphasizes the eyes, cheeks, or mouth, beauty trends emerge from the runway shows. Figure 6.21 illustrates a model getting ready for a show. Makeup, hair, and nail polish are pulled together to enhance the designer's overall creative image.

Beauty Professionals

A select group of beauty professionals is hired each season to create beauty images through makeup and hair at the fashion shows. Various makeup artists for the shows use products from Bobbi Brown, MAC, François Nars, and Pat McGrath, a makeup artist who works exclusively with Procter & Gamble, among others.

In preparation for the shows, Bobbi Brown meets with each designer before the clothes are presented. She looks at the fabrics and colors that will be used and starts to create the makeup look for the show, sometimes based upon a phrase the designer used to describe the collection or a significant color being featured. Ms. Brown reviews her plan with the designer, frequently demonstrating it on a design assistant at the designer's showroom.

MAC sends makeup artists to the four major fashion show cities to consult with designers prior to show week. Working with such designers as Badgley Mischka in

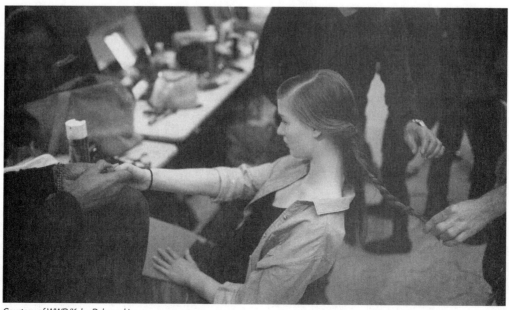

Figure 6.21
Models' hair, makeup, and nails are completed backstage before the show begins.

Courtesy of WWD/Kuba Dabrowski

New York, Roland Mouret in London, Allesandro Dell'Acqua in Milan, and Cacharel in Paris, MAC artists work under a great deal of pressure, often finishing the look just hours before the show is presented. First, the looks on the runway will be embraced by the early adopters, smaller brands, and high-end stores. However with consumers and brands better connected to one another thanks to social media and fashion bloggers, the timeframe may become even more condensed.

Hair has been worn long and straight, waved, crimped, short and messy, slicked back with gels, or in pigtails. The variety of hair looks is almost endless. Celebrity hairstylists, such as Orlando Pita at Prada, Sally Hershberger for John Frieda at Diane Von Furstenberg, Odile Gilbert at Pucci, Eugene Souleiman at Louis Vuitton, and Guido Palau at Valentino, create the runway hair images to coordinate with beauty and clothes each season.

Amateur Model Look Book

Schools or charity organizations may not have the budget to hire hair and makeup professionals. If a local hair salon or makeup studio cannot be found to volunteer its services, the model coordinator with the help of her committee is responsible for the look of the models. Students and friends with experience styling hair and applying makeup will often volunteer their services for a free ticket to the show. Figure 6.22a shows a page from a college fashion show look book and Figure 6.22b reveals how the look appeared on a model from the show.

Beauty, as created and emphasized by makeup and hair, is closely associated with presenting fashion worn by beautiful models. In order to fully coordinate the clothes, models, and beauty, we next look at the way models walk down the runway by using choreography.

(a) *Courtesy of Northern Arizona University*

(b) *Courtesy of Kristen Marie Photography*

Figure 6.22
This is from the model look book for *Get Your Fashion Fix on Route 66*, showing **(a)** Look #1 with a leaf design surrounding the eye and **(b)** a model with Look #1 during the show.

CHOREOGRAPHY

In ballet or musical performances, *choreography* refers to the art of devising movements for dances. In fashion show production, **choreography** includes the plan for the models' runway routines. The theme, merchandise, and music selected are elements that reflect the look and feel of the show and the choreography should enhance this image.

Choreography is an important aspect of a fashion show. All the runway routines for the show should be worked out before models arrive for the rehearsal. Models will either be posed on stage as the curtain opens or enter quickly and assume a position on cue. The travel patterns will ensure that the appropriate commentary or music is emphasized on cue. A **choreographer** is responsible for determining the pattern that a model will walk down the runway and the interaction of the models on the runway as they enter and exit the stage area.

Patterns of choreography include the following:

- Opening the show
- Entering the stage or runway
- Planning the runway walk with paces, pivots, and pauses
- Exiting the stage or runway
- Ending the show

Opening the Show

Perhaps the most important part of show choreography is the opening. It is critical to the success of the show to get the audience involved right from the beginning. The house lights are dark. A spotlight is focused on one model at the stage entrance. As the general lighting is raised, the model or several models enter the runway. At this point the merchandise, music, lighting, and choreography must all come together. There is a significant difference between the tempo of a fashion show

and a theatrical performance. A theatrical performance may open slowly and quietly and build to a climax and conclusion. A fashion show must start and end with emphasis.

Another possible show opening may involve some type of visual effects on the background such as a slide, video, or a light show while the models enter the stage. This can also be used to entertain and perhaps educate the audience before the models come on the runway. Each scene of the show may open using a technique similar to the one used in opening the overall presentation.

Planning the Runway Walk

The choreographer or designer will give the models specific directions regarding how to walk on the runway and describe the **pace** or relative tempo. The pace may be fast or slow depending upon the merchandise being presented and music, and where **pivots**—turns, and **pauses**—a temporary halt to movement, should take place on the runway.

Mapping

It is not necessary to create a different route for each model as he or she demonstrates each new outfit. It would be difficult for the models and choreographer to remember each separate walk. A compromise of only changing walking routes for each scene could be mapped in advance, and will allow for some variability. Then, as models are given directions, these **mapped routes**, or planned paths, can be explained and presented as visual diagrams. The route can be numbered and posted with each model's outfit in the dressing room.

Groups of Models

It generally adds more interest and variety when the show is broken up with different patterns and model groups. Having two models enter the runway wearing the same or complementary outfits creates greater impact and the repetition will help the audience remember the look.

Variations using multiple models are endless. It is common to have two, three, four, or more models on the runway at any given time. The show will be more complex in staging, but it will be more entertaining and effective in showing different colors and designs to the audience. A greater number of models will require more coordination in fittings and rehearsal.

When working with two or more models, the model on the left is considered the lead model. Stage left is considered the left part of the stage from the viewpoint of the audience facing the stage. The other models should keep pace with the lead model. Followers need to practice when to start, turn, and stop in relationship to the lead model.

Two models together may walk to the center of the runway. At the point where a pause or pivot takes place, these two models may make simultaneous turns and continue or separate, walking in different directions (Fig 6.23). Planning choreography in advance will ease the transitions.

Careful coordination during the merchandise selection process and coordination of amateur models into groups will lead to an organized appearance. The models should look good together on the runway. One fashion show featured identical horizontally striped dresses on both a petite, curvy-figured model and on a tall, slender model. The coordinator tried to make the point of featuring the same dress in the complementary colors. Although each individual model looked wonderful in the dress, the desired impact was not achieved because the models' height and shape differences did not complement each other on the runway.

"The show must go on" is one important point to emphasize to amateur models.

Figure 6.23
A fashion show with two or more models on the runway can be more interesting than a simple parade of models one at a time.

Courtesy of WWD/Robert Mitra

Despite elaborate planning and rehearsal, the model may forget the exact route. It is more important to show the garments in a professional manner than to act confused trying to figure out what to do next.

Exiting the Stage

As the model leaves the runway or stage, he or she may stop, turn, and pause, enabling the audience to take one last view of the item being presented. The model's personal flair may be revealed with some special pose or exit technique. It will also give a photographer time to take another photograph.

The plan must include directions for the models who are simultaneously entering and exiting the stage area. It must be determined if the first model will remain on the runway while waiting for the next model to enter or vice versa.

The Finale

The end of every show should be well coordinated and powerful. It should leave the audience satisfied and applauding. The finale is the last impression.

Generally, the merchandise in the final scene is the most dramatic of all that has preceded. It may be elegant hostess apparel, evening clothes, or bridal fashions. The most effortless ending is to bring all of the models, wearing their final outfit, back on stage. By bringing all of the models back on the runway, the audience is able to review the most spectacular clothing shown during the performance. This type of finale benefits from a large number of models, who by their presence on the runway provide dramatic impact.

Even though editors seated in the front row are frequently asked by photographers to tuck in their legs and feet, they quickly did so at Franck Sorbier's couture finale ("Fashion Scoops," 2001). A model wearing a wedding gown entered the runway on the back of a galloping horse. When the horse reared on its hind legs, some editors gasped in fear. No doubt that finale left a long-lasting impression!

When a show features designs from a celebrity designer, it is customary to have the celebrity join the models on stage during the finale. The show may be a charity event or a retail store promotion at which potential customers like to see and meet the creator of the garments. Personal appearances by the designer are very popular events for retail stores. If the show is held during market week, buyers and media personnel will be able to recognize and cheer the achievements of the designer's work as part of the finale.

Models wearing their last outfit applaud the designer, who enters the runway during the show's finale (Fig. 6.24). The designer recognizes his or her models, the fashion

Figure 6.24
A fashion show finale allows the audience to recognize the designer, models, and the clothing that has been presented.

Courtesy of WWD

show staff, and audience by clapping for them. The audience is also likely to show its appreciation by applauding the show and designer.

Importance of Choreography

Properly organized and performed choreography can be used to create focal points for the show. The viewer's attention is drawn to the specific merchandise or trends that the show producers want to emphasize. A poorly choreographed show looks amateurish and unprofessional, and does not leave a good impression on the audience.

Choreography can be used to reveal certain moods. Elegant and sophisticated merchandise may be accentuated through slow, deliberate movements and dramatic pauses. Athletic apparel can be highlighted through spirited and energetic gestures. Children's apparel can be stressed through

skipping, running, playing games, and so forth. The viewers should be entertained and satisfied with the show so that they will support the mission of the program, whether it is for charity or profit.

The catwalk is where all of the creative and theatrical elements of the fashion show come together. This chapter discussed the role of the fashion model in helping to create excitement on the runway. To achieve the final polished look on the runway, models have been trained to project confidence. Beauty professionals, the hair and makeup artists, have worked their magic to transform models into the dramatic creatures who strut along the runway. The choreographer contributed walking routines to emphasize the merchandise and beauty of the models. This chapter has looked at all of the contributors, making the catwalk an exciting place to be.

Inside a Modeling Agency
Sheree Hartwell

Courtesy of Sheree Hartwell

As the owner/director of the FORD/Robert Black Agency, I oversee a talent roster of over 350 people. I maintain client relationships and scout new talent, sending them overseas and to national markets, as well as manage my company's day-to-day operations. I have often been asked about the business and how to break into it. The following are some answers.

What Is a Modeling Agency?

A modeling agency is a melting pot of personalities. At any given time there may be many different people in the office: models, photographers, clothing stylists, hair/makeup artists, designers, art directors, and editors. Some come to socialize; others are there strictly for business. You never know whom you may run into.

Most major market agencies are organized in the following way:

- *New Faces:* These agents work to scout models, groom and develop them, and really hand-hold new models. They have to be patient and work well with each new model and the model's parents.
- *Scouts:* Most large agencies employ a team of scouts to do "street scouting," spending time at the mall food court or stores where teenagers shop, or scouting the crowd at concerts with a large teen following. They also travel to small modeling schools to find models in smaller markets.
- *Women's Agents and Men's Agents:* Agents who handle female models work on the Women's board. Similarly, agents who handle male models work on the Men's Board. They can be assigned to the entire female/male division or have a certain number of girls/guys to handle.
- *Art Department:* In today's fast-paced digital world, most large agencies have an art department that maintains the company image. The members of the art department work on overall company branding, social media, composing composite cards, designing and maintaining websites, as well as designing "show" packets and cards.

What Do Model Scouts Look For?

With some exceptions, the following are a few concrete traits that scouts look for:

- *Height:* Female models are generally required to be 5 feet 8 inches to 5 feet 11 inches; male models are typically 5 feet 11 inches to 6 feet 3 inches.
- *Bone structure:* The current trend is for models to have symmetrical features. Eyes are evenly spaced, cheekbones are high, noses are small, and there is an overall symmetry in the face.
- *Thin, proportionate build:* Sizing of models is determined by designers, not by agencies or agents. In today's world, high fashion models are encouraged to be no larger than a size 2/4. Desirable measurements for a 5 foot 10 inch female model are generally no larger than a bust of 34 inches, a waist of 25 inches, and hips that are 35 inches. The shorter a model is, the smaller her measurements need to be. Ideally, model bust and hip dimensions should be the same measurements.

How Does a Modeling Agency Help Prepare Its New Models?

There are many aspects of new models that we can help them to change to improve their chances for success: for example, changing hair style, color, or length. Yoga, Pilates, speed walking, and other methods of exercise that help to elongate muscles and not add bulk can help models look as long and lean as possible. To maintain hip measurements, models should avoid squats and running. One of male models' best features should be their washboard abs. We encourage many, many sit-ups!

We can help models become more polished by using good styling techniques and better posture. But we can't change a person's height or the symmetry of his or her face—at least, not without surgery!

Important tips for new models include learning how to carry themselves when they meet with a client and learning how to present themselves appropriately. Clients want to see a model's skin and hair. It is very important that a model wear very little makeup to a casting call. Hair should be clean and natural, tattoos and piercings should be hidden, and wardrobe should be fitted and flattering to a model's figure. A model is basically a human mannequin or canvas for the client or designer. The more makeup, jewelry, and accessories that the model wears, the harder it is for the client to get a true sense of what he or she really looks like.

How Soon Will I Be Able to Travel?

It is imperative for a new, budding model to travel outside the United States in order to further his or her career. Important markets are still London, Paris, and Milan; however, the Asian market has proved to be a great stomping ground for developing new models. Tokyo, Hong Kong, Singapore, and Thailand, have become popular market cities to travel to in order to garner much-coveted tear sheets necessary for a model's portfolio. Most Asian market contracts are for 60 days. Asian clients prefer quite young models, typically 15 to 22 years old. Most Asian agencies will advance the model's airfare and apartment costs, and will provide a weekly food allowance. This is a very easy market for new models to start in because minimal out-of-pocket money is needed in the beginning. Once the model starts to make money, the advanced expenses that were charged to her account will be deducted from her pay.

Are My Expectations to Become a Model Realistic?

Many times when I am interviewing new talent, I ask them why they want to be a model. Do they have a thick enough skin to handle rejection and constant scrutiny? Because the business is so competitive, the model has to *really* want it in order to make it. Some models seem as though they become overnight successes, whereas others plug away hoping to get recognized by the right client and/or photographer. So much of this business is about timing. If you don't have patience, it is very easy to become discouraged.

When I ask new female models about their goals, most answer, "I want to be a Victoria's Secret Angel." Although I appreciate their dreams, I remind them that "Angels" are supermodels—the top 1 percent of all models in the world!! The probability of any model making it into supermodel status is almost zero—not impossible, but certainly not a guarantee.

Others answer, "I want to be on the cover of *Vogue*" (or some other fashion magazine). If you take a look at magazines in the United States today, who is on the cover? Singers, actors, reality stars, and so forth. There are no longer "no-name" models on magazine covers thanks to our obsession with "celebrity." It is almost impossible for a model to make the cover or inside fashion editorial of a U.S. magazine. This is why models must travel. In Europe and Asia, there are many familiar international fashion magazines, including *Harper's Bazaar, Vogue, Elle, Marie Claire,* and *L'Officiel*. These markets are much more open to the idea of models, rather than celebrities, appearing in the magazines.

How Does an Agency Make Money?

A legitimate, licensed talent agency does not charge for classes or portfolio pictures, or have any signing fees. Agencies make money only when talent makes money. Agencies charge talent a 20 percent commission on all bookings. So, for every $100 a model makes, we make $20. We also charge our client, the person hiring the model/talent, a 20 percent agency fee. So, from each $100 billed, we make $40. It is the role of the agent to negotiate any and all talent fees. The higher that the talent rate is, the more money the agent/agency makes. It is in our best interest to get as much money for the model as possible. There are industry standard rates for most projects, but in today's economy many clients come to us with a set rate, and we can then decide if we are interested and willing to work on the project. Good agents will know whether a model will work on a project before ever having to consult with them.

Sheree Hartwell is the owner/director of the FORD/Robert Black Agency in Arizona. She began modeling with the FORD/Robert Black Agency at 12 years old. She was fortunate enough as a model to travel and work in the major U.S. markets as well as in Europe during high school and college. Hartwell earned a B.S. degree in merchandising with a minor in advertising from Northern Arizona University where she was the Model Coordinator for the fashion show *Fashions From the Closet*.

You Can Find Amateur Models Anywhere, Everywhere . . .

Karissa Keiter

Courtesy of Olivia Koehler

As a student in a fashion program and as an individual interested in models and fashion, I had my doubts about using amateur models. The models you see in print, on the runway, and in stores are professionals. When thinking about the best show one could produce or the most beautiful photograph one could take, most people would prefer to use a professional model. What many people overlook, though, is that amateur models can be just as effective as the professionals. In my experience, using amateur models is not only exciting but also rewarding. If you find people who are fun and willing to commit to the final goal, you will be surprised how incredibly wonderful the fashion show can turn out.

Using amateur models in a fashion show is a process that includes searching for them, doing the proper paperwork, getting the models excited and motivated, training, and the final show itself. One of my favorite industry quotes by Coco Chanel explains why it can be so great to use amateurs: "Fashion is in the sky, in the street, fashion has to do with ideas, the way we live, what is happening" (Madsen, 1990, p. 124). Chanel's words truly show me that fashion is within everyone and comes from anywhere, so why wouldn't we want to show fashion on normal, everyday people: amateurs?

As a student at Northern Arizona University in the merchandising program, I was selected to head the model committee for the *Get Your Fashion Fix on Route 66* fashion show. As a committee, we were to locate and then train amateur models from within the town of Flagstaff, Arizona, for our show. Although amateurs can be frustrating at times, it was amazing to see these real-life, local people become accomplished models through working with my team.

One of the hardest parts of the process is finding your models. People who do not normally model may not think that they are good enough to be in a fashion show. This part of the process must be hands-on if you are to succeed in procuring your models. Our team took three approaches to attract people to our casting calls: online social media, in-person scouting, and posters. Some of these methods turned out to be more successful than others. Although social media is becoming one of the most popular ways to communicate with people, when it came to getting people interested in modeling in a show it really did not work. Through social media outlets we had 60 people say they were coming to

NOTES FROM THE RUNWAY

the casting call, but only 15 showed up. To encourage everyday people to want to model, you have to convince them face to face, and a Facebook event page will not inspire people to come to your casting call. Whether it was asking friends if they would be interested in modeling and willing to participate in our show or physically going out on the street and talking to people about the opportunity, it worked much better to make a personal connection rather than to use online social media. Finally, we had some feedback from those auditioning at our casting calls regarding our posters, which seemed to get a fair amount of people to come try out. This second day of auditioning brought in about 30 people.

Once we had our group of models put together, it was time for the first meeting, which involved getting the models excited about being a part of the show. To do this, we presented not just the theme, date, and time of the show, but also described the fun experiences they were about to have. We discussed how we intended to make their practice fun and energetic, and also about fittings, hair, and makeup. In addition to getting them excited, we had to make sure that they knew how important this show would be to us as fashion majors. We asked them to sign an agreement, stating their commitment to the process of creating the show, in order to secure them for the show. If the models aren't dedicated to your show and vision, it will not be the success that you intended.

The process over the next couple of months included weekly training sessions for the models to learn all the necessary walks for the show. At first we made it very simple, teaching nonspecific, basic walks. If you start small and work your way up, the models will notice improvements within themselves and become more confident on the runway. This training process requires not only a lot of patience but also a willingness to give praise to each model. The more the committee members complimented the models and gave them helpful hints, the more confident they became. Then the models began to show more of their own personalities in their walks and facial expressions.

Throughout this process, I stressed to my team to let the models show their individuality, because that was what made them special as a model. In my experience, modeling is not about how pretty you are or how you can strut your stuff on a runway. It is about the energy and personality you exude. Being an individual and finding your confidence is what modeling really is about, especially with amateur models.

By the day of the show, we had worked for months putting together a unique and fabulous production with our amateur models, who beamed confidence and individuality. Many times, people would tell me that amateur models cannot make your show as great as you envision it, but that did not hold true. Throughout the whole process the most important knowledge that I came away with is that anyone can model. You can find amateur models anywhere and everywhere as long as you guide them and help them find and build the confidence they need to succeed.

Karissa Keiter is a graduate of the merchandising program at Northern Arizona University and was the model coordinator for the *Get Your Fashion Fix on Route 66* fashion show. She received the Merchandising Leaders of the 21st Century Scholarship during her junior year. In 2011, Karissa received her certification in makeup artistry from the Napoleon Perdis Makeup Academy in Hollywood, California. After graduation, Karissa accepted an internship with Nordstrom in Seattle, Washington.

1

Creative director Marc Jacobs is known for his memorable and unusual runway presentations. He turned the Paris runway into a carousel for the spring Louis Vuitton fashion show. The fully operational merry-go-round was hidden by a white curtain before the show started. When the curtain was raised, the amazed audience saw the models sitting on the horses that were painted white. One by one each model jumped off her horse and walked around the circular runway. Kate Moss was the final model to walk the innovative runway.

(Courtesy of Fairchild Archive)

2

Eight British supermodels and designers, decked out in gleaming gold dresses, were showcased at the closing ceremonies of the 2012 Summer Olympic Games in London, England. While they were only on stage for a fleeting 8 seconds, they wowed the crowd and showed that British fashion was a match for any nation, even France. From left, front row: Stella Tennant wears a Christopher Kane and Swarovski crystal pant suit; Kate Moss wears a sequined Alexander McQueen dress; Naomi Campbell wears an Alexander McQueen dress with a long train; Jourdan Dunn wears a leather dress by Jonathan Saunders and a feather headdress by Stephen Jones; Georgia May Jagger wears a Victoria Beckham cocktail dress. Above from left, back row: Lily Cole wears an Erdem embroidered and lace dress; Karen Elson wears Burberry Gold; Lily Donaldson wears a Vivienne Westwood Gold lace gown.

(Sports Illustrated/Getty Images)

In a 21st-century spin on mannequin modeling, Daphne Guinness, artist and socialite, appeared as a pseudo-mannequin model in the window of Barney's, where she undressed and dressed in the window (albeit behind a screen) into a Alexander McQueen gown for the Met's Costume Gala. The performance attracted a large audience as Guinness choreographed her preparation for the event with the aid of an attendant in a black sequined jumpsuit.

(Courtesy of WWD/Kyle Ericksen)

4

Historically, New York Fashion Week was held in tents at Bryant Park; however, in 2009, Mercedes-Benz Fashion Week in New York City moved to Lincoln Center. Here models walk a long runway through Damrosch Park at Lincoln Center.

(©2010 Kevin Mazur/Getty Images)

Various fashion weeks have emerged in many large cities around the world, expanding fashion into locations beyond New York, Paris, London and Milan. For example, Mercedes-Benz Fashion Week Berlin is Germany's most important stage for emerging talent as well as established brands. Berlin-based designer Yujia Zhai-Petrow, who was born in China, developed a distinct style that blends luxurious urban comfort with global chic for the brand 1913Berlin.

(© ROBERT SCHLESINGER/epa/Corbis)

Students enrolled in the fashion show production class and students participating in the VisualDESIGNLab at Northern Arizona University collaborated on the design of the logo used to promote the fashion show *Get Your Fashion Fix on Route 66*. The design was used on the invitations, posters, e-mail blasts, tickets, and t-shirts worn around campus to highlight the event.

(Courtesy of Patricia Murphey, Director of the VisualDESIGNLab)

The designer provides the concept and theme for the merchandise to be shown on the runway. Here is a sketch from Christian Siriano. His inspirational drawing is compared with the actual garment that was presented on the runway during fashion week.

(Courtesy of Christian Siriano, Courtesy of WWD/George Chinsee)

Color plates 8 through 11 show thumbnail photographs from a spring couture collection designed and produced by Karl Lagerfeld for Chanel. The show is featured in its entirety as we discuss merchandise flow and rhythm for a show.

(Courtesy of Fairchild Archive)

For most models, a fashion spread in *Vogue* is beyond their wildest dreams. For plus size models, it's even more of a rarity. But, American model Marquita Pring, who fluctuates between a size 12 and 14, has already been there and done that. After she walked in Jean Paul Gaultier's spring fashion show she landed the *Vogue Italia* cover. Here is Pring walking in Jean Paul Gaultier's spring ready-to-wear fashion show, which catapulted her into the world of international modeling.

(Courtesy of Fairchild Archive)

13

In his debut at Dior, designer Raf Simons launched his Christian Dior era in a grand residence in a series of intimate rooms. The walls of each room were covered in densely packed, floor-to-ceiling flowers—white orchids in one room, deep purple delphiniums in another room, and multiblooms in a third room.

(Courtesy of Fairchild Archive)

Models for the Yohji Yamamoto show were styled with a high, cotton-candy swirl of hair twisted and turned up as if the wind had just caught them. The hair and makeup made them look like Skid Row Marie Antoinettes. The mood was influenced by the most famous fashionista of the eighteenth century as envisioned by Yamamoto. The models waited backstage before putting on the hoop skirts, which were either half-covered or with their cage structure fully revealed.

(Courtesy of Fairchild Archive)

15

These models wait backstage for their turn to walk the runway for Lanvin in Paris. Alber Elbaz, artistic director for Lanvin, wanted to define the two sides of women—one, a study in graphic hardware shown in sleek, lean shapes with metal accoutrements; the other, represented in giant, full-bloom rose prints and vibrant floral colors.

(Courtesy of Fairchild Archive)

Ottavio "Tai" Missoni, patriarch of the famous Italian knitwear clan, marked his 90th birthday with a walk down the runway with his daughter Angela, the creative director of Missoni. The father and daughter team were holding their hands as they took a bow at the end of the fashion show. It was a moving moment, one rarely seen in the youth-obsessed fashion industry.

(Courtesy of Fairchild Archive)

THE CATWALK—A RECAP

- Fashion models are the individuals engaged to wear the apparel and accessories for a fashion show. They must be able to effectively promote the image of the clothing to the audience in a believable manner and are very important to the image and success of the fashion show.
- Modeling fits into two general categories: commercial—posing for catalogues, showing clothing in vendors' showrooms, doing fittings for manufacturers, or posing for television commercials and print advertisements for a wide range of goods; and editorial—walking the runways during fashion weeks and posing for editorial sections of high fashion magazines and for advertisements for prestige and luxury brands.
- Modeling agencies are companies that represent a variety of fashion models and act as scheduling agents for them.
- The negative images of modeling come from disreputable modeling agents, schools, or contests that take advantage of models who might be underage, unhealthy (anorexic), or taken advantage of as freelance workers.
- The Council of Fashion Designers of America, the Model Alliance, and the international editors from *Vogue* magazine are attempting to overcome the negative aspects of modeling.
- The decision to use professional (models trained in modeling techniques and hired through modeling agencies) or amateur models (real people selected from other resources) is often a financial one.
- The visual image and the theme of the fashion show are enhanced by beauty professionals—hair and makeup artists.
- Fashion show choreography involves the models' runway routines, which includes opening the show; entering the stage or runway; planning paces, pivots, and pauses; exiting the stage or runway; and ending the show with the finale.

KEY FASHION SHOW TERMS

advertising model	editorial model
amateur model	fit model
body parts model	freelance
bookers	go-see
booking	individual model lineup sheet
callback	look
casting call	male model
catalogue model	mapped route
cattle call	mature model
child model	model
choreographer	modeling agencies
choreography	model list
commercial model	mother agency
composite	muse

open call	request
option	runway model
pace	scouts
pause	showroom model
petite model	stats
pivot	tear sheet
plus size model	television commercial acting
portfolio	test
professional model	

Questions for Discussion

1. How does a commercial model differ from an editorial model? What kinds of jobs does each type of model perform?
2. What is the role of a modeling agency? Discuss the various terms associated with a model agency.
3. Why does Ashley Mears call modeling a bad job? Do you agree or disagree?
4. Discuss the responsibilities of a model before rehearsals, during rehearsals, and after a fashion show.
5. What does a hair stylist or makeup artist contribute to a fashion show?
6. How important is a model's walk? What does it add to a fashion show?
7. What is the purpose of a fashion show finale?

Fashion Show Activity

Break into teams of four or five members. Each team should brainstorm a theme for a fashion show. Based upon that theme, plan and discuss how you would do the following:
- Stage the opening of the show
- Create a "look" for the models' hair and makeup
- Stage the finale

The Capstone Project

The model committee should schedule a model casting. How do members of the committee suggest inviting potential models to the casting call? Discuss what music and walking techniques will be used during the auditions. Discuss who will contact the models who are selected and who will contact the models who are not invited to participate in the show. Samples of all forms, including model applications, model release forms, individual lineup sheets, personal responsibility contracts, and any other forms deemed necessary should be included in this assignment. Please refer to the CD-ROM for tools that may assist you with this section of the fashion show process.

CD-ROM

REFERENCES

About us. (2006). Parts Models. Retrieved from http://www.partsmodels.com

Bergin, O. (2012, May 4). Natalia Vodianova's six year-old daughter makes modeling debut. *Fashion Telegraph*. Retrieved from http://fashion.telegraph.co.uk

Brown, R. (2012, May 7). Kathy Ireland. *WWD In Person*. Retrieved from http://www.wwd.com

Fashion scoops. (2001, July 12). *Women's Wear Daily*, p. 5.

Feitelberg, R. (2012, March 5). Someone like you. *Women's Wear Daily*. Retrieved from http://www.wwd.com

Greenfield-Sanders, T. (Director & Photographer). (2012). *About face: The supermodels, then and now.* New York, NY: HBO Documentary Films.

Gross, M. (2011). *Model: The ugly business of beautiful women.* New York, NY: First It Books.

Hare, B. (2009, August 10). Their hands are worth $1,200 a day. *CNN Living*. Retrieved from http://articles.cnn.com

Horyn, C. (2008, October 3). In the big house. *The New York Times*. Retrieved from http://nytimes.com

Jothianandan, S. (2012, January 12). 134 minutes with Sara Ziff. *New York Magazine*. Retrieved from http://nymag.com

Krupnick, E. (2011, June 3). Carmen Dell'Orefice, oldest working model, turns 80. *Huffington Post*. Retrieved from http://www.huffingtonpost.com

Madsen, A. (1990). *Chanel: A Woman of her own.* New York, NY: Henry Holt.

Memo pad. (2012, March 5). *Women's Wear Daily*, p. 19.

Mears, A. (2011). *Pricing beauty: The making of a fashion model.* Berkeley and Los Angeles, CA: University of California Press.

The Model Alliance. (2012). *The Models' Bill of Rights*. Retrieved from http://modelalliance.org/models-bill-of-rights

Odell, A. (2012, January 26). The CFDA releases model health guidelines for fashion week. *New York Magazine*. Retrieved from http://nymag.com

Sardone, A. (2012, April 27). Big ideas at its most compelling, fashion dares. *WWD: The Collections*, p. 40.

Schell, O., & Ziff, S. (Directors). (2010). *Picture me: A model's diary* [DVD]. Los Angeles, CA: Strand Releasing Home Video.

The top 10 models. (2012, Fall). *Style.com/print*. p. 74.

Torrisi, L., & Fisher, L. (2012, February 15). Cindy Crawford stops 10-year-old daughter's career. *ABC News*. Retrieved from http://abcnewsgo.com

Wilson, E. (2012a, March 7). A minimum age? Not for this model. *The New York Times*. Retrieved from http://www.nytimes.com

Wilson, E. (2012b, May 3). Vogue adopts a 16-and-over modeling rule. *The New York Times*. Retrieved from http://www.nytimes.com

Yuan, J. (2011, August 14). I didn't think of myself as good-looking at all. But Richard Avedon did. China Machado's beginnings. *New York Magazine*. Retrieved from http://nymag.com

Yuan, J. (2012, February 12). Is there life after modeling? *New York Magazine*. Retrieved from http://nymag.com

CHAPTER SEVEN
The Framework and Sound Check

AFTER READING THIS CHAPTER, YOU SHOULD BE ABLE TO DISCUSS:

- The purposes of the stage and the runway areas visible to the audience

- The purpose of the dressing area hidden from the audience

- The uses of backgrounds and props to set the mood for the fashion show

- Options for audience seating

- The effectiveness of lighting as a mood-setting device

- The purposes of the sound designer and the music mix

- The understanding and securing of copyright permissions

- The use of an announcer for a fashion show

- The necessity of a script for a production fashion show

Jason Wu, Spring 2011. *Courtesy of WWD/Thomas Iannaccone*

When you think of Coco Chanel, what is the first image that comes to mind? A quilted bag? Faux pearls? A little black dress? Or maybe a Chanel jacket? Karl Lagerfeld honored the classic Chanel jacket by making it the backdrop of a spring couture show held at the Grand Palais in Paris. As guests arrived they were met by a 66-foot-high, stone-colored, classic jacket complete with double-C buttons and braid trim (Fig. 7.1) ("Circular Thinking," 2008). A Chanel icon in any era, the jacket was made of stone and weighed 10 tons, took 5 weeks to carve, 5 days to install—all for a 15-minute show ("Ever Since," 2008). The jacket was centered on a circular, rotating stage and opened just enough at the bottom for models to enter the stage from within it.

The soundtrack for the show was provided by an American electronic music duo, Glass Candy, from Portland, Oregon. Not only did the show feature songs from Glass Candy's *B/E/A/T/B/O/X* album, but the duo also played two songs simultaneously, creating another interesting element to the show that was praised over social media. One of the first models came out wearing a stone-colored Chanel jacket emphasizing the iconic jacket silhouette (Fig. 7.2). Both the silhouette and now the fashion show remain timeless.

Setting the atmosphere for the presentation comes together both in the staging framework—the layout of the physical facilities—and the sound check—the audio components of fashion show production. The haute couture shows each season are particularly known for their theatrical staging.

Figure 7.1
The classic Chanel jacket was the featured backdrop for a Chanel Haute Couture spring show. Both the jacket and the fashion show are timeless representations of Coco Chanel.

Courtesy of WWD/Delphine Achard

STAGING

Staging is the process or manner of putting on a performance on a stage. In fashion show production this involves all the components of set design—developing a stage and/or runway, creating a background, and setting the lights. As discussed in Chapter 3, a stage manager performs these tasks with guidance from the show director. General architectural limitations for show staging and background depend on the show type and location. Informal modeling on a sales floor generally does not require staging or background considerations. Attention to props may be sufficient. However, a large production with several scene changes may require a great deal of planning for staging and background. Showrooms, galleries, theaters, apparel mart halls, and many other locations present creative opportunities and limitations based on the physical layout of the space. Staging configurations are numerous, limited only by the creative abilities of the stage manager, show director, and staff.

The **stage** is a raised floor or platform on which theatrical productions are presented. This is a common area for models to enter and exit. In most facilities, stages are permanent fixtures that cannot be moved. The **runway**, or *catwalk*, is an extension of the stage or a freestanding unit that normally projects into the audience.

The stage and runway take on various forms according to the needs of the show and the physical facilities. Some fashion shows may have only a stage, others may have only a runway, and many shows incorporate both

Courtesy of WWD/Giovanni Giannoni

Figure 7.2
The first few models all made an entrance from the gigantic, stone-carved Chanel jacket backdrop featuring iconic Chanel jackets, complementing the color and detail evident from the back-drop.

> "The set design must act as a support and enhance a collection, improving and enlarging its spirit and identity."
> — Michael Brown, set designer

features based on the physical arrangements of the room where the show will be produced.

The **layout** is a schematic plan or arrangement of the area. The layout is often drawn as a sketch or a floor plan of the area (Fig. 7.3). It is used to give show personnel a general idea of the physical dimensions of the stage and runway, distance from the dressing area to the stage, model route, audience seating, and other details of the layout. This information will assist the model and merchandise committees in planning the timing of the show. For inexperienced show planners, a layout may be helpful in visualizing the area and planning model entrances and exits.

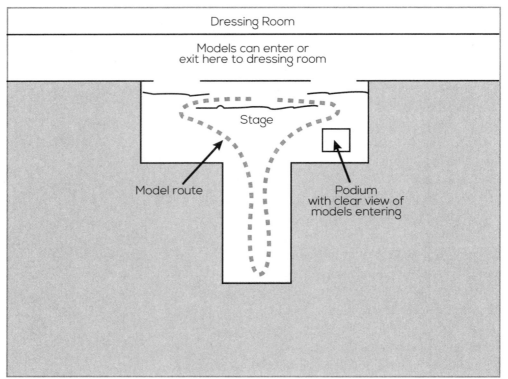

Figure 7.3
Floor plan layout.

Illustration by Carly Grafstein

The distance from the dressing area to the runway should be considered when developing the layout. The dressing areas and runway should be in close physical proximity to accommodate rapid clothing changes. In ideal settings, the dressing area and stage are adjacent to each other. A greater distance between dressing area and stage means an increased number of models to compensate for travel time between the two areas. Broadcast fashion shows, such as the Victoria's Secret annual fashion show, often show video of models hurriedly rushing off stage into a dressing area to make a quick clothing change.

Auditoriums often have dressing rooms to the side of the stage. Hotel meeting rooms frequently have suites located adjacent to the meeting room that can be used as a dressing area. Public restrooms can work, but most commercial locations will not allow their use. If suitable rooms are not available for dressing areas, temporary dressing areas can be created in the corner of a larger room with the use of screens, tables, and rolling racks.

When planning the layout, audience visibility is crucial. Every seat in the house must have an unobstructed view of the stage and the models. Attention to pillars, curtains, or other architectural obstructions must be noted on the layout.

Runway Dimensions

Runways vary in height, size, and shape based on the physical layout of the room and audience visibility. Some locations have permanent runways available for use. Other locations depend on the retailer or organization to provide a runway. Runways can be rented from local rental companies or built from plywood. Rental units have legs that lock into position for use. When renting runways, the word *stage* or *riser* is often more familiar to the rental agent. The typical size for a runway unit is 4 feet by 8 feet wide by 1 foot high. Runways are frequently multiples of these measurements (Fig. 7.4). Various height increments may also be available: 18 inches, 24 inches, 36 inches, and so on. Smaller rental agencies may carry only 1-foot-high units. A show in a small space, such as an art gallery, may use 1 or 2 units for a short runway of 8 or 16 feet. Typical trade show runways are 32 to 40 feet (4 or 5 units) in length. This provides adequate space for models to exhibit the fashions and also allows the audience enough time to review the line and make notes.

The length of the runway should accommodate the walking route and traffic flow of models on stage. Models should be on the runway long enough for the audience to adequately see the merchandise being shown. The transition area between the stage and the runway often serves as the first position where models stop and pivot. Shorter runways not attached to a stage generally have one primary focal point, at the end of the runway. Longer runways may accommodate several viewing points midway between the stage and the end of the runway (Fig. 7.5).

The width of the runway will determine the number of models who may appear side by side at any given time. If the runway is 4 feet wide, only two models should walk together. Putting two sections side by side doubles the width of the runway. When the runway is 8 feet wide or more, three or four models can walk comfortably together, adding visual impact.

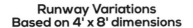

Runway Variations
Based on 4' x 8' dimensions

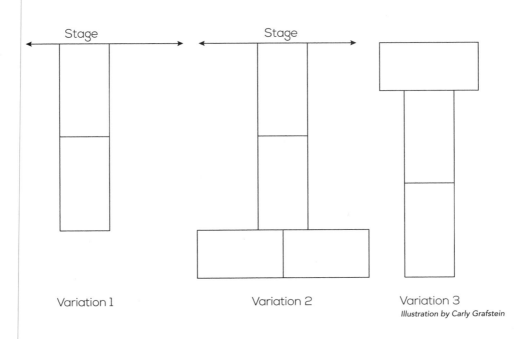

Variation 1

Variation 2

Variation 3

Illustration by Carly Grafstein

Figure 7.4
Various runway configurations based on 4-foot by 8-foot units.

Figure 7.5
In this creative stage layout, models have multiple viewing points from which to pose.

Fairchild Archive

Figure 7.6
Examples of runway shapes.

Illustration by Carly Grafstein

The height of the runway often depends upon the height of the stage and the ability of the entire audience to see the fashions. Runways are often constructed at the same height as the stage. However, if a stage is very high, one or two steps leading down may be incorporated into the layout to accommodate a lower runway. The runway must be high enough for the audience to see the fashions, but low enough so that it is not a safety hazard for the models.

Typically, the larger the room, the higher the runway must be in order for viewers at the back of the room to see. Ideal heights are between 18 and 36 inches.

Runway Shapes

The actual runway may be built in a variety of shapes, but the most common configurations include the T, I, X, H, Y, U, and Z (Fig. 7.6). The primary limitation to runway design is the size of the venue. There are advantages and disadvantages to each runway pattern.

One of the most frequently used runway shapes is the T shape, which is a combination of a stage and an extended runway. Models enter and exit from the stage and walk down the straight platform to exhibit the clothes. It is the most simple runway shape and perhaps the least exciting.

A variation of the basic T shape is the I formation. This runway shape adds a platform extension to the extended runway, parallel to the stage. This extension allows models to spend more time on the runway and closer to the audience to feature the garments in a more interesting manner. Figure 7.7 illustrates an I formation and describes from which direction models will enter, the two different routes the models will take, and where they will stop and pose.

The X- or cross-shaped runway is a unique and fascinating formation consisting of two platforms placed at 90-degree angles, generally used without a stage. Models enter and exit from doors in the room or auditorium, bringing them closer to the audience. The models generally use two or four sets of stairs set alongside the runway to ascend and descend the runway.

The H-shaped runway combines two straight runways with a connecting strip. The advantage of this type of formation is in showing several models at the same time, and may be effective in creating interest and variety. It is also useful in holding the audience's attention, particularly with large shows. Two successful examples of the use of the H-shaped runway involve French ready-to-wear designer Sonia Rykiel and the late American designer Rudi Gernreich. Because the H-shaped runway can handle many models at the same time, Rykiel brought

out 12 models identically dressed to focus attention on her simple houndstooth suits. The Fashion Group of Los Angeles used an H-shaped runway to stage a Rudi Gernreich retrospective show. The runway was so large that it incorporated three separate focal points. The models entered undetected from a secret pathway underneath the stage onto a raised platform placed in the center of the large stage.

The Y and U patterns are very similar to each other. The Y shape has two angled projections from the basic runway. The U shape has a curved extension, which brings the models out into the audience using a philosophy similar to that of the theater in the round. These formations can also be very engaging and add diversity to a show.

The Z or zigzag configuration is a simple shape conducive to a complex collection of different routines and movements. The models can turn and change

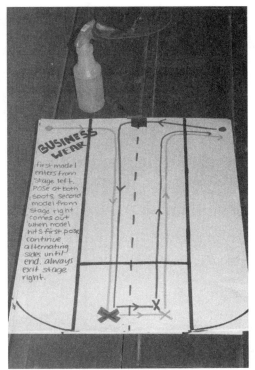

Courtesy of Christopher C. Everett

Figure 7.7
I-shaped runway pattern with instructions to models telling them which side to enter on, the path they will follow, and where they will pose and exit.

direction to effectively show different views of the garment.

The surface of the runway is another important consideration for the show planner. A carpeted or nonslip surface will help to protect models and shoes. The outside of the runway may be finished with construction materials or covered with fabric that has been tucked or pleated and tacked into place. Another type of covering is a vinyl fabric, which can be used on top of the runway and on the sides. An attractive runway can enhance the theme as well as the image of the show.

THE DRESSING AREA

The **dressing area** is a room or area designated for changing clothes, applying makeup, and styling hair. Figure 7.8 is a dressing room floor plan for approximately 20 models and 80 outfits. The dressing area should be large enough to accommodate clothing racks, accessories tables, chairs, full-length mirrors, models, and necessary support personnel. Clothing on racks needs to be evenly spaced to prevent wrinkling and to allow easy access by the dressers. One mirror should be placed near the stage entrance so that models can get a last-minute check before leaving the dressing area. If the location does not have mirrors, the fashion show producers should bring them to the site. The dressing room must be clean and free of unnecessary clutter. All unnecessary chairs and props should be removed to allow people to move around freely.

The show director and merchandise coordinator should plan the organization of the dressing area. The type of show, the number of models and dressers, and the size of the room will determine this organization. Each model should have an assigned space in the dressing area. The spaces should be assigned according to the models' order of appearance in the show; however, models who appear

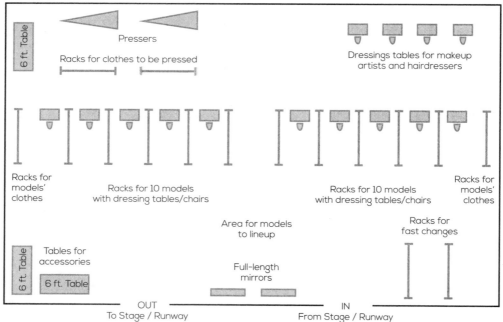

Figure 7.8
Dressing room floor plan.

Illustration by Carly Grafstein

consecutively or together in the show should not dress next to each other. Models' clothing and accessories should be placed in this area. If a model has several changes, clothing and accessories should be in correct order to help changes move more smoothly. If there is only one table for accessories, it should be placed next to the dressing room exit so that the accessories will be the last items a model puts on. Space should be reserved for models to apply makeup or style their hair, or for makeup artists and hair stylists to set up equipment. The dressing area should have a clearly defined entrance and exit to prevent awkward movements that may be seen by the audience. A list of necessary dressing room supplies is shown in Figure 7.9.

BACKGROUNDS

The purpose of the **background** is to enhance the merchandise, either with stark settings emphasizing the garments or dramatic

---

SUPPLIES NEEDED

Office Supplies
_____Tape
_____Stapler
_____Pens/Pencils
_____Paper
_____Garment tags

Alterations Supplies
_____Needles
_____Safety pins/Straight pins
_____Thread
_____Scissors

Beauty Supplies
_____Antiperspirant
_____Dress shields
_____Hair pins/hair elastics
_____Brushes/combs
_____Hair spray/mousse
_____Makeup: eyeshadows, blushes, lipsticks
_____Nail polish

Equipment
_____Extension cords
_____Mirrors
_____Table/racks/chairs
_____Iron/ironing board/steamer

Miscellaneous Supplies
_____Stocks
_____Floor coverings
_____Hangers
_____First-aid kit

Figure 7.9
Dressing room supply list.

Illustration by Carly Grafstein

backdrops emphasizing the theme. It may be decorated with a designer's, retailer's, or manufacturer's logo or some type of scenic theme. In his debut at Dior, designer Raf Simons launched his Christian Dior era in a grand residence containing a series of intimate rooms. The walls of each room were covered in densely packed, floor-to-ceiling flowers—white orchids in one room, deep purple delphiniums in another room, and multiblooms in a third (Foley, 2012). The thematically flowered background is shown in Color Plate 13.

A popular type of entryway consists of a plain white panel or screen, normally 7 to 8 feet high and 10 to 12 feet wide. Slides can be projected onto this screen to emphasize a particular theme or information. Interesting accents can also be developed with video walls. The screen may be used as a background for dramatic lighting and shadow effects created for the beginning or ending of a show segment. The show planners may have the option to use permanent or temporary movable backdrops called **flats**.

Scenery, just like a theatrical stage backdrop, may be painted to represent a room setting or an outdoor scene with natural elements. A series of doors or panels through which the models enter the stage and runway area can also be designed. The extent of the backdrop and scenery are dependent upon the type of show and the budget planned. A single backdrop can be used for the entire show, or different and elaborate backdrops can be built for each scene of the show. A revolving stage may be used to change the scene for each show segment. With a more elaborate stage setting, the expense is greater. However, the staging should never overshadow the clothes—it should be used to flatter the merchandise being displayed.

Get Your Fashion Fix on Route 66, a student-produced fashion show, was set in the 900-seat auditorium of a historic campus building. The stage was built for theatrical productions and fully equipped with lighting and sound equipment. The stage was large, approximately 38 feet by 45 feet, and had a very high ceiling. Any backdrop less than 6 feet would be inconsequential. As a result, the stage committee built a backdrop that consisted of two 12-foot-long railroad tracks (Fig. 7.10a) with large signage in the center. The backdrop was raised in place using the lighting frame (Fig. 7.10b). Figure 7.10c shows the backdrop in place, and Figure 7.10d shows models on the runway under the sign to give perspective to the very large space.

PROPS

Props are supports used to highlight the garments being exhibited. The trend for using props is cyclical. Sometimes it is popular to use props and at other times show planners want the clothes to speak for themselves.

Props may be mobile or stationary. Carrying a tennis racquet or golf club with the appropriate apparel is an example of a movable prop. There is a wide variety of this type of prop, including jump ropes and hand weights with activewear, briefcases and newspapers with career apparel, beach balls and towels with swimwear, or a notebook or apple with back-to-school fashions. Merchandise available for sale, such as briefcases, school backpacks, handbags, or glasses (Fig. 7.11), may be used as props.

Stationary props are normally immobile items that are placed as part of the scenery. These items might include furniture for a room setting, one or two beach umbrellas for a swimwear segment, a motorcycle or car for a teen or menswear show, or a gazebo for a

(a)

Courtesy of Christopher C. Everett

(b)

Courtesy of Christopher C. Everett

Figures 7.10 (a–d)
Backdrops need to be in
proportion to the staging
area: **(a)** large signage
is being put in place; **(b)**
the signage is raised in
place using the lighting
frames. *(Figure continues
on following page.)*

(c)

Courtesy of Kristen Marie Photography

(d)

Courtesy of Kristen Marie Photography

Figures 7.10 (cont'd)
(c) The entire stage is shown to illustrate the overall size, and **(d)** the backdrop is shown with models to illustrate proportion.

bridal show. Although these props are typically heavy and bulky, they can be changed with scene changes. Figures 7.12a and b

show the size and proportion of the stationary props used for *Get Your Fashion Fix on Route 66.*

SEATING PATTERNS

Two styles of seating arrangements are used to accommodate the audience. They may be seated in a theater pattern or luncheon or dinner style at tables.

Theater Seating

Theater seating involves placing chairs side by side and next to the stage and runway (see Fig. 7.13). This style is best used for fashion shows without meal service. The audience may have assigned or open seating on a first-come, first-served basis. Programs, gifts, or promotional materials may be placed on the seats before the guests arrive. Theater seating generally provides the best view of the fashions in the show because all the members of the audience are seated facing the runway.

Table Seating

A **table seating** arrangement is used at a show when meal service is provided (Fig. 7.14). A buffet or sit-down meal may be served prior to or after the fashion show. There are some visibility problems with this type of seating. Often a round table is set, holding as many as eight to ten people. Some people will not be able to see the stage or runway. Chairs will have to be turned in order to fully view the presentation and some members of the audience may find this kind of seating awkward.

Combination Seating

Depending upon the location, available space, and budget, a show may combine both seating styles. The lunch or dinner can be served in one banquet room using table seating. After the meal, the audience can move to another location where the stage, runway, and theater seating are set up.

LIGHTING

Lighting is the method and/or equipment used to provide illumination (Fig. 7.15). Good lighting is necessary to show clothing to its best advantage, set the mood of the show, and accentuate the theme of the show. Raising and lowering the house lights adds to the theatrical nature of fashion shows. Spotlights or track lighting placed above the runway can be used to highlight models while they are on the runway. Spotlights in a darkened room can be used to introduce, emphasize, or close a segment. Spotlights should be located as high up as possible.

Figure 7.11
Handbags and designer frames are common props.

Courtesy of WWD/Stephane Feugere and Giovanni Gionnoni

> "Light is a powerful tool that transforms reality."
> — Tierry Dreyfus, art director

They should not "blind" the audience. Care and practice with lighting should take place before the show to prevent any potential lighting problems. Lighting cues should be practiced during rehearsals.

There may be limited lighting in the area where the garments are shown. One fashion show held in the carriage house of a historical site had virtually no lights over the area where the runway was placed. Photographers' spotlights were used to illuminate the runway.

(a)

Courtesy of Christopher C. Everett

Figures 7.12 (a–b) Stationary props used for the *Get Your Fashion Fix on Route 66* fashion show.

(b)

Courtesy of Kristen Marie Photography

Strobe lights were popular effects used to create a mechanical look during the 1960s. In the 1970s and 1980s, theatrical productions such as *Phantom of the Opera*, *Cats*, and *Starlight Express* influenced others to create dramatic lighting and staging effects. These influences can be seen in some of the more complex and expensive fashion shows held during this period.

The 1990s brought more creative lighting effects. John Galliano used unique lighting for one of his couture collection shows. The show was held under lantern-shrouded chandeliers in an old Paris mansion. Karl Lagerfeld used lighting as the focus for one show of his ready-to-wear line (Fig. 7.16).

Many designers incorporate colored lights into their shows. Colored gels have been used to accentuate a particular look.

Figure 7.13
Seats are placed side by side in theater seating.

A fashion presentation by Enrico Coveri used pink runways and, to further enhance this look, pink-gelled lamps. Along with his colorful and youthful collection, the presentation popped!

Strings of small, white Christmas tree lights are another popular and effective way to light runways. Stringing lights around the entire perimeter of the stage and runway creates a glamorous appearance for the audience. When the house lights are darkened, this type of lighting also allows models to see the edge of the stage so their safety on stage is increased.

The atmosphere of the show is largely determined through the appropriate use of the physical facilities and effective use of the staging framework. The stage or runway, background, props, seating, and lighting must be planned and coordinated for the most striking and successful presentation to excite the audience and generate sales.

Figure 7.14
Tables became part of the runway for this Chanel show. Guests were served champagne or other beverages along with miniature cakes and sandwiches as the models strutted around them.

Figure 7.15
Technicians make adjustments to lighting equipment.

Courtesy of WWD/Thomas Iannaccone

Figure 7.16
Neon lights illuminate the runway for Louis Vuitton.

Fairchild Archive

MUSIC

Music has always been an essential element in fashion shows. The first retailer to set fashion shows to music was Stanley Marcus, who in the 1920s used the Ted Weems band as background music for his weekly fashion show (Diehl, 1976). Music was as important in the 1920s as it is today in setting ambiance and creating excitement for fashion shows.

In current times, the media is full of examples of the fusion of music and fashion. Musicians are front-row celebrity guests at fashion shows (Fig. 7.17). Fashion designers are teaming up with musicians for fashion events. Tommy Hilfiger, with his brothers as musicians, has always had his hand in music and entertainment. He has joined the cast of *American Idol* as image adviser (Medina, 2012). Justice, a French electronic music duo, did a mix for a runway show for Dior and then released it. According to

Mia Moretti, a popular fashion show D.J. (she was the D.J. for Chelsea Clinton's wedding) considers releasing a fashion show mix as the ultimate runway song (Ortved, 2011). Kanye West is a further example of the merging of music and fashion. He is a musician and the designer for his own clothing line.

Music is considered the pleasing or harmonious sounds, or combination of sounds, used to heighten the atmosphere of the show for the audience and models. Many fashion show producers believe the right music is essential to the success of a show. "If the clothes are the meat of the show, music is the soul that brings it alive," according to fashion designer Prabal Gurung. "Each season we want to tell a story for 12 minutes or so on the runway. That story can be successfully told when there is a perfect harmony between clothes and the music" (Ortved, 2011, ¶ 1). The right music can get an audience excited about what they are going to see more rapidly than any other element of preshow ambience.

There are as many different options for music as there are different items of merchandise to choose from for a fashion show. Blues, classic rock, jazz, classical, mashup, or many other styles can be successful in influencing an audience. The key to choosing the right music is to match the music style with the designer's inspiration and the audience. Runway show music is becoming so important that fashion media regularly report on popular playlists of the collections. Models, too, depend on music to set the pace of the show. They listen to the music to move easily and rhythmically on the stage and down the runway. If the music has a fast beat, models will walk faster.

Figure 7.17
Entertainers, such as Nicki Minaj, seated next to Anna Wintour, editor of *Vogue*, are often front-row guests at fashion week collection openings.

Getty Images

Sound Designer

The **sound designer** (*sound illustrator, music director,* or *D.J.*) (Fig. 7.18) is the person responsible for researching and selecting the appropriate music, obtaining permissions to use copyrighted music, mixing the music at the show, and preparing the sound system at the show venue. The use of music may be limited to the show itself, or played as background as the audience enters and leaves the show site. Silence in a room can frequently make people feel uncomfortable talking or moving around before the show begins. Background music will make an audience feel more comfortable and at ease.

Sound designers, music directors, or technicians are hired to prepare and play music during the show. They may be a professional affiliated with the fashion show site or a freelancer. Michel Gaubert is a well-known sound designer who, for over three decades,

Courtesy of Christopher C. Everett

Figure 7.18
Sound designers and
fashion designers work
very closely in planning
music for the show.

has created fashion week show sound backdrops in New York, London, Milan, and Paris for labels such as Rodarte, Thakoon, Oscar de la Renta, Michael Kors, Diane von Furstenberg, Gucci, Fendi, Jil Sander, Balenciaga, and more. Clients happily "pay Mr. Gaubert $10,000 to score the mini-narrative that, in essence, is a fashion show" (Trebay, 2011, ¶ 5). Frédéric Sanchez created the title "sound illustrator" to reflect his sensitivity for providing music that perfectly fits the designer's outfits on the runway. He has worked for Martin Margiela, Marc Jacobs, Calvin Klein, Prada and Rue du Mail (Vilaseca, 2010).

Local theaters and auditoriums often have their own technical staff whose members know the specifics of the equipment at the location (Fig. 7.19). A technician is more

> "I'm not a musician but I'm not a D.J. either. Music can tell a story and that is what I do: I tell stories using music."
>
> — Frédéric Sanchez,
> sound illustrator

aware of problems that can occur with the sound system and can make any needed corrections. Although these technicians are provided by the facility, the fashion show producer is responsible for their wages for working the show. Technicians should attend all rehearsals in which music is needed to note cues from the announcer, starter, and models.

Music Mix

Music mix is the combination of different musical styles to create a specific mood. The music should match the merchandise, starting with a strong musical selection to capture the attention of the audience and finishing with a strong finale that they will remember. The middle segments of the show should have music that flows so easily that

Figure 7.19
Location staff technicians are often more attuned to equipment capabilities and problems.

Courtesy of Christopher C. Everett

the audience is unaware they are listening to anything.

When planning music, many more songs will be reviewed than will be used to match the merchandise grouping. Mr. Gaubert, highlighted earlier, has an archive of 60,000 CDs, 20,000 vinyl records, and over 340,000 songs stored on a MacBook (Trebay, 2011). A variety of music should be used. Music may become monotonous if there is not enough variety in the selections. Ideally, each scene should have music specifically mixed for its merchandise selection. Sportswear requires fast tempo, upbeat music, whereas evening wear requires slower, sophisticated, and subtle music. Kris Bones, D.J. for Donna Karan, suggests "The Rolling Stones' 'Sympathy for the Devil' in all its mash-up and remix forms as the ultimate runway song" (Ortved, 2011, ¶ 9), and cautions that "avant-garde is for doing drugs, not catwalking" (¶ 7), and should be avoided.

Get Your Fashion Fix on Route 66, a student-produced fashion show introduced earlier in this chapter, was themed around the play on words of the Nat King Cole song "Get Your Kicks on Route 66." The students were quick to comment that they wished to include the iconic song but didn't want to appear too cliché or have the song clash with the rest of the music mix, so they selected a revamped and remixed version of the song that played during the show's introduction.

During the show, songs were selected to accompany each segment because their sound or lyrics fit either the title or contents of the segment. The segment music progressed chronologically, beginning with remixes of 1960s tunes, and ended with a very futuristic medley. After the show, a mellow playlist was used to ease the audience out of the auditorium after the intense finale segment. The students had the music mixed by a professional. Although each segment lasted only 6 to 7 minutes, the students instructed him to create 12-minute segments in case any one segment went longer than expected. The extra music turned out not to have been needed, but the extra length was a good solution to avoiding potential problems.

Music Playlist

All of the music selections to be used for the show are listed on the **music playlist** (or *soundtrack*) (Fig. 7.20). The title of the song, recording artist, and length of the song are included. The initial list will have more selections than will actually be used. Music edited for the final show will be slightly longer than the length of the show.

Live or Mixed Music

Music may be performed live or mixed for a show. Each form has benefits and drawbacks, which should be evaluated before a style is chosen. **Live music** is performed by musicians during the show (Fig. 7.21). Live music can provide excitement and can be more personal than mixed recorded music, but it requires a budget large enough to pay

MUSIC PLAY LIST

Get Your Fashion Fix on Route 66

Song	Artist
Scene 1: Easy Rider Road (casual wear)	
• *(I Can't Get No) Satisfaction*	The Rolling Stones
• *Satisfaction*	Benny Benassi
• *San Francisco Dreaming*	Benny B vs. Global DJs
• *California Dreaming*	Benny Benassi
• *Purple Haze*	Jimi Hendrix
• *Tighten up*	The Black Keys
Scene 2: Wheelin' Dealin' Drive (business wear)	
• *Black and Gold*	Sam Sparrow
• *Paris*	Friendly Fires (Aerosmith remix)
• *Don't Look Back*	Telepopmusik (John Tejada remix)
• *Add Suv*	Pharral Williams and Uffie (Armand Van Helden Club remix)
Scene 3: Snow Bird Blvd (outerwear)	
• *Black and White*	The Raveonettes
• *Ready for the Floor*	Hot Chip
• *Ghosts on Fire*	Deadmau5 vs. Cut Copy
• *Heads Will Roll (Yeah Yeah Yeah)*	Atrak remix
• *Dance Yourself Clean*	LCD Soundsystem
Scene 4: Tourist Attraction Ave (date wear)	
• *Crave You (featuring Giselle)*	Flight Facilities
• *Valerie (Amy Winehouse)*	Mark Ronson Mix
• *Time Stands Still*	Cut Copy
• *I'm good, I'm gone*	Lykke Li
• *Rill Rill*	Sleigh Bells
Scene 5: Road Warrior Way (student designs)	
• *1940*	The Submarines (Amplive remix)
• *Kids*	Sleigh Bells
• *Supermassive Black Hole*	Muse
• *Odessa*	Caribou
• *Not Exactly*	Deadmua5

Figure 7.20
Music playlist from *Get Your Fashion Fix on Route 66.*

Illustration by Carly Grafstein

professional musicians for their time, both during the show and at rehearsals. Musicians can be limited to a soloist or a small group to minimize expenses, while still providing diversity within the musical style. Although live music may be expensive, the musicians are able to adapt to the show's pace by viewing the actions on the stage. John Galliano once hired the entire string orchestra from the National Opera of Paris to play live in the background at a Christian Dior haute couture show (Limnander, 2001).

Live mixed music is an alternative to live music. A D.J. uses playback equipment to play music live during show segments. A D.J. may be less expensive than hiring musicians, and timing problems associated with prerecorded music are eliminated.

Mixed music is prerecorded music played during the show. This music type is more popular for fashion shows because of its convenience. Costs involve fees to mix the soundtrack professionally or privately by a knowledgeable committee member. It is more cost effective than live music because it has a one-time cost, regardless of the number of rehearsals needed. Mixed music allows for the most trendy and familiar songs of the moment to be used, adding to audience excitement. Using mixed music may add more musical categories, which live musicians may not be able to recreate. Music for each scene may be completely different to provide added theme emphasis.

At the beginning of a scene the music should fade in, starting very softly and gradually accelerating to the volume to be used throughout the scene. Fading out the music is used at the end of a scene to reverse the process, gradually lowering the volume of the music until it is inaudible. Unless a dramatic effect is desired, music should not start out loud, as this may startle the audience. Just

Figure 7.21
Live musicians are often used to ramp up the excitement at Victoria's Secret televised fashion shows.

Courtesy of WWD/Steve Eichner

as variety is required in musical selections, volume of the music should also be varied to avoid monotony. Fading in and out allows for longer or shorter scene transitions as needed by the models or behind-the-scenes staff without making the audience aware of any problems.

Vocal Music

Some thought should be given about whether to use vocal music or instrumental music to accompany a fashion show. In the past, vocals were never used because it was thought that the audience could be distracted by the lyrics. Today, music with vocals is so popular that it is hard to ignore this music when planning a fashion show. Vocals can have a positive or negative influence on a show. If the vocals are popular with the audience they can add familiarity to the show. If vocals are too loud the audience may forget the fashions and become preoccupied with the music.

Copyrighted Music
If a commercial song or CD is used, copyright permission must be obtained. **Copyright permission** is authorization from the owner of the copyright to use copyrighted materials. According to the American Society of Composers, Authors and Publishers (ASCAP, n.d.) the law provides a few limited exemptions for performances associated with teaching activities of a nonprofit educational institution. Purely nonprofit performances may be exempt if (1) there is no direct or indirect commercial purpose; (2) there is no payment to the performers, promoters, or organizers; and (3) there is no admission charge or, if there is a charge, all proceeds after deduction of costs are used exclusively for educational or charitable purposes. However, do not take our word for it. If you have any questions concerning copyrighted music that your team may want to use, read the requirements at http://www.ascap.com and make your own legal inquiries.

To acquire permission to play copyrighted material, it is necessary to determine who owns the copyright. Usually the record producer or the artist holds the copyright. An e-mail or letter to the recording company should be sent asking for specific permission to use selected songs. It is advisable to allow enough lead time to obtain the necessary permissions before the materials are needed. Ask for permissions as far in advance of the show as possible to guarantee that the music chosen can be used at show time. If you do not receive a response to your request for permission, you cannot assume you have been granted the necessary permission. For *Get Your Fashion Fix on Route 66*, Kaci Shields was the stage manager and served in the role of sound designer. Her story is profiled in Notes from the Runway: Copyrights and Permissions.

> "For more than 70 years courts have consistently held that those who operate facilities or sponsor events at which copyrighted music is performed publicly may not avoid their responsibilities under the United States Copyright Law by attempting to shift those responsibilities to their entertainers."
> — American Society of Composers, Authors, and Publishers

SOUND SYSTEM

In addition to preparing music for the fashion show, the music coordinator must arrange to have a sound system and public address system available for the announcer or master of ceremonies. The **public address system** consists of the microphone, amplifiers, and speakers. The **sound system** is the equipment needed to play the music, and may include a computer, turntable, or CD player; and speakers, equalizer, and necessary wiring to allow the sound to be heard at the location (Fig. 7.22). Certain locations will have sound systems available for use. If a sound system is not provided at the site, the components may be rented from local rental companies. The rental fee must be included in the budget.

It is important to test the sound system with the music system before rehearsing

Figure 7.22
The sound system and a qualified technician are critical to the success of a fashion show.

Courtesy of WWD/Steve Wrubel

with the models. Often a technical run-through with lights and sound is necessary to learn cues. If the music or script is inaudible, the audience will lose interest in the show. Annoying hums or shrill microphone whistles will also detract from the fashions presented in the show.

VERBIAGE

Commentary

Historically, most fashion shows had a commentator who narrated descriptions to the audience as they viewed the fashions. However, as we said in Chapter 1, Mary Quant led the trend to eliminate commentary from press and trade shows in the 1960s. In contemporary society, audiences are so attuned to interpreting images visually, and music has grown so important as a communication and entertainment device, that verbal narration has become unnecessary. Music has replaced commentary as the element that puts the audience and models at ease and creates a welcoming environment.

Script

Production shows use a script, treating the show as a theatrical performance and the announcer (or master of ceremonies) as an actor performing specifically scripted narration to introduce the show and welcome guests, transition between scenes, close the show, and thank the audience for attending. The **script** is the printed version of a show narration and includes the words to be spoken and important technical directions. The announcer and production personnel often use the script to set the pace of the fashion show. Starters and models must have knowledge of the script. Models, announcers, and starters must know narrative signals for entrances, called **cues**, to send models out.

Figure 7.23 is an example of a script from a student-produced show, *Runway to Wonderland*. This script is narrated by the character Alice, who appears between segments and creates transitions. The script was developed using the story of *Alice in Wonderland* to engage the audience in the dreamlike atmosphere of the show.

SCRIPT
Runway to Wonderland

Pre-show:

"Alice on Wonderland" soundtrack plays while audience is being seated

Lights should be up for this

2 cards with makeshift trumpets announce the show:

> **Card #1:** "Welcome to RUNWAY TO WONDERLAND! The show will begin in five minutes! Please enjoy the show!"

> **Card #2:** "Please be sure to check out the silent auction! Located to my right (point). This show, as well as our auction, supports the Merchandising Leaders of the Twenty-first Century Scholarship for merchandising students!"

Show Opening: Scene 1: Stuck in a Dream

House lights down, spot on Alice with book in hand

She is wandering around, obviously distracted from her lesson

> **A:** "How doth the little bumble bee improve his shining..."
> "UGH! How can one possibly pay attention to a book with no pictures in it?! In a world of my own, books would have nothing but pictures. Fashion pictures full of bright colors, different textures, and the hottest trends! I feel like that would only happen in a dream...there is no such thing as a Runway to Wonderland.

Alice begins to falls asleep.

Emy with microphone from sound booth talks as if you could hear Alice dream.

> **Emy as A:** Oh no I'm really dreaming about Wonderland. I'm **stuck in this dream**, and the dream is all about sleepwear. There are many different styles in pajamas and robes, and slippers and even fuzzy socks! I'm stuck in this wonderful dream with sleepwear from Target, Old Navy, and PJ Chilcottage. I'm dreaming away about wonderful fashions.

Alice falls asleep under the tree and all lights go down.

Clocks begin to tick tock, growing louder and eventually fading into the backbeat of the music for the segment.

In the darkness, Alice exits.

Scene 2: Chasing the White Rabbit:

Alice reappears as the final models are exiting the stage. She wanders around as if examining new surroundings.

Rabbit scampers across the stage, making some noise.

> **A:** [small gasp] Oh, silly me! It's just a rabbit with a waistcoat [turns head suddenly in surprise in the rabbit's direction] and a watch!

> **R:** Oh, my fur and whiskers! I'm late! I'm late! I'm late!

> **A:** But what could a rabbit possibly be late for? Please, sir!

Figure 7.23
Script example for
Runway to Wonderland.

Illustration by Carly Grafstein

SCRIPT (continued...)
Runway to Wonderland

R: I'm late! I'm late for a very important date! No time to say hello, goodbye! I'm late! I'm late! I'm late!

A: Oh, it must be something awfully important, like a party or something! Oh, Mr. Rabbit!

R: I'm late! I'm late for a very important date! No time to say goodbye, hello! I'm late! I'm late! I'm late!

A: Sir! Where are you going?

R: I'll be fashionably late to see the latest trends in Active and Outdoor Wear. I don't want to miss this segment, **Chasing the White Rabbit**, that has been generously sponsored by Deckers Corporation sporting Ugg footwear and accessories.

A: You'll be late to see hiking boots, ski wear and those trendy puffy vests of the season. You'll be late to see retailers Decker's, Aspen Sports, Mountain Sports, and Babbitt's! Why am I standing here Chasing the White Rabbit?...let's go...

Alice and the rabbit chase each other back and forth, hiding behind sets, and using the runway. They finally run off stage as Alice yells one final "Mr. Rabbit!"

Models enter to complete the active wear section.

Scene 3: An Afternoon with the Caterpillar
Swirling music will set the tone.

Card comes out and starts reading from the book.

Emy reads from sound booth.

Emy as Card: "The Caterpillar and Alice looked at each other for some time in silence: at last the caterpillar addressed her in a languid, sleepy voice."

Have the card pretend to be the caterpillar. Still reading but reading as a character.

Emy as Caterpillar: Whoooooooooooooooooooo are you?

A: I hardly know sir, just at present – at least I know who I was when I got up this morning, but I think I must have been changed several times since then.

C: What do you mean by that? Explain yourself.

A: You see sir, I am caught up in a Runway to Wonderland, fashions are swirling before me. This **Afternoon with a Caterpillar** I am seeing casual wear including fedoras, leggings, cardigan sweaters and more...I'm seeing casual wear from retailers including Gap, Raci Threads, Basement Marketplace and Shoes and Such.

A: Oh, now I'll never find my way out of here!

Card: Well let's try. Follow me...

Alice and the card move off stage...

Figure 7.23 (cont'd)

Illustration by Carly Grafstein

SCRIPT (continued...)
Runway to Wonderland

Scene 4: A Mad Tea Party
Mad Hatter and Alice enter.

MH: Would you like a cup of tea? I'm the Mad Hatter and I'm having a Tea Party. It's my un-birthday, you know!

A: ...Un-birthday...? What's that?

MH: Statistics prove, prove that you've one birthday. That's just one birthday every year. Ah! But there are 364 UN-birthdays, and that is why I'm standing here to cheer!

A: Ah, well then today is my un-birthday too!

MH: It is?! What a small world this is! And speaking of small worlds, WHAT IN THE WORLD ARE YOU WEARING? Have you never heard of fashion? Please, please my dear you can NOT wear that out to a party!

A: Oh no you're right! I can't wear this to a birthday party, not when everyone is so fashionable, dressed in top hats, bow ties, and cocktail dresses!

MH: Why, of course! All these wonderful styles are from Dillard's, Blackhound Gallerie, Basement Marketplace, and Premier Designs Jewelry! But, what are you waiting for, my dear? Let's get dressed up and come alive for After 5! Let's join the Mad Tea Party!

Alice takes Mad Hatter's arm and they both exit.

Scene 5: Meeting the Queen:
Cards start a procession marching down the stage, and off the runway, looping around to line up along the back drop of the stage.

Queen follows and takes her place dead center. Alice runs out, still looking for the rabbit.

Q: Hello, my dear. Tell me, do you play croquet?

A: (to audience) Oh, my! I'm meeting the queen! I hope she's nice! **(To the Queen)** Why, yes, your majesty.

Q: Then let the games begin!

One card from each side comes up the stairs and leans into each other to make a wicket. Alice bumps into the Queen.

Q: That does it. OFF WITH HER HEAD!!

A: Wait a minute! Don't I get a trial first?

Q: Trial?

A: Just a little trial?

Figure 7.23 (cont'd)

Illustration by Carly Grafstein

SCRIPT (continued...)
Runway to Wonderland

Q: Hmmm...well, you are not dressed properly for that sort of occasion. No blazer, no vest, no professional attire at all! TAH!

A: But where would I find an outfit at this time?

Q: Watch this, my dear! Here are some classy examples fit for a **meeting the queen!** These outfits from Dillard's and Carol Anderson will certainly impress anyone. Maybe this will teach you to properly dress for all things business! THEN LET THE TRIAL BEGIN!

Cards, Queen, and Alice exit as models enter in business attire.

Segment ends, lights go black.

Scene 6: A Twisted Dream:
Alice and Rabbit come back on stage.

R: How dare you follow me into my house! You touched my things, you ate my carrots, you drank my tea and you still won't leave me alone.

A: But I knew something interesting was sure to happen.

R: Just go home dear. You look tired.

A: But that's just it! I am stuck in a dream...A Twisted Fantasy! And now, I feel dizzy. I'm seeing original designs from students Tina Gillespie, Cristy Auble, Lexee McLendon, Bloodwash, Karissa Lee Keiter, Ramara Nardone, and Caitlin Holliday.

Emy from sound booth.

Emy: Now introducing student designers Tina Gillespie, Cristy Auble, Lexee McLendon, Bloodwash, Karissa Lee Keiter, Ramara Nardone, and Caitlin Holliday.

As designers are introduced they take a bow on the runway.

All lights and music for effects.

End in a loud BANG and lights down immediately.

End of Show:
Lights come back up for final model procession, and character bows, class members and thank-you's.

Alice comes out onto the stage.

A: You woke me up from such a wonderful dream! I was stuck in the dream about sleepwear. And I was chasing a white rabbit in active and outdoor wear. Then I spent the afternoon with the caterpillar with all the latest casual wear. After that, I went to the mad tea party with the mad hatter himself. And then I had a meeting...with the Queen of Hearts. She critiqued my business attire. Lastly, my head was spinning in a twisted fantasy of student designs. Was it a dream...Or did it really happen?

Figure 7.23 (cont'd)

Illustration by Carly Grafstein

Figure 7.23 (cont'd)

> ### SCRIPT (continued...)
> ### *Runway to Wonderland*
>
> *Model procession begins.*
> *Announcer from sound booth.*
>
> **Announcer:** Please hold your applause until the end.
>
> **Announcer:** We would also like to thank the Northern Arizona Merchandising Association for all of their support along with Prince for DJing, Brandon Neumann for the lighting and video, and Sky Anderson for assistance at the duBois Center and Michael's for their role in the stage production.
>
> **Announcer:** Without the retailers this show would not have been possible, thank you –Mountain Sports, Deckers, Aspen Sports, Babbitt's, Target, Old Navy, PJ Chilcottage, Gap, Raci Threads, Basement Marketplace, Shoes & Such, Dillard's, Blackhound Gallerie, Premier Designs Jewelry and Carol Anderson. Along with the retailers, we would like to thank the student designers for all their hard work and allowing us to show off their talent.
>
> **Announcer:** We would like to say a special thanks to the Merchandising 434 class. Put your hands together for the Model committee lead by Michelle Marchi; Merchandise committee lead by Caitlin Morgan; Promotion committee led by Lexee McLendon; Stage committee led by Megan Austin; budget committee led by Katie Schmalzel; Student director Tiffany Carlyon; Faculty Consultant Dr. Kris Swanson and Faculty Director Professor Judy Everett.

Illustration by Carly Grafstein

Announcer or Master of Ceremonies

The **announcer** (or *master of ceremonies*) is an individual responsible for delivering the script lines during the show. Although the announcer delivers the script, it is the responsibility of show staff to prepare the script. In some instances, a well-known celebrity may be used as an announcer to add newsworthiness to the show, draw a larger audience, and increase enthusiasm. Ryan Seacrest is a popular celebrity that is often called upon to be the master-of-ceremonies at Hollywood events to increase enthusiasm. Shows may choose to use one or two announcers. Working in pairs, announcers often put each other at ease to overcome their nerves and stage fright.

The best announcers are comfortable as public speakers and have the ability to put the audience at ease. The announcer must understand the purpose of the show and use the script to entertain the audience as well as monitor the pace of the show. Like models, announcers should at all times act in a professional manner, spotlighting the fashions, not themselves. Egos are checked at the door. Most important, announcers must rehearse in the same manner that all other show participants rehearse. Sometimes individuals who have had other public speaking roles take for granted their ability to read a script or ad-lib at a moment's notice. However, sometimes these individuals may say or do something that reflects poorly on the show staff, models, and retailers. The ability to rehearse, rehearse, rehearse is the most important quality of a good announcer.

Copyrights and Permissions
Kaci Shields

Courtesy of Kaci Shields

As creative director of *Get Your Fashion Fix on Route 66*, I coordinated staging and the creative elements that set the tone and mood of the entire show. For our production, we borrowed and constructed props, selected and mixed music, and even attempted to incorporate video clips that related to Route 66. Therefore, understanding copyright was a big concern for our team.

When you produce your own fashion show, you will likely want to set your show to music and perhaps incorporate video or other imagery. If you or a member of your team is able to compose your own music or shoot your own video footage, you will not need to worry about copyright laws (unless you wish to copyright your own work). However, if you are like me and my team and do not have the means to orchestrate your own score or record your own video, you will need to use existing art to enhance your show. In this case, you should be aware of copyright protection and laws, public domain, the fair use rule, how to obtain permission, and the consequences that you could face if you do not obtain permission.

Copyright is an exclusive legal right to artistic or intellectual property. It is established by law and enforced in the courts. Copyright applies to all sorts of media including music, movies, television, books, poetry, photographs, software, sculpture, architecture, choreography, and more. To receive copyright protection, a work must exist in tangible form, be creative, and be original. Copyright, however, does not protect the ideas contained within a work, only the work itself. Generally, copyright lasts at least 70 years. A work does not need to contain notice of copyright to be copyrighted. Even if you do not see the word *copyright* or the symbol ©, it is likely that the work is protected by law (Stanford University Libraries, 2010).

Some works, however, are no longer protected by copyright. These items are considered to be in the public domain. Everything published before 1923 is in the public domain and does not require any permission to use. However, you must still be careful with publications you suspect are part of public domain. Sometimes in situations of modifications, compilations, trademarks, or works created or protected outside of the United States, complications can arise (Stanford University Libraries, 2010). Typically, to avoid legal trouble it is best to assume that a work is copyrighted unless you can prove without a doubt that it is not.

If everything is copyrighted, how can you use music or video in your production without creating it yourself? The simplest way is through the fair use rule. If you are taken to court, it is difficult to know exactly what a court will deem fair use. However, the court looks at whether your use competes with sales of the material, how much of the work you have taken, and how you have used the work. If the material is used to educate, inform, criticize, or comment and is not used for profit, then the use is probably fair (Stanford University Libraries, 2010). If you think that your use of protected material is fair, feel that you are not a worthy target for litigation, and are willing to accept the risk of using the material without obtaining permission, you can do so.

There are five basic steps to obtaining permission to use protected material. The first is to determine if permission is actually necessary. Remember, there is a chance that the material in question may be in the public domain. Second, you must identify the owner of the work. This may be an individual, an artist, a corporation, or even multiple owners. Next, you need to determine what rights you need. For example, you may need permission to reproduce, distribute, or modify the work. The fourth step is to contact the owner or owners of the material that you wish to use. At this point, you will negotiate terms and payment. Finally, once you have come to an accord, you should put details of the agreement in writing for both parties (Stanford University Libraries, 2010).

When we began work on *Get Your Fashion Fix on Route 66*, we intended to introduce each segment of the fashion show with a 1- to 2-minute video clip from films shot on Route 66 and in Route 66 destinations. These films included *Easy Rider* (1969), *Meet Me in St. Louis* (1944), *Casablanca* (1942), *Sixteen Candles* (1984), and *Rebel without a Cause* (1955). Despite the fact that all the proceeds would benefit a scholarship, because we were going to charge admission to our fashion show we determined that we should formally request permission to broadcast these clips during the production.

After much research, I was able to track down the studios that currently have rights to each of these five films. Some of the films had been sold several times, or their original distributor had merged with another company. After finding the owners of the movies, I located contact information for their clips and stills licensing departments. I wrote a well-composed e-mail to each studio, requesting permission to use a brief clip of the film. Sony's Columbia Tri-Star replied quickly and in the affirmative that we could use a 2-minute clip of *Easy Rider* without payment. This was promising. However, Universal responded next, quoting us $500 to $1,000 to use a 1- to 2-minute clip from *Sixteen Candles*.

Because *Get Your Fashion Fix on Route 66* was a not-for-profit college production, we clearly could not afford to pay for licensing rights to use film clips. We consulted with FBI agents in Phoenix who told us that if we were caught showing protected film clips without permission at our fashion show, it was likely that the harshest punishment we would be dealt was an order to cease and desist playing the clips. However, if this was not the case, we could be sued for lots of money.

We decided not to risk the use of protected material and went another route, creating scene titles such as "Road Warrior Way" for student designs to introduce the scenes of our *Route 66* fashion show. If you doubt that your use of copyrighted material is fair use, you should also consider seeking permission or finding another way to enhance your fashion show!

Kaci Shields graduated summa cum laude with a B.S. degree in merchandising from Northern Arizona University. She was the stage manager and creative director for *Get Your Fashion Fix on Route 66*. In addition to her academic work, Kaci was president of Sigma Alpha Iota, an international music fraternity for women. She has also worked as an assistant sales manager and buyer in the bridal industry.

The Framework and Sound Check—A Recap

- Staging is the process or manner of putting on a performance on a stage.
- The stage is a raised floor or platform on which theatrical productions are presented. The runway is an extension of the stage or a freestanding unit that normally projects into the audience.
- The layout is a schematic plan or arrangement of the area.
- Runways vary in height, size, and shape based on the physical layout of the room and audience visibility, with the most common configurations being the T, I, X, H, Y, U, and Z shapes.
- The dressing area is a room or area designated for changing clothes, applying makeup, and styling hair.
- The purpose of the background is to enhance the merchandise, with either stark settings emphasizing the garments or dramatic backdrops emphasizing the theme.
- Props are supports used to highlight the garments being shown.
- The audience may be seated in a theater pattern or at tables.
- Lighting is the method and/or equipment used to provide illumination.
- Music is an essential element in fashion shows.
- The sound designer is responsible for selecting music, obtaining permissions, mixing music, and preparing the sound system at the show venue.
- Music mix is the combination of different musical styles to create a specific mood.
- All of the music selections to be used for the show are listed on the music playlist or soundtrack.
- Live music can provide excitement and adds personal touch
- Mixed music is prerecorded music played during a show.
- Copyright permission is authorization from the owner of the copyright to use copyrighted materials.
- The public address system consists of the microphone, amplifiers, and speakers.
- The sound system consists of a computer, turntable, or CD player; speakers; equalizer; and the necessary wiring to allow the sound to be heard at the location.
- Music has replaced commentary as the element that puts the audience and models at ease and creates a welcoming environment.
- The script is the printed version of a show narration and includes the words to be spoken and often any important technical directions.
- The announcer is an individual responsible for delivering the script during the show.

Key Fashion Show Terms

announcer	flats
background	layout
copyright permission	lighting
cues	live mixed music
dressing area	live music

mixed music	script
music	sound designer
music mix	sound system
music playlist	stage
props	staging
public address system	table seating
runway	theater seating

Questions for Discussion

1. Describe a simple staged fashion show. What kinds of fashion shows require simple staging? Describe an elaborately staged fashion show. What types of fashion shows require elaborate staging?
2. Why is it important to have the dressing area close to the staging area?
3. What is the purpose of using props in a fashion show?
4. Discuss the pros and cons of theater seating. Discuss the pros and cons of table seating.
5. Discuss the differences between live music, mixed music, and live mixed music.
6. What does a master of ceremonies contribute to a fashion show?
7. What is the purpose of a fashion show script?

Fashion Show Activities

1. Use YouTube or other media websites to view the spectacular shows of the current and past seasons. Specifically, watch a show from the current season and a show from a past season. Write up a two-page report comparing and contrasting the two shows. Be prepared to discuss your report.
2. Break into teams of four or five members. Each team should brainstorm a fashion show theme. From that theme brainstorm three different stage options, from simple to elaborate. For each staging option, plan and discuss the following:
   - Runway configuration: include where models would enter and exit, the path they would take, and where they would stop and pivot for the audience
   - Audience seating
   - Background
   - Props
   - Lighting
   - Music

The Capstone Project

The stage committee should schedule visits to potential venues on campus or in your community. Take specific notes about the opportunities that each venue provides, including costs, date availability, audience seating, potential backgrounds, runway configurations, dressing areas, and lighting equipment. Discuss the possibilities among the team members and then

CD-ROM

present your top three choices to the class. Determine which venue is best for your show and proceed through the process to secure the location. Once a contract has been signed, start brainstorming about the show. Discuss runway configurations, backdrops, props, music, and lighting. Determine who will take charge of the various parts. Discuss what elements should be included in the script, including the model and merchandise committees as necessary. Start writing the script. Hold auditions for the announcer(s). Samples of all forms, including contracts, layouts, receipts for building supplies, and any other forms deemed necessary, should be included in this assignment. Please refer to the CD-ROM for tools that may assist you with this section of the fashion show planning process.

References

American Society of Composers, Authors and Publishers [ASCAP]. (n.d.). *Using copyrighted music*. Retrieved from http://www.ascap.com

Circular thinking. (2008, January 23). *Women's Wear Daily*, p. 4.

Diehl, M. (1976). *How to produce a fashion show*. New York, NY: Fairchild Books.

Ever since Lagerfeld put a parrot on the runway, designers have loved stunts. (2008, April 18). *New York Magazine*. Retrieved from http://nymag.com

Foley, B. (2012, July 3). A new master of the house. *Women's Wear Daily*, pp. 1, 4.

Limnander, A. (2001, July 7). Style.com: Fall 2001 haute couture—Christian Dior. Retrieved from http://www.style.com

Medina, M. (2012, March 8). A new "idol": Tommy Hilfiger. *Women's Wear Daily*, pp. 4, 13.

Ortved, J. (2011, September 15). Music to strut the collection by. *The New York Times*. Retrieved from http://www.nytimes.com

Stanford University Libraries. (2010). *Copyright and fair use*. Retrieved from http://fairuse.stanford.edu

Trebay, G. (2011, March 4). Not paying the piper, but calling the tune. *The New York Times*. Retrieved from http://www.nytimes.com

Vilaseca, E. (2010). *Runway uncovered: The making of a fashion show*. Barcelona, Spain: Promopress.

8

CHAPTER EIGHT
The Show

AFTER READING THIS CHAPTER, YOU SHOULD BE ABLE TO DISCUSS:

- The purpose and types of rehearsals.

- Developing a creative opening, presenting the show, and ending with a memorable finale.

- The importance of professionalism in keeping the event fun and stress free.

- Why a show might have to be cancelled and ways to do it.

- The evaluation process, including assessing personnel, theme and title, location, audience, budget, promotion, merchandise, models, music, staging, and script.

Karl Lagerfeld told his models, "It is Coco Rock, not rococo," according to Miles Socha (2012, p. 4). The 2012 *Chanel Resort Collection* fashion show was held in the gardens of Versailles; 400 guests were in attendance. The clothes were given a nod to Marie Antoinette with a 21st-century twist. Mr. Lagerfeld told models to put their hands in their pockets to avoid any resemblance to a historical look. It wasn't supposed to be 18th century—it was to be very modern. Figure 8.1 shows a model with her hands in her pockets, stomping down the gravel pathway to M.I.A.'s music—"Live fast, die young, bad girls do it well."

Models, designers, celebrities who will sit in the front row, stylists, hair and makeup artists, boyfriends, girlfriends, journalists, tailors, dressers, photographers, bloggers, and the public relations staff are all backstage with the clothes before any fashion show starts. It is organized chaos—or just chaos—behind the scene on the show day. This chapter profiles the days leading up to and presenting the show and how the show is evaluated.

REHEARSING

The **rehearsal** is a practice performance, held in private, in preparation for a public performance (Fig. 8.2). The fashion show director takes this opportunity to solve any problems prior to the public presentation of the show to the audience. The rehearsal may be a simple run-through or a full dress rehearsal. The **run-through** is a rehearsal of the show sequences and involves showing models the choreography. At this stage, the models wear casual clothing similar to items worn to a casting. A **dress rehearsal** consists of a walk-through with complete garment changes. A **full dress rehearsal** is held to check all theatrical aspects of the show including timing, music, garment changes, and all other technical aspects.

The need for a rehearsal is dependent upon the type of show being produced and whether professional or amateur models are being used. When to hold the rehearsal is also dependent on the type of show, availability of the venue, and the number of staff people involved. A rehearsal may take place 1 week prior to the show, the day before the show, or the day of the show. An elaborate production show may need a rehearsal far ahead of time. A show set in a retail department store may be rehearsed immediately prior to show time.

Figure 8.1
Karl Lagerfeld gives Marie Antoinette a 21st-century makeover.

Courtesy of WWD/Giovanni Giannoni

(a)

Courtesy of Christopher C. Everett

(b)

Courtesy of Christopher C. Everett

Figure 8.2 (a–d)
The rehearsal is an opportunity for models and production staff to polish lineup and choreography, in addition to checking the timing of the show with the music and lighting. (*Figure continues on following page.*)

(c)

Courtesy of Christopher C. Everett

Figure 8.2 (cont'd)

(d)

Courtesy of Christopher C. Everett

During fashion week shows, models are often booked for several shows each day. In this case, there is only enough time to give simple verbal directions prior to the start of the show.

A full dress rehearsal is ideal to check every aspect of the show from lighting and music to overall fashion show coordination. This will show the most efficient traffic flow from the dressing area to the stage. Another important reason to hold a dress rehearsal is to determine show length. The fashion show director should record the actual time of the full dress rehearsal. Knowing how long the dress rehearsal takes will help coordinators set the pace and assist models to understand cues.

A tentative lineup is created as the fittings take place. After the rehearsal, any problems with what each model is wearing or the order in which garments are presented on the runway are ironed out and the final lineup is established. Copies of the final lineup are given to the announcer or master of ceremonies, the stage manager, music and lighting technicians, and the show director, and are also made available in the dressing room for the models, dressers, and starters. The final lineup will help everyone to know what is expected and when to expect it.

Rehearsal Preparation

There are many considerations that must take place prior to the dress rehearsal. First, all the spaces, including dressing areas, storage areas, and restrooms, must be reserved. Then the stage and runway are set up. The cost for using the venue for a rehearsal is included in the budget. Because there are many costs involved in holding a rehearsal,

it is necessary to keep rehearsals as short as possible.

The show director should inform all personnel of the designated rehearsal time and when they should arrive. Figure 8.3 is an example of a show day schedule distributed to all participants as they get ready for rehearsals and the show. Music technicians, stage personnel, and lighting personnel may need to arrive earlier to have the stage set and ready when the models arrive.

Clothing and accessories should be organized and labeled in the dressing room before models arrive. The merchandise committee organizes clothing according to each model, not according to scene. All the elements of each outfit, including accessories, should be pulled together for each model and placed on clothing racks in the order they will be worn by each model. Models and dressers can refer to the final lineup to verify the order and placement in the lineup.

Because the first walk-through involves the models wearing their own clothes, the choreographer gives the models directions regarding entrances, groupings, turns, and exits (Fig. 8.4). If the show involves amateur models, the choreographer may also give some additional modeling tips and techniques, along with encouragement. This first walk-through is done with the benefit of music and lighting.

Dressers

The **dressers** are the individuals who help the models change in the dressing room. They play an extremely important behind-the-scenes role, limiting the chaos in the dressing room. Dressers for professional shows are often fashion students or interns looking for

Get Your Fashion Fix on Route 66
Schedule for November 18, 19, & 20

Times and activities most likely will change as the days progress. Please check with your coordinators and directors throughout the day!

November 18—Thursday
    Merchandise committee—pick up garments and organize clothing by model

November 19—Friday
8:30 AM Fashion show production class members at Prochnow Auditorium
    Turn in ticket money to budget committee
    Dressers and merchandisers organize dressing rooms
    Final view of stage
    Test music
    Tickets available for sale until 5 pm

9:30 AM Models arrive

10:00AM–
12:00 PM Run-through to clarify choreography

12:15–
1:15 PM Break for lunch backstage

1:30–
3:30 PM Full dress rehearsal

4 PM Kid models arrive for run-through

12- 6 PM Hair and makeup

5:30 PM Doors open for silent auction

7 PM Showtime

8:30 PM Cast and crew dinner at Taverna

November 20—Saturday
9:00AM Models arrive for hair and makeup

11:30 AM Doors open for silent auction

1:00 PM Show time

3:00 PM Stage strike
    All members of the class must stay until the auditorium is returned to its original condition, clothing and props organized to return to stores/designers.

Figure 8.3
A show day schedule keeps models, fashion show staff, and venue professionals aware of what, where, and when things need to be done to make the show go smoothly.

Illustration by Carly Grafstein

Figure 8.4
The choreographer reviews the walk for the first scene of the show.

experience in fashion show production or they may be modeling agency staff. No matter how big or small the show, dressers make the show run smoothly (Fig. 8.5).

Ideally, each model should have a separate dressing area, which is clearly identified, and a personal dresser. A good dresser can handle more than one model if the changes are not back-to-back and the models are spaced far enough apart in the dressing room. The dresser must be completely familiar with the lineup. Both the dresser and the model must know the order of the garment presentation—exactly what outfit comes first, second, third, and so forth.

The model's responsibility for her outfits is discussed in Chapter 6, but the dresser is also responsible for getting the clothes ready to be worn. Zippers are unzipped, buttons are unbuttoned, and tags are hidden. Speed

in dressing is essential and wasted motions should be avoided. The dresser may wish to make special notes for accessories and/or props to be carried on the individual model lineup sheet. A sash, scarf, or pin may need to be worn in a certain manner. Simple written directions help to keep the appearance just as it was planned by the fashion stylist.

Protecting garments is essential. Horror stories about entire racks of clothes stained by food or beverages circulate around fashion offices. Although catastrophes of this sort are rare, the dressers need to be concerned with protecting the clothes. Placing a sheet on the floor where the model changes and hanging garments up immediately after they are worn will help to keep the clothes fresh and in good condition. Using a scarf over the model's face will protect clothes from being stained by makeup.

(a)

Courtesy of Christopher C. Everett

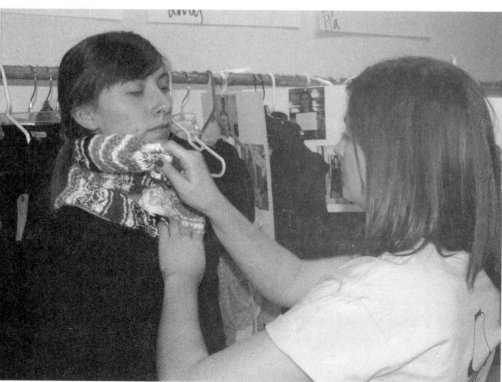

Figure 8.5 (a–c)
Dressers help the models
get ready for the show
and make changes
quickly.

(b)

Courtesy of Christopher C. Everett

(c)

Courtesy of Philadelphia University

Figure 8.5 (cont'd)

Starters

The **starter** (*cue* person) is responsible for cueing the models onto the stage in the correct order at the right time using the final lineup (Fig. 8.6). The starter should work closely with the fashion show director at the dress rehearsal and during the show. Cues, such as a D.J. starting a specific song, someone making an announcement to silence phones, or a technician dimming the lights, are established to let the starter know when to send models onto the runway. During the rehearsal, the starter will make necessary written notes that she will refer to during the show. The starter will be out of sight of the audience, but will be able to signal the director if a model misses a cue in the lineup. The starter will know in advance how fast the models' changes should take and have the authority to replace a model if he or she is not ready. The starter is also responsible for the final inspection of the models as they go on stage. Tags should be out of sight, hair and makeup should be appropriate, and undergarments concealed.

At minimum, one starter should be used. Depending on the distance between the dressing area and the stage, two or three assistants can be used—at the stage, at the dressing area, and any area in between. Communication between the stage and the dressing area is vital. Most fashion show starters will have headsets to communicate between all necessary backstage personnel.

The rehearsal often appears very rough. Although participants may feel discouraged at this point, the rehearsal points out problems that even the most experienced staff may not have anticipated. The staff should take this opportunity to rearrange the

Figure 8.6
The starter gives a model the cue to start walking down the runway.

Veer/Ocean Photography

sequence of models, replace merchandise, finalize timing, or solve any other problems that might surface during the rehearsal. The successful presentation of the show is dependent on working out the last-minute details during the rehearsal, and this helps to build confidence for the show personnel after the rehearsal.

PREPARING BACKSTAGE

The stylist or merchandise committee members should set up the dressing area. Mirrors should be available. Racks of clothing organized by model should arrive in the dressing area at least 2 hours prior to the show. The people moving the clothing should be given specific directions concerning the delivery location. Although this may seem obvious, there are stories of clothing being delivered to the wrong location.

Final preparation of the garments should include pressing, making sure tags are hidden, and taping soles of shoes to prevent models from slipping. The models should arrive at the designated time, well before the start of the show, to have makeup applied and hair styled before putting on their first outfit. Figure 8.7 shows models getting hair styled and makeup applied before the show starts. (See also Color Plates 14 and 15.)

The script is placed at the speaker's podium. The announcer should be ready, checking the sound system and script for any last-minute changes at least 30 minutes before the show.

The floor plan should be consulted to be sure that the stage, runway, and seats are ready. Many large charity shows and fashion week events require elaborate seating charts, developed in the planning stages, rather than

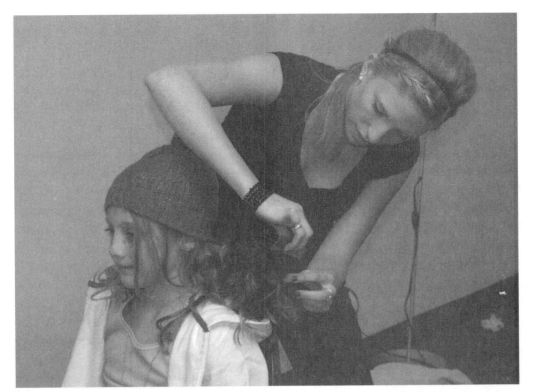

(a)

Courtesy of Christopher C. Everett

(b)

Courtesy of Christopher C. Everett

Figures 8.7 (a–c)
Models get into hair
and makeup backstage
before the show starts.
*(Figure continues on
following page.)*

Figure 8.7 (cont'd)

(c)

Courtesy of Philadelphia University

Figure 8.8
A staff member places reserved signs and programs on the fashion show seats before the audience arrives.

©Masterfile

"at large" seating. Seating charts show where celebrities, editors, retailers, and front-row ticket holders should be seated. Names of these people are placed on the seats. Remember the 2 a.m. phone call telling an audience member her seat assignment from Chapter 1!

Skirting or trim on the runway should be examined. Stage sets or props should be in place. Cues should be reviewed with the starter. Lighting should also be tested and lighting cues should be reexamined. The sound system should be tested for volume and potential feedback noises before the audience starts to arrive. The microphone should be tested at the same time that the sound system is checked.

Programs are placed on the chairs (Fig. 8.8) or tables, or left with the ushers to hand out

Courtesy of Christopher C. Everett

Figure 8.9
A silent auction may feature items from donors or creative items. "Alice" places a bid on a flower pot decorated at the silent auction for *Runway to Wonderland.*

as audience members arrive. If hostesses or ushers are to be used, they are given any specific instructions. They should be ready at least 20 minutes before guests arrive.

Any door prizes or giveaways should be displayed. If a drawing for a gift is to take place, the procedure for tickets should be in place. A designated person should be responsible for following through with this activity. If a silent auction (Fig. 8.9) is planned, it should be set up at least 30 minutes before the audience starts to arrive.

Special introductions or verbal acknowledgments should be written in advance and rehearsed prior to the audience's arrival. The show director or charity chair may wish to have everyone who took part in the show stand for applause at the end of the show. Show staff should be informed about this in advance and rehearsed.

If refreshments and food service are to be included as hospitality, it should be in place,

away from the stage or runway. The audience should not be confused by the food service. Signage and programs should make the audience aware of the time that refreshments are to be served, prior to or after the show.

Prior to the arrival of the audience, last-minute details are wrapped up. These checks will help to ensure a smooth, professional presentation. After all the hours of preparation the production is ready to show to the audience.

PRESENTING THE FASHION SHOW

It's time to start the show. The opening moments of the show are critical. First impressions will influence the show's success or failure. All of the advance planning pays off with a show, featuring beautiful clothes on attractive models, that is well paced with appropriate stage settings, lighting, and music. In Figure 8.10, the best

Figure 8.10 (a–c)
University of Philadelphia student designers Thomas De Jesus **(a)**, Rachel Wendling **(b)**, and Gretchen Harris **(c)** present their collections in a gala fashion show staged at Philadelphia's Academy of Music.

student designers from Philadelphia University are showcased in a fashion show to a wide-ranging audience of students, family, faculty, trustees, professional designers, and fashion and apparel industry leaders.

Estel Vilaseca shares the excitement on the day of the show, "The big day has arrived and the most important details are already decided. Now all that is needed is to supervise, help and let nature take its course."

It is important to be ready to start the show on time. A 5-minute delay is not disastrous, but too many shows, both professional and amateur, start as long as 30 minutes or more late. If the announcer comes on stage at the appointed time and says the show will start in 15 minutes, the organization looks disorganized and unprofessional and the audience may become restless.

Signals to the technical staff are necessary if there are any problems. If music is too loud or soft, a signal to change volume is sent. The spotlights may be blinding the models or someone in the audience. Even though these points were considered during rehearsal, some conditions may not have been obvious and need to be corrected when the show is under way. A wireless communication system or phone texting system may be required for a fashion show using complex music, lighting, and staging. In this case the communication system is used to link the fashion show director, cue personnel, and dressers with the technical staff.

The show producers need to be aware of audience reaction throughout the show's production. Audience reaction will reveal technical problems in lighting, sound, and music that were not detected earlier. Adjustments in music and public address system volume or in lighting direction may be made to make the audience more comfortable. Flexibility is important. Everyone must be able to adjust to changing conditions.

CLOSING THE SHOW

The finale should provide a visual closing to the show. Music and lighting, combined with the most dramatic clothing, should signal the end of a well-produced fashion show. Betsey Johnson always ends her shows with an energetic cartwheel, as illustrated in Figure 8.11. The show may end with closing remarks by the director or by bringing the

Courtesy of WWD/Giovanni Giannoni

Figure 8.11
Betsey Johnson shows her excitement by doing a cartwheel on the runway at the end of her show.

designer onto the runway for recognition. A charity show may close with acknowledgments (see Color Plate 16). The show director or master of ceremonies may draw the winning tickets for door prizes while the audience watches. All this creates excitement at the end of the show. If refreshments are planned after the show, the audience will be invited to share food or be served.

STRIKING THE SHOW

A misconception held by many people involved in fashion shows is that when the curtain goes down, the show is finished and their responsibilities have been fulfilled. People with this delusion have not yet realized that cleanup and stage strike must occur. **Stage strike**, a term taken from the theater, refers to striking, or physically disassembling, the set. Strike takes place at the close of all fashion shows (Fig. 8.12).

An in-store strike includes taking down the stage, replacing all props and equipment in the appropriate locations, and leaving the location as it was found. In addition to these activities, a remote show will require transporting the garments and accessories back to the selling location.

Retail Shows

Shows within a retail department should be disassembled immediately after the show. Runways should be returned to storage. Backdrops must come down to be stored or disposed of, and chairs and tables should be removed from the selling floor. Retailers frequently have a prop room where visual display equipment, including props and runways, can be stored. Sales areas should be returned to their normal arrangement to accommodate customers eager to try on the garments they have just seen. Crowded sales racks must be spaced properly to allow customers to review the merchandise. Safety is also a concern within a retail department. With customers wanting to enter the sales area soon after the show, it is important to

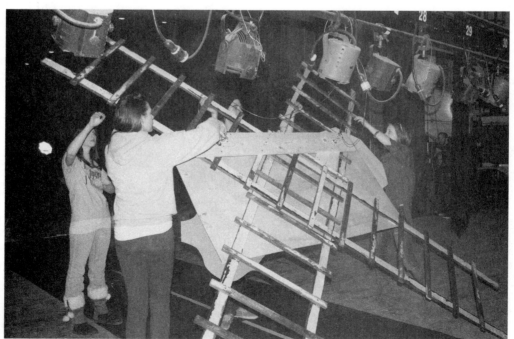

Figure 8.12
Stage committee disassembles the set after a show.

Courtesy of Christopher C. Everett

remove props and electrical footage (cords, plugs, and equipment used for the sound system and lights) and secure the area against hazards as quickly as possible after the show.

Auditorium Shows

If the show is executed at any location other than a retail department, arrangements were made with the venue personnel and the stage manager prior to the show. The use of lighting, sound equipment, and public address systems, and the return of these items, were discussed at the time of rental. Stacking and returning chairs used for audience seating, hostess tables, and skirting for the tables and stage take place as part of stage strike.

Fashion shows presented in auditoriums or other locations with permanent stages have different requirements during stage strike. Mobile stages, orchestra pit covers, curtains, podiums, lights, and all permanent props of the stage area must be replaced in the position where they were located when show personnel arrived on the site. Sound barriers, often used in auditoriums to bring the action on stage closer to the audience, must be returned to the proper location off stage. Sound barriers are fragile and expensive and should always be moved by stagehands familiar with them. Curtains and orchestra pit covers also require special help from knowledgeable stage crew to replace them after the show.

If technical assistance is required to dismantle the sound or lighting systems, the professional technicians used during the show should be responsible for the task. This responsibility was discussed with these individuals at the onset of employment and compensation budgeted, with all parties in agreement. Rented equipment should be returned as soon as possible after the show to avoid added expenses.

The venue of the show should be thoroughly cleaned and left in the order in which it was found unless custodial services were contracted in advance. Dressing areas, restrooms, or offices should be left in their original state. Programs or giveaways not taken by the audience should be gathered. Pins, tape, tags, and so forth should be collected by show personnel and not left for venue personnel to clean up. All trash should be disposed of properly. The show staff is responsible and must remain at the location until all equipment and garments have been removed. A final check should be completed to make sure no item was left behind.

Personnel

Stage strike should include as many people as possible to make the task easier for everyone. Models and others who are paid hourly rates are excused to avoid added costs, but all volunteer staff should help. Often in the frenzy of a successful show, many individuals leave the show to celebrate, leaving the show director to strike alone. It should be stressed in the planning stages of the show that all individuals will participate in stage strike. Good show directors turn the task into a fun atmosphere by providing refreshments to an exhausted staff to entice the volunteer crew to follow through.

Merchandise Return

Garments and accessories should be moved from the show location and returned to the retailers as quickly as possible after the show. The retailers need time to prepare the merchandise for customers. If the show is performed during the daytime, clothing and accessories may be returned before the business day is over. If the show is a night performance, the clothing and accessories may have to be stored at a secure location until the following morning, when they can be returned.

Garments should be returned to the retailers in the condition they were borrowed, ready for sale. They should be pressed or steamed, examined for soil or damage, and hangtags should be replaced. Arrangements for soiled or damaged garments and accessories were prearranged between the merchandise coordinator and the retailer in advance of the show.

Garments, upon arrival back to the retail store, should be inventoried by both the retailer and a member of the merchandise committee so that both parties are aware of soiled or damaged merchandise. The inventory should be completed and the merchandise loan record signed off by the store representative and the show representative. In situations where cleaning is required, the merchandise coordinator should request from the retailer the name of the preferred dry cleaner. If repairs are needed, the same policy should be implemented with the retailer's choice of an alterations' service. It is the responsibility of the fashion show personnel to compensate the retailer for any cleaning or repair that needs to be performed. These expenses were included in the budget.

Accessories should also be returned in saleable condition. Accessories—including bracelets, necklaces, pins, hair accessories, and scarves—should be replaced in the packaging (cards, boxes, bags, tissue, etc.) in the way they were borrowed. Some states have health regulations prohibiting the sale of earrings that have been worn. For this reason, models may need to provide their own earrings or perhaps not wear any. The tape applied to shoes should be removed before they are returned.

BEING PROFESSIONAL

Professionalism is acting in a manner accepted by the occupation. Simply acting in a manner that respects other people's feelings and the merchandise being shown is considered professional. Planning and executing a fashion show is often done on a tight schedule. Murphy's Law

("whatever can go wrong will go wrong") seems appropriate. Tempers often flare and personality conflicts are often magnified during this stressful time. All participants must keep in mind the goal—a coordinated, well-executed, entertaining fashion show.

The director of the fashion show must be able to resolve problems diplomatically during the planning process and the production. One important attribute of the fashion show director is tact—the ability to do or say the right thing while not offending anyone.

Flexibility, the ability to adjust to change, is also necessary for a successful fashion show. Last-minute changes in the merchandise, models forgetting an accessory or prop, garments being soiled or damaged, and misplaced music are all a part of fashion show production. Flexibility and a sense of humor help the crew to get through all of the little problems.

Positive working relationships between people involved in fashion show production must be maintained. In a small town, many student and charitable groups compete with each other to borrow merchandise from local retailers. Retailers will continue to allow outside groups to use their merchandise for fashion shows if the following occur:

- The merchandisers and models act professionally at in-store fittings.
- The merchandise is kept in a clean, ready-to-sell condition upon return to the store.
- The merchandise is returned in a timely manner.

A fashion show is just like any theatrical or musical presentation. The audience should not be aware of behind-the-scenes operations. Backstage should be quiet and efficient in its operation. Members of the audience are likely to enjoy the show, buy merchandise, and return to future shows if the quality of the production is at a professional level.

In Notes from the Runway: Nothing Can Beat the Feeling of Watching Fashion Unfold!, Emilee Dunn looks back at her experience as a fashion show student director and shares how her three significant lessons—communication, preparation, and quality—shaped her experiences as a student and as a professional in the fashion industry.

CANCELING A SHOW

It is extremely rare to cancel a fashion show, but certain situations call for this action. Severe weather that makes travel for the audience and staff hazardous is the most likely reason to cancel a show. Announcements should be made through local broadcast media.

Show planners may be hesitant to cancel a program after they have completed so much work putting the show together. Regardless, the safety and well-being of the audience and staff must be considered. News releases and e-mails should be sent and phone calls made as quickly as possible to inform participants and audience members of the cancellation. For example, the local radio and television stations should be e-mailed or called as soon as the decision to cancel the show is made. An alternative date may be arranged if a show is postponed. If this is not possible, refunds must be given to ticket holders, and somehow expenses must be covered by other means.

In an unprecedented move, New York Fashion Week shows were cancelled in September 2001 (Horyn, 2001). Immediately after the horrific destruction of the World Trade Center, normal activities in New York City came to a halt (Fig. 8.13). The impact of this unbelievable incident and cancellation of fashion week led to informal presentations by designers such as Calvin Klein, Michael Kors, and Narciso Rodriguez, which were attended by retailers and members of the press. The British Fashion Council in London, the Chambre Syndicale in Paris, and the Camera Nazionale della Moda in

Figure 8.13
On September 11, 2001, New York Fashion Week shows were abruptly cancelled after the World Trade Center was attacked. The American flag was quickly hoisted in front of the tents.

Milan decided to proceed as normal, despite a decidedly somber international mood.

WRAPPING UP

Thank you notes should be written as soon as possible after the show. Retailers who loaned merchandise or accessories should be thanked along with other businesses or individuals, including the amateur models, who provided services or time to the show production. Celebrities or personalities who helped promote the show should also be thanked in writing. Professional models and paid technicians will not expect a thank you note. If the show used volunteers or was an exceptional success, a written message of appreciation is a nice gesture on the part of the show staff. Figure 8.14 shows a sample thank-you note.

EVALUATING

Evaluation is an important but often overlooked aspect of fashion show production. Each element of the show (including participants, theme and title, venue, audience, budget, promotion, merchandise, models, music, staging, and script) should be reviewed. Any recommendations for future shows should be included.

The Evaluation Process

The fashion show is not complete until personnel involved in the production come together one last time to evaluate the performance. **Evaluation** is an appraisal of the performance, people, places, and processes. Although evaluation should be ongoing through the entire development of the show, it is given special emphasis at the conclusion of the event. Evaluation may seem anticlimactic after the excitement of the show but

> "I never believe what people tell me. . . . When one finishes, the next one begins."
>
> —Mark Jacobs, fashion designer

it can provide critical information for the procedures and strategies of future shows.

Evaluation takes place on several levels. On one level, the reaction of the audience must be analyzed. On another level, designers, retailers, manufacturers, and suppliers must evaluate the show based on sales or services generated. And on yet another level, fashion show coordinators and committee members must evaluate each team's contributions as well as each team member's contributions. Insight into how traditional media (journalists trained in criticism) and new media analysts (bloggers) view the show are also sources of evaluation.

When to Evaluate

The best time to complete the evaluation process is immediately following the show, when successes and problems are fresh in everyone's mind. The fashion office of a retail store may pull staff together the following day. A community group may set a meeting within a week of the production, and students generally evaluate the show at the next class meeting or during a final exam.

Everyone who participated in the show production should complete an evaluation. The process should be headed by the show director and all committee coordinators, models, technicians, suppliers, retailers, and anyone else involved should be asked for input in the evaluation process. In addition, employees who viewed the show from the audience or the sidelines should be invited to participate in the evaluation process. An outside observer can provide a perspective that may not have been touched on by personnel closely involved in the production. If the show was sponsored by a charitable organization, members of the

**NORTHERN
ARIZONA
UNIVERSITY**

COLLEGE OF SOCIAL AND BEHAVIORAL SCIENCES
School of Communication
Box 5619 Flagstaff, AZ 86011-5619
928-523-2232

November 28, 2010

Stacie Avelar
Threadz
201 Aspen Street
Flagstaff, AZ 86001

Dear Ms. Avelar:

The Fashion Show Production (MER 434) class produced its fashion show, *Get Your Fashion Fix on Route 66,* on November 19 & 20, 2010. We don't know how we could have done it without you. Your merchandise was perfect for our target audience. Your continued support is greatly appreciated.

Our projects are entirely student-developed in order to raise money for the *Merchandising Leaders of the 21st Century Scholarship* fund at NAU. This show gives students an opportunity to gain experience in fashion show production yet also helps them give back to hard-working peers. All of the money raised from the event goes directly towards the scholarship. This fund benefits many merchandising students who have demonstrated their commitment to academic work.

We know that you are aware of the challenges and rewards that come from doing our fashion show. We hope to work with you again in the future. Thanks for helping us make this show successful.

Sincerely,

Abbei Brown
Merchandise Coordinator
acb@nau.edu

Figure 8.14
Thank-you notes should be sent as soon as the fashion show is over.

group should be asked for their input as well. In rare cases, an outside firm may be hired to evaluate a show. Using an outside firm to evaluate a show is costly. However, it reduces the workload burden on staff and removes prejudices that might affect the process.

Evaluation Form

An **evaluation form** is a document with blanks provided for the insertion of details or information. An evaluation form should be developed and used to summarize the evaluation process. Figure 8.15 provides an example of a simple evaluation form that lists all components of the show on one form for a general summary. Another approach may be to develop a more detailed evaluation form for a specific show component, such as models.

After the evaluation of the show has been completed, the forms should be filed with other documentation regarding the planning and presentation of the show—show budget and actual expenses, planning, fitting and model lineup sheets, and correspondence—and kept on file for reference.

Evaluation Based on Goals

Evaluation should begin with a review of the goals of the show. In Chapter 2, we outline the various reasons retailers produce a fashion show. These include selling merchandise, presenting fashion trend information, introducing

---

EVALUATION FORM

Type of Show

Participants

Theme/Title

Audience

Show Budget (attach Final Budget)

Summary of Publicity and Advertising

Merchandise

Models

Commentary & Commentator

Notes for Improvement

Figure 8.15
A general evaluation form gives the fashion show staff an outline for its post-show report.

Illustration by Carly Grafstein

new lines, building store traffic, establishing fashion authority, offering goodwill to the community, or providing training for employees. Frequently, the success of a fashion show is tied directly to generated sales. How much of the merchandise presented was actually sold within a specific period of time? Sales may be encouraged in general themes or categories of merchandise. Customers may also be stimulated by color trends or new classifications of goods similar to ones introduced in the show.

The presentation of fashion information or trends is also an important goal of fashion show production. In the evaluation, processing audience reaction is a way to identify if the audience successfully recognized the new trends. Did they clap or offer other appropriate feedback? More important, did they buy the intended trend-setting pieces? Retailers look for immediate sales, but they also will follow sales trends after the show. With Universal Product Code (UPC) and scanner technology, retailers can accurately determine styles and colors that are rapid sellers, as well as those trends that are slow to take off with the public.

Evaluation Based on Strengths and Weaknesses

Based on show goals, event personnel should determine what the strengths of the show were and how problems or weaknesses of the show should be corrected or replaced for the next time. Look for strengths of the event. Even if the team is very satisfied with the fashion show, look for ways to make the show stronger in the future. Build on show elements that were popular with the audience. Did they like the music mix? Was the seating arrangement comfortable? Did the merchandise match the audience?

Similarly, look for show weaknesses. Do not dwell on the negative aspect of show weaknesses, but rather brainstorm to turn the weaknesses into opportunities to improve the next

show. For example, was the lighting too dark for the audience to adequately see the fashions? Was communication between team members as good as it could have been? Review of weaknesses is difficult but necessary for adequate evaluation and improvement in the future.

Statistics

In evaluating the success of a fashion show, show personnel should secure available statistics about the show. Statistics may include cash intake from ticket sales, audience counts, media coverage, sales generated from the show, or other numeric measures. Statistics provide objective measures. For example, if the goal was to bring in 100 people to a before-store-hours show of new seasonal fashions, and 110 people turned out, the show staff exceeded its goal.

Audience count is the number of attendees. It is an easy statistic to calculate. In controlled situations, audience count can be determined by the established seating capacities or number of tickets presented at the door. In uncontrolled situations, hosts, ushers, security, or personnel involved in crowd control may be able to make reliable estimates.

Media coverage, or the number of exposures generated in the media, can also be quantified. Count the number of news releases distributed and the number of media impressions that resulted from the news releases. Multiply this by the circulation or number of viewers and listeners to determine total media impressions. Figure 8.16 shows media coverage for *Runway to Wonderland* in *The Lumberjack*, a campus newspaper.

Any time a numeric measure can be compared against the same numeric measure from a previous show, a nonsubjective assessment can be made. For example, a charity show that generated $2,000 toward breast cancer research last year may have generated $2,500 this year. The $500 increase in contributions is an objective numeric measure.

SPECIFIC ELEMENTS TO EVALUATE

Evaluation may take the form of a general summary or detailed analysis. Each committee—budget, merchandise, model, public relations, and stage—as well as the fashion show director, should put together a detailed show diary outlining the committee's steps from planning to implementation of the show. The show diary includes planning documents; calendars; copies of letters, e-mails, or other communication; forms such as fitting sheets, model lists, and media lists; and evaluation of the personnel involved in producing the show (Fig. 8.17).

This document serves as a recap and as an outline for the next class or fashion show committee. Regardless of the depth of the evaluation, the following questions and considerations should be reviewed. There will always be a future show and providing as much detail about the present show can only help to make the future show better.

Participants

Community clubs and novice fashion show production personnel find it helpful to maintain lists of all people who participated and what their responsibilities were. These lists can include names, addresses, telephone numbers, and e-mail addresses. Having a framework of what needs to be done, when, and by whom assists in running a future production smoothly.

Theme and Title

Also, as part of the evaluation, the theme and title of the show should be reviewed. Were any special strategies used to capture the mood of the merchandise? Was coordination of the theme and merchandise using music, lighting, props, or any other devices evident? Ask the following questions:

- How did the scenes coordinate with the overall theme?
- Was the theme chosen to correlate with the merchandise?
- Was merchandise readily available to develop the theme and scenes?
- How could the theme be improved?

Venue

The *venue*—where the fashion show is produced—should be thoroughly described. The description should include not only the physical address, but also features such as the proximity of the dressing rooms to

Figure 8.16
This article appeared in *The Lumberjack,* a campus newspaper, as a result of the media kit that was sent to the paper.

Courtesy of The Lumberjack Newspaper.

Budget Committee Fashion Show Diary

Cynthia Tripathi Coordinator

Breann Aldridge

Marcella Lara

Katherine Reband

Figure 8.17
A fashion show diary documents all of the planning and activities that took place during a particular fashion show.

the show area, seating, runway accessibility, helpfulness and cooperation of the venue employees, availability of parking, and any special ambience or amenities. Typical questions relating to the physical location are as follows:

- Was the facility adequate for the show production staff and the audience?
- Were there any problems getting models from the dressing area to the stage and runway?
- Were the audiovisual technologies adequate and appropriate?

- Were there plenty of restrooms for the audience and show participants?
- Were the hospitality services adequate?

Audience

Audience reaction should also be evaluated. First, the staff should consider the size of the audience:

- Was the audience an appropriate size for the location?
- Was the audience large enough to cover expenses?
- Was the audience small enough so that everyone had a good view?

To gauge audience reaction, a **survey**—a questionnaire distributed to ask people their opinions or reactions—can be printed before the show and distributed to the audience as individuals arrive at the show. Show planners might ask the audience members to comment on their demographic information (age, gender, income, etc.) and their attitudes toward show elements (merchandise selection, music, lighting, stage set). In addition, the audience should be asked how they learned about the fashion show to help assess the quality of show promotion.

The following guidelines should be considered when developing a survey. First, make sure the instructions are easy to understand. It is best to keep survey questions short and easy to answer. As questions are formulated, establish an easy way to tabulate the answers to better quantify them. Avoid asking questions that lead the respondent to an answer. Each question should ask about only one item. Finally, pretest the questionnaire to make sure it works. Figure 8.18 is an example of an audience reaction survey.

It is also important to consider the appropriateness of the audience to the merchandise and the type of show produced and how the audience reacted to both elements. Consider the following:

- Was the desired audience attracted? If not, describe the audience that did attend.
- Was the promotion campaign targeted to the right group?
- Did the merchandise and theme match the type of audience desired?
- Was the audience enthusiastic?
- Did the audience appear to be interested and entertained by the production?
- Did members of the audience ask where to find the merchandise?

Budget

Despite careful planning, the actual expenses may differ from the figures projected in the budget. The actual expenditures must be recorded and compared to the budget. This is important for community groups trying to raise funds for some altruistic or operational project. Ask the following:

- Was the budget realistic?
- What were the unforeseen expenses?
- Were there profits?
- Did ticket sales and donations exceed costs?

Promotion

A recap of the activities relating to advertising and public relations should be included in the show evaluation. Copies of advertisements, flyers, invitations, news releases, names of media personnel contacted, and other relevant information should be included in the fashion show diary. These samples serve as illustrations and examples for the future.

Merchandise

A description of the quantity and types of merchandise presented should be included. Names of store contacts at retail stores or fashion businesses and their helpfulness can be included. It may also be helpful to include the length of time required to show the number of outfits presented to serve as a guideline for timing future shows.

Fitting sheets and final lineup charts enhance this basic information. The relationship of the merchandise to the scene theme and fashion show theme should also be discussed:

- Was the merchandise appropriate to the theme, audience, and company image?
- What departments or stores participated in a retail show?

AUDIENCE REACTION

Age:
24 or under ☐
25-44 ☐
45-64 ☐
65+ ☐

Sex:
Male ☐
Female ☐

Family Income:
$24,999 or lower ☐
$25,000 – 49,999 ☐
$50,000 – 74,999 ☐
$75,000 – 99,999 ☐
$100,000 or more ☐

Rate the following:

	Like				Dislike
Clothing	☐	☐	☐	☐	☐
Stage Set	☐	☐	☐	☐	☐
Music:					
Style	☐	☐	☐	☐	☐
Loudness	☐	☐	☐	☐	☐
Lighting	☐	☐	☐	☐	☐

How did you find out about the show?
Newspaper advertisement ☐
Radio advertisement ☐
Poster ☐
Personal Contact ☐
Other _____

_____
_____

Additional Comments;

Figure 8.18
This is an audience reaction survey that is distributed at the fashion show.

Illustration by Carly Grafstein

- Were any departments or stores overlooked that should have been included?
- Were any departments or stores used that would not be recommended for future shows?

Models

Any organization utilizing models on a regular basis should set up evaluation criteria. Models who do not receive a favorable evaluation should be eliminated from future

---

MODEL EVALUATION FORM

Name:_____

Show:_____

Date:_____

Model Type:_____

Measurements and physical characteristics:

_____

_____

Contact Information:

_____

_____

Attended fittings:	_____on time	_____late	_____no show
Attended rehearsal:	_____on time	_____late	_____no show
Attended show:	_____on time	_____late	_____no show
Prepared at fittings:		_____yes	_____no
Prepared at rehearsal:		_____yes	_____no
Prepared at show:		_____yes	_____no
Professional attitude:		_____yes	_____no
Would use this model again:		_____yes	_____no

Comments:

Figure 8.19
A detailed model evaluation form provides information about the model's performance.

Illustration by Carly Grafstein

consideration. The model coordinator or fashion director should create a file that includes all contact information on the models featured in the show. Information should include name, address, telephone and fax numbers, e-mail addresses, and relative statistics for each model regularly employed. Measure of performance should be recorded after each show to help show personnel in selecting models for future shows. If a modeling agency is used, that information should also be recorded.

Figure 8.19 illustrates a model evaluation. For evaluation purposes, models should be on time for fittings, rehearsals, and the show. They should be cooperative, provide their personal supplies, take care of merchandise, and dress quickly. A model should expect to do his or her own makeup and hair unless told otherwise. The models should be well groomed and polished, providing the ideal image to exhibit the clothing and accessories.

Music

As stated earlier, music has become extremely important as an element of fashion show production. Therefore, it should also be critiqued:

- Did the music mix match the audience?
- Were the sound levels of the music appropriate? Too loud? Too soft?

- Was the equipment coordinated properly?
- Were the technicians easy or difficult to work with?

Staging

The staging is intended to enhance the fashions without overpowering them. The staging also sets a background for theme emphasis. Consider the following:

- Was the staging appropriate for the fashions presented?
- Were there any difficult elements of the staging that tripped up the models, such as platform height or stairs?
- Did the background and the stage blend together in a coordinated look?
- Was the model entrance and exit convenient and obvious for the models?
- Was the entrance and exit hidden from the audience?
- Could starters see the stage adequately?
- Were the lighting levels appropriate?

Script and Announcer

Copies of the script should be included in the fashion show evaluation. The announcer's performance should also be assessed:

- Was the script interesting?
- Did the announcer strengthen the theme of the show?
- Did the announcer deliver the script effectively?

Evaluate Other Shows

As part of evaluation, show personnel should evaluate shows that others produce. Note what others do differently and effectively. It is always good to change some show elements to keep the event fresh and growing. Identify strategies that work well. Keep these techniques fresh for the future.

The media is an important evaluator of fashion shows. Journalists evaluate shows using **tone**, which is the manner of expression used in speech or writing. If the journalist likes the show, the tone in the article will be positive and upbeat. If the journalist is not pleased with the show, the tone of the evaluation will be negative and critical. Worse, a journalist may evaluate a designer show as boring or just ignore the show all together.

Suzy Menkes is the fashion editor of the *International Herald Tribune*; she is both loved and feared for her critiques. Designer Albert Elbaz will not start his shows until Menkes takes her seat in the front row.

> "When we designers do a good collection, Suzy [Menkes] is so happy for us, and when we do a bad one she seems almost to get angry."
>
> —Albert Elbaz, fashion designer

Evaluate Media Coverage

According to David Graham of the *Toronto Star* (2012), there was a time when fashion designers feared the critics who sat in the front rows of their fashion shows. A bad review could mean a designer's collection was ignored by the fashion magazines or that stores might turn to another designer for its merchandise. Newspapers and magazines sent their fashion experts around the world to critique the biannual ready-to-wear collections and bring back important news to discerning readers. These journalists were tough critics, harsh when they were disappointed with the collection and flattering when complements were deserved. Fashion critics walk a fine line. If they are too critical, they are not invited back to see the shows. Unlike a movie critic, who can buy a ticket to the next movie, a journalist who offers a harsh criticism of a designer's show may be banned from attending the next presentation.

Some traditional media outlets still have journalists covering the fashion industry. Cathy Horyn, fashion critic and blogger for the *New York Times* since 1999, is a trained reporter with a master's degree in journalism from Northwestern University ("Cathy Horyn," 2012). As the Art Critic in Residence at Stanford University, Ms. Horyn said that you have to know what you are doing: be a reporter, go backstage, try on the clothes to see if they are wearable (Haven, 2010). As an early adopter of blogging, she was intrigued by the immediacy of the Internet and the ability to interact directly with readers in her *On the Runway* blog. Ms. Horyn believes a good fashion critic is a good observer, with the ability to think analytically and ask the right questions. Should the story be written about conformity or originality of design? Additional *New York Times* fashion writers—including Eric Wilson, Guy Trebay, and Simone S. Oliver, among others—contribute to the *On the Runway* blog.

The *Wall Street Journal* fashion blog is called *Heard on the Runway*, which provides news about the worlds of fashion and retail, as well as dispatches from and analyses of the biannual fashion shows in New York, Milan, and Paris. Among the journalists writing for the *Wall Street Journal* are Christina Binkley and Teri Agins.

Other well-respected fashion journalists include Suzy Menkes and Robin Givhan. Suzy Menkes is the fashion editor of the *International Herald Tribune*. This globally distributed newspaper features her articles on the international collections, which are read by fashionistas around the world. Robin Givhan is the special correspondent for style and culture for *Newsweek* and *The Daily Beast*. Ms. Givhan started her career with the *Detroit Free Press* and won a Pulitzer prize for her work as a fashion critic at the *Washington Post*.

One of the reasons fashion criticism has decreased in recent years is that print-media budgets have been reduced. This has resulted in fewer fashion critics sitting in the fashion show audience and more bloggers—often young women untrained in the craft of criticism—taking fashion editors' places at the shows. According to some, bloggers are the new critics. However, not everyone believes this.

Ms. Givhan has expressed her doubts about bloggers' abilities to analyze fashion (Graham, 2012). She is concerned that bloggers are too dazzled by celebrity culture, offering simplistic reviews and personal opinions—not criticism. Because bloggers typically use fictitious names, it is hard to trust their anonymous opinions. These writers are too cozy with some designers who pay for their trips and gifts, and as a result Ms. Givhan believes they are engaged in advertising rather than fashion criticism.

Whether the review comes from a trained journalist or a blogger with an online fan base, fashion show personnel can anticipate hearing about the good as well as the bad opinions about the merchandise and the show.

MEASURING SUCCESS

A fashion show is not truly over (Fig. 8.20) until the staff completes an evaluation to measure the success of the show. It is difficult to measure the success of any particular show. Some people gauge the achievement by the dollar volume of

"People outside the industry think it's crazy. You work for six months for something that lasts for ten minutes? . . . Everyone is hypersensitive to what you are saying. They're all looking at your stage sets, the models you've been able to pull in, your front-row celebrities, whether Anna Wintour has turned up. You are gauged hot or not every six months."

—Joseph Velosa, co-founder of Matthew Williamson fashion design

the sales; others assess the accomplishment by the reaction of the audience, participants, and media. No matter how the success is defined, producing a fashion show can be an exciting and rewarding experience and reviewing the successes and problems will help ease some of the stress when the staff produces the next show.

Figure 8.20
The audience's reaction helps the fashion show producers measure their success.

Courtesy of WWD/Stephan Feugere, Giovanni Giannoni, and Davide Maestri

Nothing Can Beat the Feeling of Watching Fashion Unfold!

Emilee Dunn

Courtesy of Emilee Dunn

I was the student director for my college fashion show, one of the most challenging and rewarding experiences of my college career. Accepting the position was extremely exciting. However, I wasn't aware of all the lessons to be learned throughout the semester. The three most applicable lessons involved communication, preparation, and quality. These were vital to the fashion show production process. Then these valuable lessons became key components in molding my professional, post-college career in the fashion industry.

After college, I landed a job working for a fashion designer based in Los Angeles, California, as a consultant account manager for a direct selling company marketing an exclusive designer collection of women's clothing. My role has become more defined and has grown to include additional responsibilities as communications manager on the field development team. In a short time, I have already been exposed to many different facets of the company and worked on a variety of tasks and projects, ranging from event setup and planning to field development communication.

Having the ability to wear many different hats throughout a typical workday is a lesson learned while balancing the duties of student director, student, president of the school's student fashion association, and other commitments outside of academics. In my new job in the professional world, I see how important multitasking is. The importance of communication skills is more significant than I first realized.

As student director, I was required to communicate important deadlines, words of advice from previous fashion show experiences, and important instructions for tasks to be completed and steps to be taken. It did not take long to learn that it was key to communicate thoroughly and in a timely manner. Now I am in constant communication with a variety of people. It is important to understand whom you are communicating with and what information needs to be communicated. As both a student director and a professional, I need to be knowledgeable. Confidence is key when establishing trust with students and consultants alike. It is vital to be able to distinguish what information is most important and what method will be most effective to communicate your message.

Preparation was another key skill I took away from my experience as student director and brought into my job in the fashion industry. Organization and prioritization were very helpful in making sure I was prepared for each task that was required of me. I still find myself writing down important dates to remember and jobs to complete. Twice each year, my company coordinates a convention at which the new line is introduced through a fashion show, and consultants are educated about the new merchandise for the upcoming selling season. I work closely with the marketing team to prepare this event. Tasks range from preparing floral arrangements to setting up the main tent stage and training rooms. Our team works for a week on sight preparing for over 3,000 consultants, making sure everything is in order so that the convention can go off without a hitch. It is vital for each person to know his or her show day responsibilities and complete as many tasks as possible before we arrive on site. That helps the event flow smoothly. Using my experience as student director has helped me to understand the importance of preparation, as well as being able to think on my feet and react quickly when a problem or crisis arises. Keeping calm in last-minute crises is directly related to how much preparation is done beforehand, and how confident I am in my team's, coworkers', or students' preparation as well.

Finally, one of the most important lessons carried over from my student director experience to my fashion career is understanding what quality means. The company I work for has four values, one of which is quality. We view quality as the concept of leaving something better than you found it—doing the best you are able to do, always pushing toward excellence, and holding yourself to the highest standard. As student director, I was held accountable for the show's quality.

In the fashion show production class, the quality and success of the show are completely up to the students and how much drive they put behind the show. As student director, I encouraged the students to follow the steps of producing a fashion show, from planning through to strike. That way, they could see the best results in their show. It was exciting to see how much my encouragement as student director influenced the quality of the students' work.

While working in the fashion industry, it is sometimes hard to hold yourself to such high standards. It is different from school, working without grades or teachers to hold you accountable. However, I find that I have used that drive I learned to use in school in making sure my writing is nothing but the highest quality work.

My experience as student director for *Get Your Fashion Fix on Route 66* was a great teacher. I learned so many valuable lessons throughout both negative and positive experiences surrounding the class and fashion show. Words cannot express how rewarding it is to see the show come together after a full semester of hard work. The day of the fashion show can be stressful, but once the lights go down, and the music starts, nothing can top the feeling of watching fashion unfold! Fashion shows are always exciting to watch, but knowing your planning, coordinating, and teamwork contributed so much to the end result makes the show even more exhilarating. These experiences helped to form my work habits in the fashion industry after graduating from Northern Arizona University. Although I am still growing professionally, I know the lessons I learned as student director in communication, preparation, and quality will continue to be foundational pieces in my career.

Emilee Dunn was the Student Director for *Get Your Fashion Fix on Route 66* and a member of the Model Committee for *Runway to Wonderland* at Northern Arizona University, where she earned a B.S. in merchandising. She currently works for a direct sales company that markets an exclusive designer collection of women's clothing.

The Show—A Recap

- Fashion shows use the rehearsal as a way of practicing the performance in private before the show is publically presented. It is especially important as a way of preventing mistakes on the runway with an inexperienced production staff.
- The merchandisers or designers work with the model committee to prepare the dressing rooms to facilitate quick and easy changes for the models.
- Dressers and starters work to get the models changed and back on the runway as soon as possible.
- First impressions at the beginning of the fashion show and final impressions at the end of the show will influence the audience's opinion of whether the show is a hit or a miss.
- At the end of the show the stage and set are physically disassembled, all props and equipment are returned to the appropriate locations, merchandise is returned to the sales floor or designer, and the location is left as it was found.
- Acting in a professional manner that respects other people's feelings and respects the merchandise being shown leaves all of the people involved with a pleasant impression.
- Participants and their contributions, as well as an analysis of the theme and title, venue, audience, budget, promotion, merchandise, models, music, staging, and script, should be evaluated. Any recommendations for future shows should be included.
- Media coverage can give designers and show producers an outside opinion of how well the show and merchandise were perceived.

Key Fashion Show Terms

audience count	professionalism
dresser	rehearsal
dress rehearsal	run-through
evaluation	stage strike
evaluation form	starter
full dress rehearsal	survey
media coverage	tone

Questions for Discussion

1. What is the purpose of a walk-through, rehearsal, and full dress rehearsal? Why are they important?
2. How should the dressing room be set up? Who is responsible for getting the dressing room and garments ready for the rehearsal and show?
3. What are the responsibilities of the dresser and the starter?
4. What is the importance of the opening and the closing of the show?
5. Why is it important to have everyone involved in striking the stage?
6. What does being professional mean to you? Give some examples of fashion show participants acting in an unprofessional manner.

7. What are some of the reasons a fashion show should be cancelled?

8. How should fashion show success be measured? Why do so many fashion show teams fail to evaluate a show?

9. What is a show diary and why is it important?

FASHION SHOW ACTIVITY

Break into teams of four to five. Each team should pick a show theme and brainstorm how to close the show. Be prepared to share your ideas with the other teams.

THE CAPSTONE PROJECT

All of the hard work comes together on the day of the show. After the show is over, each team, budget, merchandise, models, promotion, and stage, as well as the fashion show director must create a show diary. Pull together any examples of work produced, from planning documents and calendars to evaluations that have taken place during the semester. Each team member should identify his or her contributions to their team and to the show as a whole. Each participant should write a memo to future students or fashion show participants from a charitable organization discussing the strengths and weaknesses of your team and personal contributions to the event.

CD-ROM

REFERENCES

Constant, F., & Mazaud, P. (Producers), & Prigent, L. (Director). (2007). *Marc Jacobs & Louis Vuitton* [DVD]. Paris, France: ARTE.

Graham, D. (2012, March 7). Fashion week: The beleaguered art of fashion criticism. *Toronto Star*. Retrieved from http://www.thestar.com

Haven, C. (2010, October 21). The Times' fashion critic talks about the business. *Stanford Report*. Retrieved from http://news.standford.edu

Horyn, C. (2001, September 16). Fashion week cancelled, designers plan small showings. *The New York Times*. Retrieved from http://www.nytimes.com

Horyn, C. (2012). Times Topics. *The New York Times*. Retrieved from http://topics.nytimes.com

Prigent, L. (Director), (2007). *Marc Jacobs & Louis Vuitton* [DVD]. France: Anda Media.

Seabrook, J. (2001, March 17). A samurai in Paris. *The New Yorker*. Retrieved from http://*www.newyorker. com*

Socha, M. (2012, May 15). Marie gets punked. *Women's Wear Daily*. Retrieved from http://www.wwd.com

Tungate, M. (2008). *Fashion brands: Branding style from Armani to Zara* (2nd ed.) Philadelphia, PA: Kogan Page.

Vilaseca, E. (2010). *Runway uncovered: The making of a fashion show*. Barcelona, Spain: Promopress.

Glossary of Fashion Show Terms

7th on Sixth Nonprofit organization created by the Council of Fashion Designers (CFDA) to centralize the American runway shows.

A

action shot Photograph of a product in action.

advertising Nonpersonal message, paid for and placed in the mass media, and controlled by the sponsoring organization.

advertising content Paid announcements run in the media.

advertising model Individual used to display and enhance products for publication in newspapers, magazines, point-of-purchase displays, and other media.

amateur model Individual not trained as a professional.

announcer Individual responsible for delivering the script during the show.

app Mobile applications used by smart phones and tablets.

apparel mart Wholesale center located in a major U.S. city leasing space to manufacturers.

art Illustrations or photography of an advertisement.

audience count Number of attendees.

B

background Dramatic backdrops emphasizing the show's merchandise or theme.

backgrounder Fact sheet in media kit describing historical facts about the show.

banner ad Advertisement embedded into a web page.

basic fact sheet Page in a media kit offering details about the fashion show and explaining its significance in a factual manner.

biographical information Page in a media kit to explain the principal contributors.

body Important details of the advertisement or news article.

body parts model Men and women with attractive hands, legs, feet, and/or hair highlighting these strengths as a sub-industry within the modeling industry.

booker Individual who is hired by the modeling agency to promote, coordinate schedules, and negotiate fees for models.

booking Job for a runway show or a photo shoot.

brand Name, term, design, symbol, or any other feature that identifies one seller's good or service as distinct from those of other sellers.

British Fashion Council Organizers of London Fashion Week.

budget Estimate of the revenues and expenses necessary to produce the fashion show.

budget coordinator Person responsible for keeping track of all the income and costs of a show.

C

callback Invitation from a client for a model to return for a second look.

Camera Nazionale della Alta Moda Italia Governing body of the Italian couture overseeing the activities of couture designers, ready-to-wear, shoe, and accessory manufacturers.

casting call Event at which various models audition for a slot on the runway or for print work.

catalogue model Individual who is photographed wearing clothing and accessories that will be sold through direct response media.

cattle call Group setting casting call at which a client sees a variety of possible looks.

celebrity stylist Individual responsible for dressing his or her clients for special events.

child model Young person who displays merchandise for the baby, toddler, children's, boys, girls, and preteen markets.

choreographer Individual in charge of determining the pattern that a model will walk down the runway and the interaction of the models on the runway as they enter and exit the stage area.

choreography Plan for the models' runway routines.

clip art Prefabricated illustrations generated on a computer or purchased in clip art books.

closing date Designation when ad copy must be received by a magazine.

commercial advertising Paid promotion with the purpose of making a profit for the firm.

commercial model Individual who works in the mass market or for-profit side of the fashion business.

composite Printed promotional card that includes the model's name, measurements, and agency contact information with various photographs.

consumer show Event directed at the consumer.

cooperative fashion show Retailer and manufacturer show in which both parties share expenses.

cooperative promotion (co-op) Multiple channel representatives partnering in financial support and production of a fashion show.

copy 1) Written material in an advertisement; 2) Actual material or content for a news story within a new release.

copyright permission Authorization from the owner of a copyright to use copyrighted material.

cost per click Money earned by an affiliate every time a unique user clicks on its ad.

Council of Fashion Designers of America (CFDA) Nonprofit trade organization for North American designers of fashion and fashion accessories.

cover letter Introduces media kit and informs editors or producers why the event deserves attention in the media.

created audience Individuals who will attend a fashion show as a result of promotional activities.

cue Signal on or off the stage for an entrance.

cutline Photo caption placed directly below or next to a photo, describing what happened in the photo.

D

dateline Opening of a news report that indicates where and when the story was written.

defiles des createurs Paris designer runway shows.

demographics Statistics, including age, gender, education, income, occupation, race and ethnicity, and family size, used to study a population.

design piracy Stealing designs and creating "knockoffs."

diary Written record of all plans and evaluations for the show.

direct mail Direct response communications sent through the mail.

direct marketing Process by which organizations communicate directly with target customers to generate a response or transaction.

direct response media Distribution method requiring a direct reply from traditional or digital media.

directrice/directuer French term referring to the male or female head of the couture salon.

documentary video Film that focuses on the behind-the-scenes activities of designers or manufacturers, runway shows, magazine production, and other aspects of the fashion industry.

dresser Individual responsible for helping models to change.

dressing area Room or area designated for changing clothes, applying makeup, or styling hair.

dress rehearsal Walk-through with garment changes.

E

editorial content Communication that is initiated by public relations personnel.

editorial model Individual who works the runways during international fashion week shows and poses for editorial sections of high fashion magazines.

editorial stylist Individual who is responsible for providing creative input and planning how to highlight key pieces of the collection through editing and accessorizing and who supervises the merchandise and dressers for a fashion designer.

evaluation Appraisal of the performance, people, places, and processes.

evaluation form Document used to summarize the evaluation process.

F

Fashion Calendar Schedule updated daily online with hard copy issues mailed every other week, which lists American and international fashion events.

fashion director Individual responsible for creating the fashion image for a particular retailer.

fashion dolls Historic miniature, to scale figures wearing replicas of the latest clothing.

fashion show Event where the latest fashion, fabric, and color trends in apparel and accessories are presented to an audience using live models.

fashion show director Individual charged with the responsibility of producing the show, planning all arrangements, delegating responsibilities, and accepting accountability for all details.

fashion show plan Document that describes the preliminary decisions made to produce the fashion show.

fashion trend show Event produced to introduce consumers to the latest trends in silhouettes, fabrics, colors, and themes of new seasonal merchandise.

fashion week Designated time when many designer collections are brought together and shown as a series of fashion shows.

feature story Journalistic story in a media kit to provide insight into the event.

Fédération Française de la Couture, du Prêt-à-Porter des Couturiers et des Créateurs de Mode France's governing body for fashion.

finale Exciting conclusion of the show.

final lineup Complete listing of models and outfits in order of appearance.

fit model Person with a particular attitude and specific body measurements that meet a manufacturer's ideal standard size.

fittings Matching models to merchandise.

fitting sheet Information sheet coordinated to the merchandise, including size, order number, and detailed description of the garment.

flat Temporary movable backdrop.

formal runway show Conventional presentation of fashion similar to a parade, featuring a series of models who walk or dance on a runway in a sequential manner.

freelance Modeling on a per-project basis.

full dress rehearsal Practice with garment changes to check all aspects of the show, including timing, music, and other technical aspects.

full-run Advertising that runs in all editions of a newspaper.

G

go-see Invitation to a model to meet the client.

graphic design Art or profession of using design elements, including typography and images, to convey information or create an effect.

gratuity Cash tip given to service people, such as wait staff, or attendants in the coat check area and restrooms.

grip-and-grin Photograph of people receiving awards, passing out scholarships or fund-raising checks, or cutting ribbons.

group shot Photograph of several people lined up.

guaranteed audience Individuals who will attend the show regardless of the fashions displayed.

H

haute couture French word for "high fashion" and the name of the French industry that produces high fashion garments.

headline 1) Part of an advertisement or news article used to attract the attention of the reader and create interest; 2) First sentence of the news release, which sets the tone with a strong and appealing synopsis of the purpose of the release.

headshot Small photo of a person's face, typically a portrait, cropped from the chest or bottom of the neck to the top of the head.

home-shopping channel Multi-platform shopping site on television and digital media.

host Person who greets audience members and shows them where to sit.

I

ideal chart Plan listing all categories of merchandise that will be represented in the show.

illustration Image created by pen, pencil, brush, or crayon, as the artwork for a printed advertisement.

individual model lineup sheet Form used in organizing the specific model's order of appearance, outfit, shoes, hosiery, accessories, props, and grouping.

infomercial Commercial presented as if it was a regular television show.

informal fashion show Casual presentation of garments and accessories.

institutional advertising Paid promotion focused upon building the reputation and fashion leadership of the company or sponsoring organization.

in-store training fashion show Event presented to educate sales associates about trends and related promotions intended to highlight new merchandise.

instructional video Film created for in-store training for store personnel.

Internet sponsorships Organization that subsidizes a section of a website or provides content to a website.

interstitial Ad that appears on a screen while a website's content is loading.

K

knockoff Copy of designer originals at lower prices.

L

layout Schematic plan or arrangement of the fashion show floor plan.

lead First paragraph in a news release that summarizes the importance of the story, which should be created to grab the attention of the editor.

lease agreement Contract between leasing agencies and users drawn up prior to the show.

lighting Method and/or equipment used to provide illumination.

link Underlined reference within Web text that takes the viewer to additional information or related material on another website.

list of participants Page within a media kit to explain the participants.

live mixed music Use of a D.J. and playback equipment to change music during various segments of the show.

live music Performance provided by musicians during the show.

local advertising Time bought on local television stations.

logo Copyright-protected symbol or phrase used by an incorporated organization.

look Reference point, a theme, a feeling, an era, or an essence given off by a potential model.

M

magazine tie-in show Cooperative fashion show between major fashion publication and individual retailer.

male model Men who are hired to display clothing and accessories.

mannequin Live model used to present merchandise in fashion shows or a stationary doll or dummy used as a display fixture.

mannequin modeling Presentations in a store window or on a display platform by live models who strike poses similar to the stationary display props for which they have been named.

mannequins du monde High society women, wives of millionaires, and popular actresses from stage and screen who became the fashion models in the 1930s.

mapped route Path planned for models to follow on the runway.

market calendar Published dates of trade shows known as market weeks.

market week Time designated for producers of a specific category of merchandise to open sales on the season's new styles.

mature model Women who continue doing modeling jobs well into their 30s, 40s and 50s—and sometimes beyond.

media coverage Number of exposures generated in the media about the show.

media kit Collection of public relations materials delivered or mailed to the media, often in a colorful folder with pockets.

media list Inventory of media outlets that might be used to publicize the fashion show.

media show Event specifically held for members of the media prior to present the fashion story to the public.

merchandise categories Divisions of merchandise within the show.

merchandise coordinator Individual in charge of the selection of merchandise for each scene and the entire show.

merchandise loan record Standardized form used by fashion show producers to record details of the merchandise borrowed from retailers.

merchandise pull Physically removing merchandise from a retailer's sales floor to an area reserved for fashion show merchandise storage.

merchandise selection Designation of apparel, shoes, and accessories for presentation in a fashion show.

mixed music Prerecorded music played during the show.

model Individual employed to display clothing and accessories by wearing them.

model coordinator Individual responsible for selecting and training the models and coordinating activities that involve the models.

modeling agency Company that represents and acts as a scheduling agent for a variety of fashion models.

model list Form that includes the model's name, telephone number, and garment and shoe sizes.

model order Rotation in which the models will appear throughout the show.

mother agency Business that serves as the model's home agency.

multimedia production show Digitally produced show using video or interactive technology.

muse Designer's inspiration for his or her ideal customer, be it fit model, friend, or celebrity.

music Pleasing or harmonious sounds, or combination of sounds, used to heighten the atmosphere of the show for the audience and models.

music mix Combination of different music styles to create a specified mood.

music playlist Inventory of music selections, including title, length of song, and recording artist.

N

national promotion Primary and secondary promotion activities directed at the consumer.

network advertising Time bought on one of the major networks.

news release Article on a newsworthy event sent to editors or news directors for publication or broadcast in the media.

news story Journalistic story in a media kit that gives basic information about the fashion show in an announcement news approach.

noncommercial advertising Paid promotion directed toward gaining support for charitable work.

nonprofit organization Business or group with 501(c)(3) status as designated by the Internal Revenue Service.

O

online commercial Online equivalent to a traditional television commercial.

open call Event hosted by a modeling agency to look for new faces.

option Agreement between the client and booker that reserves the model's availability.

P

pace Model tempo during the show.

paid search Payment when a consumer clicks on an advertiser's ad or on a link from a search engine page.

paste-up Rough draft of an advertisement.

pause Planned hesitation when models stop and pose on the runway.

personal selling Direct interaction between customer and seller with the purpose of making a sale.

petite model Individual typically between 5 feet 2 inches and 5 feet 7 inches tall.

photo credit Identification of photographer or owner of a photo.

photograph Image prepared specifically for use in media to accompany news releases or to be included in a media kit.

photography Reproduction of prints created by a camera.

photo opportunity Any photo or video that serves as a visual enhancement to the news story.

pivot Turn executed by models on a runway.

planning All aspects of preliminary preparation necessary to present a well-executed show.

plus size model Person who typically wears from a size 10 to 20 plus.

point-of-purchase video Film placed on the sales floor of a retail store.

pop-under Advertisement that appears underneath a website after a viewer leaves the website.

pop-up Advertisement that appears as a window when a website is opened.

portfolio Book of photographs that shows a model in the most flattering way, showing the model's versatility.

preferred position Newspaper advertisement run at a specified page or position within the newspaper.

premier/premiere French term referring to the male or female head of the couture workroom.

prêt-á-porter Ready-to-wear fashion industry in France.

primary resource Raw materials producer such as a textile firm or color agency.

product advertising Promotion of specific good or service.

production show Most dramatic or theatrically produced type of show.

product shot Photograph emphasizing the fashion item by itself or with other fashion items.

professionalism Acting in a manner accepted by the profession and/or occupation.

professional model Person trained in modeling techniques and hired through a modeling agency.

program editor Individual responsible for all activities related to creating a program.

program of events Page in a media kit that provides detailed information about the scheduled activities.

promotion Communication activities initiated by the seller to inform, persuade, and remind the consumer about products, services, and/or ideas offered for sale.

promotion coordinator Individual responsible for the creation and distribution of promotional materials required for the show.

prop Item used in fashion shows to highlight the garments exhibited.

psychographics Characteristics of consumers based upon activities, interests, and opinions.

public address system Microphone, amplifiers, and speakers used to project voices.

publicist Individual hired to publicize a client or client's products in the media.

publicity Information with news value, uncontrolled by the source because the source does not pay the media for placement, and is provided by public relations specialists to be used in the mass media.

public relations (PR) Management function that establishes and maintains mutually beneficial relationships between an organization and the public on whom its success or failure depends.

public service announcement Print or broadcast spot run free of charge to charitable organizations.

R

rate card Published rates for the advertising units in all media.

ready-to-wear Mass-produced fashion.

rehearsal Practice performance, held in private, in preparation for a public performance.

release date Designation when the news release is written.

request Client's call for a specific model.

responsibility sheet Form used in planning a show and delegating responsibilities to all participants.

retail promotion Store promotion directed at the consumer.

run-of-paper Newspaper advertisement run at any location in the newspaper.

run-through Rehearsal of the show sequences and involves showing models the choreography.

runway Extension of the stage or a freestanding unit that normally projects into the audience.

runway model Men and women who find work at trade shows and major fashion centers.

S

scout Model agency representative who searches public areas, such as shopping districts, school events, or sports venues, looking for potential models.

script Printed version of a show narration including the words to be spoken and technical directions.

secondary resource Clothing and accessory manufacturer.

show producer Individual hired to bring all fashion show elements together, including translating the designer's vision into a three-dimensional live show.

showroom model Men and women who work freelance or as a manufacturer's house model during market weeks.

slogan Catchy phrase that is appealing when spoken or viewed in print.

social media Web-based and mobile technologies to turn communication into interactive dialogue.

sound designer Person responsible for researching and selecting the appropriate music, obtaining permissions to use copyrighted music, mixing the music at the show, and preparing the sound system at the show venue.

sound system Equipment needed to play music.

spam Unsolicited and unwanted e-mails.

special event One-time occurrence with planned activities, focused on the specific purpose to bring attention to a brand, manufacturer, retailer, or organization, or to influence the sale of merchandise.

special interest show Event presented to consumers that have special affinity with each other or a unique vocation.

specialty market show Event geared to a specific, narrowly defined group of consumers.

sponsorship Supporters who lend their name to an event and/or underwrite production costs of an event.

spot advertising Time bought on independently owned broadcast stations.

stage Raised area or platform on which theatrical productions are presented.

stage manager Individual responsible for overseeing the venue and organizing the equipment and people providing services used behind the scenes.

stage strike Physically disassembling the set.

staging Process or manner of putting on a performance on stage.

standard advertising unit Space designated in print media by column inch.

starter Individual responsible for "cueing" the models to go on stage in the correct order at the right time.

stats Models' height, weight, suit or dress size, measurements—bust, waist, hips for women and waist, shirt, and inseam for men, as well as shoe size and hair and eye color.

subheadline Part of advertisement that further explains the headline.

survey Questionnaire distributed to ask people their opinions or reactions.

T

table seating Chair arrangements used at a show with some sort of meal service.

tea-room modeling Informal fashion show presented in a restaurant where models walk from table to table displaying garments.

tear sheet 1) Advertisement torn directly from the newspaper to show proof of publication to the advertiser; 2) Editorial work included in a model's portfolio.

television commercial model Individuals who make the transition from modeling to acting in television advertisements.

tentative lineup Order of models and merchandise designed from the ideal chart and model order.

tertiary resource Retail organization.

tests Variety of photographic shots that show a model's versatility and are put in a model's portfolio.

theater seating Chairs placed side by side next to the stage and runway.

theme Creative title that tells the audience the nature of the fashion show.

tone Manner of expression in speech or writing.

trade Any activity aimed at distribution of fashion and related products within the industry.

trade association Group of individuals and businesses acting as a professional, nonprofit collective in meeting common interests.

trade fair International trade shows.

trade promotion Activities designed to promote products from one business to another.

trade show Groups of temporary exhibits of vendors' offerings for a single merchandise category or group of related categories.

trunk show Informal fashion show that features garments from one manufacturer or designer at a retail store.

U

usher Person who escorts members of the audience to their seats and hands out programs.

V

venue Location where the fashion show is held.

video on demand Use of video clips of various types of entertainment or sports activities.

video opportunity News story that is captured on digital video.

virtual tear sheet Online advertising tear sheet that appears as a PDF file.

visual merchandising Physical presentation of products in a nonpersonal approach, including window, interior, or remote displays.

W

webisode Short film created by an advertiser and shown on the Internet.

white space Area between the copy and art of an advertisement.

Z

zoned edition Advertising run in selective editions.

Index

5th/58th blog, 130–131
7th on Sixth, 47–48

A

Action shot, 122, 123f
Actors' Equity Association, 185
Advertising
    definition and classification of, 106–107
    direct marketing as, 126–127
    for fashion shows, 107–108
    magazines for, 111–112
    media kit and news release as, 117–118
    for Mercedes-Benz Fashion Week, 110f
    newspapers for, 108–109
    online environment, 126–127
    publicity versus, 105
    purpose of, 178
    radio for, 113–114
    rate card for, 108
    television for, 112–113
Advertising content, 114–115, 115f
Advertising model, 178
Age. *See also* Child model
    of audience, 71–72
    of models, 172–173, 185
Agent, 180
    men's and women's, 204
Amateur model
    "no show", 194
    training, 188f, 189–190, 205
    traveling and, 205–206
    use of, 188–189, 207–208
Amateur model look book, 199
Ambrosio, Alessandra, 24
American Apparel and Footwear Association, 53
American Fashion Press Week, 19
American Guild of Musical Artists, 185
American model, 11–12
American Society of Composers, Authors, and
    Publishers, 234
Announcer, 240
    evaluation of, 275
Antoinette, Marie, 6
    Karl Lagerfeld show and, 248, 248f
Apparel mart, 51
Application (App), 127
Art, 109
Art department, in modeling agency, 204
Atmosphere, 227

Audience
    demographics and psychographics for, 71–72
    guaranteed versus created, 69
    reaction of, 271–272, 273f, 277f
    targeting, 69, 71
Audience count, 269
Audience security, 89
Auditorium show, striking, 263

B

Babushka, 9
Backdrop, 222, 223f, 224f
Background, 221–222
Backgrounder, 122
Banner ad, 128
Barbie, as fashion model, 8, 9f
Barry, Ben, 49, 55–56
Basic fact sheet, 122, 124f
Beauty
    coordination of, 199
    on runway, 197, 198f
    trends in, 198
Beauty professional, 199
Bébé, 7
Bendel, Henri, 17–18
Benz, Chris, 150
Bérard, Christina (Bebé), 7
Bergdorf-Goodman, 130–131
Bernier, Olivier, 6
Bertin, Rose, 6
Biannual press show, 11
Biographical information, 122
Blogging, 131
    5th/58th blog, 130
    branding and, 143
Body, 109
Body parts model, 178
Bonabel, Eliane, 7
Booker, 180
Booking, 182
Brand, 105
Branding, 105–106
    of fashion shows, 140–141
    social media and, 143
    stages of, 107f
Bridal show, merchandise categorizing for, 153
British Fashion Council, 48
B-roll, 122
Brown, Danny, 43

Budget, 79–80, 83, 84–87
  evaluation of, 272
  expenses, example of, 81f, 82f
  for fashion show, 96–98
  for venue, 83
Budget coordinator
  responsibility sheet, use of, 70f
  role of, 66f, 68
Bündchen, Gisele, 24, 84
  picture of, 171f
Burberry, 106, 129
  live stream of, 130f
Business-to-business promotion, 38

C

Cable television advertising, 112–113
California Market Center, 51
Callback, 182
Camera Nazionale della Moda Italiana, 48
Campus venue, 76
Cancellation, of fashion show, 265–266
Career, after modeling, 174
Career Day Dallas, 18
Cartwheel, 261, 261f
Casting call, 180
Catalogue model, 178, 179f
Catering
  expense for, 84
  at fashion show, 76, 78, 259
  for Ralph Lauren show, 77f
  working with, 78
Cattle call, 180
Catwalk, 216f
  choreography and, 203
  forms of, 215
Celebrity
  fashion designers and, 26–27
  fashion shows and, 4, 4f, 24–26
    music, 228–229, 229f
  fashion stylist for, 93
Celebrity stylist, 65
Chambre Syndicale de la Haute Couture
  Parisienne, 7
Chandelier, 226
Chanel jacket, 214, 214f, 215f
Chanel show, 154–155
Charm school, 24
Chase, Edna Woolman, 17, 17f
Chicago Garment Manufacturers Association, 17
Chicago trade show, 53f
Child model, 175–177

Choreographer, 200
Choreography
  in fashion show, 200
  finale and, 202
  importance of, 203
  model and, 199
Choreography pattern, 200–202
Christmas tree lighting, 227
Classic model, 173
Classified rate, 108
Clip art, 109
Closing date, 111
Clothing, as tool of power, 36
Clothing care, 195
Clothing designer. *See* Fashion designer
Coco Chanel, 214
Cole, Nat King, 231
College. *See* School
Color scheme, 105
Combination seating, 225
Commentator, 235
Commercial advertising, 107
Commercial model, 172, 173f, 179f
  men as, 177
Composite, 180
  example of, 181f
  importance/use of, 182
  in show package, 184
Condé Nast International, 185, 187
Consumer show, 53–54
  leadership for, 65–67
  merchandise for, 156
Cooperative advertisement, 46f
Cooperative fashion show, 37
Cooperative promotion, 37
Coordination, of merchandise, 151f
Copy, 109
Copyrighted music, 234
  permissions and, 241–242
Corinth, Kay, 6
Corporate sponsorship, 135
Cost per click (CPC), 128
Costa, Francisco, 197
Costume Institute of Metropolitan Museum of Art,
  8, 19–20
Cotton Incorporated, 53
  24-hour runway show advertisement for, 54f
Council of Fashion Designers of America (CFDA),
  47–48
  health initiative by, 185
Cover Girl, 22

Cover letter, 122, 124f
Coveri, Enrico, 227
Crawford, Cindy, 175–176
Created audience, 69
Critic, 275–277
Cross-shaped runway, 219
Cue person, 255–256
Cutline, 120
Cutrone, Kelly, 64f

D
The Daily Beast, 276
Dallas Market Center, 51
Dateline, 118
Decorations, 86
Defiles des creaeurs, 48
Dell'Orefice, Carmen, 173
    picture of, 174f
Demographics, 71
Demoiselle de magasin, 10
Design piracy, 88
Diary, 271
Digital fashion show, 27
    purpose of, 47
Dior, Christian, 13, 13f
Direct mail, 126–127
Direct marketing
    on online environment, 129
    process of, 126
Direct response media, 126
Directrice/directeur, 11
Diversity, in fashion show casting, 55–56
DKNY PR Girl, 104, 104f, 129
Documentary video, 40
Door prize, 135
Dovima, 22
Dress rehearsal, 11, 248, 251
Dresser, 251, 253, 254f
Dressing room, 216, 216f
    floor plan for, 220–221, 220f
    supplies needed in, 221f
Dressmaker, 5

E
Eating disorder, 185, 187
Editorial content, 114
Editorial model, 172, 173f
    boys/men as, 177
    as edgy, 180
    opportunities for, 177–178

Editorial stylist, 64
Education show, leadership for, 65–67, 66f
Elbaz, Albert, 275
Entryway, 222
Environmental shot, 122
Equipment, security for, 88–89
Ethnic model, 23–24
    diversity in, 56
European monarch
    fashion trends during, 5
Evaluation
    basis for
        goals, 268–269
        statistics, 269
        strengths and weaknesses, 269
    elements of, 270–276
    process and timing for, 266
Evaluation form, 268, 268f
An Evening of Innovation poster, 137f
Evite, 142
Execution-at-dawn, 121
Expense, 86
    budgeting for, 79–80, 84–87
    examples of, 81f, 82f
    for venue, 83

F
Fabergé, 22
Facebook, 131
    branding and, 143
Fact sheet, 122, 124f
Fashion association, 17–20
Fashion calendar, 74, 74f
Fashion collection, presentations for, 44
Fashion designer
    applauding models and staff, 202–203
    celebrities and, 26–27
    as controversial, 44–45
    fashion shows and, 5
    inspiration sources for, 150
    merchandes de modes as, 6
    submitting designs, 157f
Fashion director, 65
    responsibility sheet, use of, 68, 70f
Fashion doll, 5, 5f
    fashion show of, 7
    history of, 6
    in Théâtre de la Mode, 7, 8f
Fashion Fête, 17
Fashion Group International, 18
Fashion model. *See* Model

Fashion parade, 6
  fashion shows as, 12–13
Fashion presentation, types and location for, 44
Fashion publicist, 18
Fashion show. *See also* Planning; Runway fashion
  show, 65–67
  advertising for, 107–108
  audience targeting in, 69, 71
  backstage preparation for, 256, 258
  branding, 106
  branding of, 140–141
  budgeting for, 79–80, 83, 96–98
  calendar for, 74f
  cancellation of, 265–266
  as carnival, 14
  categories for, 39–43
  celebrities and, 4, 4f, 24–26
  changes to, 13
  choreography in, 200
  clothing designer influencing, 9
  commentator for, 235
  definition of, 5
  as digital, 27
  dress rehearsal for, 11
  expenses for, 81f, 82f
  as fashion parades, 12–13
  fashion stylist for, 93
  finale of, 10, 261, 261f
  food and beverage at, 76, 77f, 78
  giveaways and door prizes at, 135
  as grand productions, 15–16
  image on, 197
  informal, 42
  in-store training, 38
  for international clients, 54
  on Internet, 40, 40f
  leadership for, 66f
  length of, 74
  media coverage and, 104, 105f
  merchandise selection for, 150–151
  model diversity in, 55–56
  model responsibility during, 196, 197
  niche markets for, 54
  opening moments of, 259
  planning for, 62
  producer of, 63–64
  production of, 4
  promotion for, 106
  as promotional tool, 36
  purpose of, 36, 38–39
  at retail stores, 20–21
  sequences of, 154–155
  for students, 38–39
  success of, 277
  themes for, 78–79
  timeline/scheduling for, 72, 73f, 74
  transitions within, 154–155
  of twenty-first century, 16
  unfolding of, 278–279
  University of Philadelphia, 260f, 261
  venue for, 74–76, 77f
  wrapping up, 266
  at WWDMAGIC, 50, 50f
Fashion show diary, 271
Fashion show director, 65–66
  role of, 66f
Fashion show plan
  calendar for, 91f
  example of, 90f
  parts of, 89, 92
Fashion stylist
  business aspects of, 94–95
  definition and types of, 93
  skills and traits of, 94
Fashion trend show, 54
Fashion week, 45–46
  Los Angeles, 132f
  Mercedes-Benz, 38, 47
  newcomers to, 48–50
  staging for, 46, 46f
Fashion writing, fashion stylist for, 93
Father of haute couture, 10
Feature story, 126
Fédération Française de la Couture, du Prêt-à-Porter
  des Couturiers et Créateurs de Mode, 45
Filipowski, Ed, 47
Final lineup, 159, 160f
  use of, 161f
Finale, 10, 261
  cartwheel at, 261f
  choreography and, 202
Fit model, 179
Fitting. *See* Merchandise fitting
Fitting sheet, 162, 162f
Fitting supply, 162–163
Fit-to-confirm, 182
Five Ws, 63
Flat, 222
Flyer, as promotional material, 135
Font, 105
Food and beverage. *See* Catering
Ford, Eileen, 24

Ford, Tom, 88
Ford Modeling Agency, 24
Formal runway show, 41, 41f, 42f
Framel, Kelly, 131
Freelance, 184
Freelance publicist, 116
Full dress rehearsal, 248, 251
Full-run, 108–109

G
Galliano, John, 14–15, 16
Garland, Judy
    as inspiration, 150
    photograph of, 150f
Gaubert, Michael, 229–230
Gerber, Kaia, 175–176
Get Your Fashion Fix on Route 66, 107f
    backdrops for, 223f, 224f
    Kaci Shields and, 234
    look book for, 199f
    model application for, 190f
    model committee for, 190
    music mix for, 231
    radio-advertising script for, 114f
    schedule for, 252f
    stationary props for, 226f
Girl with the Dragon tattoo, 197, 197f, 198
Girls. *See* Model
Giveaway, 135
Givhan, Robin, 276
Glamourai, The, 131
Goldstein, Lori, 65
Gollidge, Sylvia, 24
Google AdWords, 128
Go-see, 180
Grand Divertissement à Versailles, 14, 15f
Graphic design, 109
Gratuity, 86
Grip-and-grin, 121
Group shot, 121, 121f
Guaranteed audience, 69
Guinness, Daphne, 43

H
Hair styling, 56
    budgeting for, 84
    on runway, 199
Haute couture
    as controversial, 44–45, 45f
    criteria for membership, 45
    definition of, 44

father of, 10
    location for, 44
Haute couture show, 44–45
Headline, 109
Headshot, 121
Health initiative, 185
    six-point pack, 187
Hemingway, Margeaux, 22
High society woman, 22
Historical fact sheet, 122
Home-shopping channel, 129
Horsting, Viktor, 9, 16
Horyn, Cathy, 276
Hospitality, 86–87
Host, 86
Hotel, 75–76
House model, 179
H-shaped runway, 219
Hughes, Leonore, 11f
Hutton, Lauren, 22, 22f
Hyperlink, 128

I
Ideal chart, 151, 152f, 153
Illustration, 109
Image, branding and, 106
Iman, 23–24
IMG Fashion, 50
Income, of audience, 72
Individual model lineup sheet, 192, 192f, 193f
Infomercial, 129
Informal fashion show, 42
    audience for, 71
Informal modeling, 42
In-house publicist, 116
Inspiration
    muse as, 179
    sources of, 150
    Women's Wear Daily and, 150f
Instagram, 130
Institutional advertising, 106
In-store training fashion show, 38
Instructional video, 38
Insurance, 87
International Ladies Garment Workers Union
    (ILGWU), 19
International model, 16
Internet. *See also* Online environment
    fashion shows on, 40, 40f
    as promotional strategy, 139
Internet sponsorship, 128

Interstitial, 128
Interstoff trade show, 52f
Invitation, as promotional material, 135
Ireland, Kathy, 174–175
I-shaped runway, 219f
Italian ready-to-wear industry, 48

J
Jacob, Marc, 16
    Luis Vuitton fashion show inspirations, 123f
    show planning and, 62
Johnson, Betsey, 150
Journalist, 11, 12f
    American Fashion Press Week and, 19
Jumeau, Bébé, 7
Jungle Jap label, 14, 14f

K
Kenzo, 14, 14f
Kim Dawson Agency, 51
Klein, Calvin, 45
    Girl with the Dragon tattoo and, 197, 197f, 198
Klum, Heidi, 24
Knockoff, 88
Kors, Michael, 150
Kroenig, Brad, 176
Kroenig, Hudson, 176, 176f

L
Laboratory Institute of Merchandising (LIM), 28
Lagerfeld, Karl, 154–155, 176
    lighting, 226, 228f
    Marie Antoinette and, 248, 248f
Lambert, Eleanor, 18–19
Lawley, Robyn, 175, 175f
Layout, 215, 216f
Lead, 120
Leadership
    for consumer/education shows, 65–67
    development of, 63
    for industry shows, 63
    organizational chart for, 66f
    responsibility documentation and, 68, 70f
Lease agreement, 88–89
Length, of fashion show, 74
Les Incroyables, 14–15
Licht, Aliza, 104, 104f
Lighting, 225–227, 228f
Lima, Adriana, 24
Lineup sheet, 192, 192f, 193f

Link, 128
List of participants, 122
Live music, 232, 233f
Live stream, 3D, 130f
Local advertising, 112
Logo, 105, 109
London Fashion Week, 48
Look book
    amateur model, 199
    for Get Your Fashion Fix on Route 66, 199f
Los Angeles Fashion Week, 132f
Lucie Clayton, 24

M
Machado, China, 173
    picture of, 174f
Made Fashion Week, 127–128
Mademoiselle A, 19
    first fashion show, 28–29
Made-to-order garment, 10
Magazine advertising, 111–112
    WWDCollections as, 111f
Magazine tie-in event, 37
Mailing list, 135–136
Makeup artist, 56, 198–199, 198f
    budgeting for, 84
    volunteering services, 199
Male model, 177, 177f
Mallis, Fern, 19
Mannequin. *See also* Model
    history of, 10
Mannequin du monde, 22
Mannequin modeling, 43, 43f, 132f
Mapping, choreography and, 200
Mara, Rooney, 197, 197f
Marilyn Agency, 24
Market calendar, 50
Market week, 50
Marketing, levels of, 37, 37f
Marque déposée, 105–106
Marque Luis Vuitton Desposée, 105–106
Maryhill Museum of Art, 8
Master of ceremony, 240
Mattel Toy Company, 8
Mature model, 172–173
McQueen, Alexander, 44, 45f
Media coverage, 104, 105f
    evaluation of, 275–277
    from media kit, 270f
    statistics for, 269

Media kit, 117
 ancillary materials for, 122, 126
 article written from, 270f
 basic fact sheet in, 124f
 cover for, 118f
 cover letter in, 124f
 photography in, 120–122
 as public relations, 142
 for Tampa Bay Times, 108f
Media list
 definition and information on, 116
 example of, 116f
Media show. *See* Press show
Membership list, 135–136
Menkes, Suzy, 275, 276
Mercedes-Benz Fashion Week, 38, 47
 advertisement for, 110f
 in Berlin, 48
 locations for, 50
Merchande de mode, 6
Merchandise
 evaluation of, 272–273
 feminine versus masculine, 72
 return of, 263–264
 security for, 87–88
Merchandise Buyers Exposition and Fashion Show, 17
Merchandise category, 151
 active and leisure, 153
 retailers and, 156
 themes for, 155–156
Merchandise committee, 87
Merchandise coordinator
 fittings and, 162
 merchandise categories and, 156
 responsibility sheet, use of, 70f
 role of, 66f, 68
Merchandise fitting, 159
 fitting sheet and, 162, 162f
 lineup sheets and, 161f
 model responsibility during, 194
 pre-fitting organization, 163
 scheduling for, 161
Merchandise flow, 153–155
Merchandise grouping, 153, 154f
 for consumer show, 156
Merchandise lineup, 158–159
Merchandise loan, 158
Merchandise loan record, 158, 159f
Merchandise planning chart, 151, 153f

Merchandise pull, 158
Merchandise selection, 150–151
 coordination and, 151f
Metropolitan Museum of Art, Costume Institute of, 8, 19–20
Milan Fashion Week, 48
Minister of Fashion, 6
Mixed music, 233
Mobile prop, 222
Model. *See also* Mannequin
 Americans as, 11–12
 applauding designer, 202–203
 career opportunities for, 177–179
 careers after, 174
 characteristics of, 170–172, 174–175
 choreography and, 199
 classifications of, 172–173, 173f
 diversity in, 55–56
 as ethnic, 23
 evaluation of, 273–274, 274f
 at fashion show, 21f
 fittings and, 161–163
 health initiative for, 185
 high society women as, 22
 highest-paid, 24
 informal, 42
 international, 16
 mannequin, 43, 43f, 132f
 "new face" of season, 170
 number and rotation of, 191–192
 option on, 182
 personal responsibility contract, 87
 picture of, 171f
 portfolio of, 180
 posing on runway, 218f
 professional versus amateur, 187–191
 request for, 180
 responsibilities of, 194, 196f
 during fittings, 194
 during show, 196
 rock stars and, 22
 runway versus photographic media, 13
 schools for, 18
 security for, 87
 selection/booking of, 193
 status of, 21–22
 tear sheets for, 110
 television commercial acting and, 178
 training, 205
Model Alliance, 185, 186f

Model Alliance Support, 185
Model application, 190f
Model committee
    for Get Your Fashion Fix on Route 66, 190
    selection/booking of models, 193
Model coordinator
    responsibility sheet, use of, 70f
    role of, 66f, 67
Model grouping, choreography and, 200–201, 201f
Model list, 194, 195f
Model order, 158
Model portfolio development, fashion stylist for, 93
Model Release form, 191f
Model stat, 180
Modeling
    as bad job, 184
    downsides of, 182–183
    scams in, 183–184
Modeling agency, 24–25, 203
    disreputable, 182
    history of, 179
    income of, 206
    model diversity in, 55–56
    purpose and structure of, 180
    staff of, 204
Modeling fee, 84
Modeling scam, 183–184
Modeling student, 38–39
Models' Bill of Rights, 185, 186f
Money, 97–98
Monick, Caroline, 154f
Montana, Claude, 16f
Moss, Kate, 24
Mother agency, 180
Mug shot, 121
Mugler, Thierry, 15
Multimedia production show, 40, 43
Muse. *See also* Inspiration
    for Calvin Klein, 197f
    designers using, 179
Music
    copyrighted, 234
    evaluation of, 274–275
    importance of, 228–229
    live, 232, 233f
    mixed, 233
    sound designer for, 229–230, 230f
    sound system for, 234–235, 235f
    vocal, 233–234
Music mix, 230–231
Music playlist, 232, 232f

N
National Chamber for Italian Fashion, 48
National promotion, 37
National Retail Federation, 53
Neon lighting, 228f
Network television advertising, 112–113
"New face" of season, 170
New faces division, of modeling agency, 180, 204
New York Fashion Press Week, 19, 47, 69f
    model pay for, 184
New York Times, 276
News release, 117–118
    example of, 119f
    guidelines for, 118–119
    photography in, 120–122
    writing and distribution of, 120
News story, 126
Newspaper advertising, 108–109
    preparation for, 109
Newsweek, 276
"No show" model, 194
Noncommercial advertising, 107
Nonprofit organization, 83
    retailers and, 156

O
Occupation, of audience, 72
Online commercial, 128
Online environment. *See also* Internet
    advertising on, 127–128
    direct marketing on, 129
    public relations on, 129
Open call, 180
Option, putting model on, 182

P
Pace, of choreography, 200
Paid search, 128
Paquin, Jeanne, 10, 12
Paris fashion show, 45
    ready-to-wear, 48
Parker, Suzy, 22
Participants, list of, 122
Paste-up, 110
Patou, Jean, 11–12, 11f
Pause, 200
Personal responsibility contract, 88f
Personal selling, 131–132
Petite model, 175
Photo credit, 120
Photo opportunity, 120–122

Photo shoot model, 177–178
Photographic media, models in, 13
Photography
   as expense, 85
   in media kits/news releases, 120–122
   in newspaper advertisement, 109
Picture Me: A Model's Diary, 184
Pivot, 200
Planning. *See also* Fashion show plan
   five Ws of, 63
   leadership and, 65–67, 66f
   show purpose and, 62
Plaster head, 7
Plus-size model, 175
Point-of-purchase video, 40
Poiret, Paul, 10
Polyvore, 131
Pop-unders, 128
Pop-ups, 128
Portfolio, 39
   of model, 180
Posen, Zac, 150
Poster, as promotional material, 135, 137f
Poupées de mode, 6
Power, clothing as tool of, 36
Powers, John Robert, 24
Prada, actors wearing, 36f
Prada, Miuccia, 36
Preferred position, 108
Pre-fitting organization, 163
Premier/premiere, 11
Press kit. *See* Media kit
Press release, 117–118
   example of, 119f
   guidelines for, 118–119
   photography in, 120–122
   writing and distribution of, 120
Press show, 11, 12f
   American Fashion Press Week and, 19
   purpose of, 47
Prêt-à-porter, 48
Primary resource, 37, 37f
Product advertising, 106
Product shot, 121–122
Production show, 39–40, 42f
   audience for, 71
Professional model, 187–188
Professionalism, 264–265
Program editor, 68
Program of events, 122
   as promotional tool, 138

Promotion
   advertising versus editorial content, 115
   budgeting for, 84–85
   definition of, 36, 104
   evaluation of, 272
   for fashion show, 106
   importance of, 132
   market levels of, 37, 37f
   media coverage and, 104
   social media and, 143
   strategies for, 139
   types of, 131–132
Promotion coordinator
   responsibility sheet, use of, 70f
   role of, 66f, 67–68
Promotional material, creative development of,
   135–139
Prop, 224
   handbags and designer frames as, 225f
   as mobile or stationary, 222
PSA (Public service announcement), 117
Psychographics, 71
Public relations, 63–64, 64f
   communication and, 114–115
   importance of, 114
   on online environment, 129
Public relations director, 65
Public service announcement (PSA), 117
Publicist, 115
   in-house versus freelance, 116
Publicity
   advertising versus, 105
   definition of, 115
   press material delivery, 117
   types and outlets for, 116

Q
Quant, Mary, 13

R
Radio advertising, 113–114
   script for, 114f
Rate card, 108
Ready-to-wear show, 45–50
Rebull, Joan, 7
Rehearsal. *See also* Dress rehearsal
   model responsibility during, 195–196
   preparation for, 251
   purpose of, 249f
   run-through versus full-dress, 248, 251

Release date, 119
Répétition générale, 11
Request, 180
Responsibility sheet, 68, 70f
Restaurant, 76
Retail promotion, 38
    public relations and, 142–143
Retail show, 20–21
    striking, 262–263
Retailer
    advantages/disadvantages of using,
        156–157
    relationships with, 158
Ribbon, 153, 154f
Rizer, Maggie, 9, 9f
Rock star, models and, 22
Run-of-paper (ROP), 108
Run-through rehearsal, 248
Runway. *See also* Catwalk
    dimensions of, 216–217, 217f
    height of, 218
    shapes of, 218–219, 218f
        I-shaped, 219f
    surface of, 220
Runway fashion show. *See also* Fashion show
    actors in, 36f
    audience for, 71
    formal, 41, 41f, 42f
    history of, 10
    models in, 13
    production of, 41, 41f
Runway model, 177
Runway rehearsal, 56
Runway to Wonderland
    ideal chart for, 152f
    media kit cover for, 118f
    model release form for, 191f
    news release for, 119f
    script for, 235, 236–240
    silent auction for, 259f
    sponsorship pitch for, 133f–134f
    tentative/final lineup for, 160f
    themes for, 155–156
Russian court dress, 5f

S
Sanchez, Frédéric, 230
Scam, modeling, 183–184
Scenery, 222
Schedule of activities, 122

Scheduling, of fashion show, 72, 73f, 74
School
    fashion shows and, 38–39, 76
    for models, 18
School show. *See* Education show
Scout, 180
    purpose of, 204
    traits of interest by, 205
Script
    definition of, 235
    evaluation of, 275
    for Runway to Wonderland, 236–240
Search engine advertising, 128
Seating chart, 258, 258f
Seating pattern, 225, 227f
Secondary resource, 37, 37f
Security
    for audience and staff, 89
    for merchandise and personnel, 87–88
    personal responsibility contract, 88f
    for venue and equipment, 88–89
Sequence, of fashion show, 154–155
Shannon Rogers and Jerry Silverman School of
    Fashion Design and Merchandising, 39
Shell, of media kit, 117, 118f
Shields, Kaci, 234
    copyrights and permissions, 241–242
Shopgirl, 10
Show producer, 63–64
Showroom model, 179
Shrimpton, Jean, 22
Silent auction, 259, 259f
Simons, Raf, 222
Slogan, 109
Snoeren, Rolf, 9, 16
Social media, 104
    brands using, 129–130
    types of, 129, 130f
A Soul Brought to Heaven, 150f
Sound, 105
Sound designer, 229–230, 230f
Sound system, 234–235, 235f
Spam, 129
Special event, 132
Special events director, 65
Special interest show, 54
Specialty market show, 54
Sponsorship
    corporate, 135
    definition of, 132

importance of, 133
  pitch example for, 133f–134f
Spot advertising, 112
Spotlight, 225
Staff security, 89
Stage, 215, 216f
  example of, 224f
  layout of, 216, 216f, 218f
Stage manager
  responsibility sheet, use of, 70f
  role of, 66f, 67
Stage strike, 262–264, 262f
  merchandise return, 263–264
  personnel for, 263
Staging. *See also* Runway
  background for, 221–222
  dressing room, 216, 220
  evaluation of, 275
  lighting for, 225–227
  props for, 222, 224
  seating patterns for, 224–225
  stage and layout, 215
  striking, 262–264, 262f
Staging framework, 214
Standard advertising unit (SAU), 108
Starter, 255–256
Stat, of model, 180
Stationary prop, 222, 224, 226f
Statistics, 269
Striking. *See* Stage strike
Striking the show, 262–264
Strobe light, 226
Strut: The Fashionable Mom Show, 37–38, 38f
Studio shot, 122
Stylebook, 112f
Styling, 56
Stylist, 64–65
  budgeting for, 84
Subheadline, 109
Success, measurement of, 277
Supermodel, 23, 23f, 170
Support staff expense, 85–86
Survey, audience evaluating fashion show, 272
Symbol, 105

T

Table seating, 225, 227f
Tabletop product shot, 122
Tampa Bay Times, 108–109
  media kit for, 108f

Tear sheet, 110, 180
Tea-room modeling, 21
Technical staff salary, 85–86
Television advertising, 112–113
Television commercial acting, 178
Tentative lineup, 158, 160f
  creation of, 251
Tertiary resource, 37f
Test, 180
Thank you note, 266, 267f
Theater seating, 224–225, 227f
Théâtre de la Mode, 7
  fashions dolls in, 8f
Theatrical staging, 214
Theme, 78–79
  decorations and, 86
  evaluation of, 270
Theme, of merchandise, 155–156
Ticket, as promotional material, 138
Tiegs, Cheryl, 22
Timing/timeline
  for design presentations, 88
  of fashion show, 72, 73f, 74, 74f
Tone, 275
Toronto Fashion week, 49, 49f
Toronto Life, 112f
Trade association, 53
Trade promotion, 38
Trade show, 17, 50–51
  models in, 52f–53f
Transition, within fashion show, 154–155
Transmedia storytelling, 130
Transportation cost, 86
Trunk show, 42–43, 43f
T-shaped runway, 219
Twiggy, 22, 150
Twitter
  branding and, 143
  DKNY PR Girl and, 104, 104f
  transmedia storytelling and, 131

U

University of Philadelphia student show, 260f, 261
U-shaped runway, 219
Usher, 86

V

Venue
  evaluation of, 270–271
  expense for, 83

for fashion show, 74–76, 77f
    security for, 88–89
Verbiage
    announcer or master of ceremonies, 240
    commentary, 235
    script for, 235, 236–240
Vernet, Marie, 10, 21
Versace, Gianni, 23f
Versailles, 14
    restoration of, 19–20
Victoria's Secret, 153
Video expense, 85
Video on demand, 128
Video opportunity, 122
Virtual tear sheet, 110
Visions Couture, 43
Visual merchandising, 132
VisualDESIGNLab (VDL), 140
Vocal music, 233–234
Vogue, 17–18
    closing date for, 111
    magazine tie-in events and, 37
Vuitton, Georges, 105

W
Waiver, for missing/damaged merchandise, 87
Wall Street Journal fashion blog, 276

Wang, Vera, 65
Wardrobe, fashion stylist for, 93
Webisode, 129
Wen, Liu, 170, 170f
Westwood, Vivienne, 14
White space, 109
Women's Wear Daily, 150f
Worth, Charles Frederick, 10
Wrapping up, 266
Ws, five, 63
WWDCollections, 111f
WWDMAGIC, 50, 50f

X
X-shaped runway, 219

Y
Y-shaped runway, 219

Z
Ziff, Sara, 184, 185
Zigzag-shaped runway, 219
Zoe, Rachel, 65
Zoned edition, 109
Zoran, 16
Z-shaped runway, 219